CYFARTHFA SCHOOL

THE FIRST 100 YEARS

1913-2013

CYFARTHFA SCHOOL

THE FIRST 100 YEARS

1913-2013

EDITED by

JOE ENGLAND

Published by Cyfarthfa High School
2012

CYFARTHFA HIGH SCHOOL

Cae Mari Dwn

Queen's Road

Merthyr Tydfil CF47 0LS

All proceeds from the sale of this book will go to
Cyfarthfa High School

A CIP catalogue record for this book is available from the British Library.

ISBN: 978-0-9514580-9-9

Design: jenksdesign@yahoo.co.uk
Printed and Bound by Cambrian Printers, Aberystwyth

CONTENTS

PREFACE

LORD ROWLANDS CBE

The acquisition of Cyfarthfa Castle in 1909 by the newly incorporated Merthyr Tydfil County Borough Council is a defining moment in the political and social history of the Borough. William Crawshay II had built the castle to be a physical manifestation of ironmaster power. Now, in a symbolic transfer of power, Merthyr's great capitalist family gave way to the newly elected civic democrats.

Ironmasters and coal owners had fought, since the passing of the Municipal Corporations Act of 1834, a long rearguard action against civic incorporation and the drive for Merthyr to have its own Council. But eventually the increasingly powerful voice of the local business and professional community had prevailed. In 1905 incorporation was achieved and in 1908 Merthyr Tydfil gained the powers of a County Borough.

The new County Borough Council set about establishing long overdue civic institutions and amenities including new libraries, parks and the great Taff Fechan water project. Ownership of the castle and park was part of that drive to make Merthyr a more pleasant town in which to live.

And so, with the acquisition of the castle for the purpose of free secondary education, began a century of opportunity for generations of young Merthyr citizens, albeit restricted by the 11 plus until the school's transformation into a comprehensive high school.

I did not have the pleasure, as contributors to this volume did, of attending Cyfarthfa School. I went to a rival valley's grammar school, Porth County. But our three children attended Cyfarthfa, and Janice and I enjoyed a 30-year close working relationship with its two heads, Dennis Bennett and Alan Pritchard. Many of the staff became our friends and acquaintances.

I especially recall the school's contribution to the wonderfully successful Urdd Eisteddfod in 1987. Janice chaired, but had as her vice-chair someone very close to our hearts, Ray Gethin.

As the school celebrates its centenary it again faces the challenge of change with the introduction of a tertiary system and, a first for Cyfarthfa High School, a Headmistress.

I know we all wish Carolyn Meade and her staff every success in meeting this new challenge and are confident that they will successfully do so.

.

RHAGAIR

YR ARGLWYDD ROWLANDS CBE

Mae caffaeliad Castell Cyfarthfa ym 1909 gan Gyngor Bwrdeistref Sirol Merthyr Tudful, oedd newydd ei sefydlu, yn foment diffiniol yn hanes gwleidyddol a chymdeithasol y Fwrdeistref. Adeiladwyd y castell gan William Crawshay II i fod yn ymgorfforiad o rym meistr y gwaith haearn. Nawr, mewn trosglwyddiad symbolaidd o rym, ildiodd teulu cyfalafol mawr Merthyr i'r democratiaid dinesig oedd newydd eu hethol.

Ers pasio Deddf y Corfforaethau ym 1834 'roedd perchnogion y gweithfeydd haearn a'r pyllau glo wedi ymladd yn hir yn erbyn corffori dinesig a'r ymgyrch i Ferthyr gael ei chyngor ei hun. Ond yn y pen draw fe orchfygodd llais cynyddol y gymuned fusnes a phroffesiynol lleol. Daeth corffori i rym ym 1905 ac ym 1908 fe enillodd Merthyr Tudful rymoedd Cyngor Bwrdeistref.

Aeth y Cyngor Bwrdeistref Sirol newydd ati i sefydlu cyrff a chyfleusterau dinesig yr oedd angen dirfawr amdanynt yn cynnwys llyfrgelloedd a pharciau newydd a phrosiect d☐r mawr Taf Fechan. Roedd perchnogaeth o'r castell a'r parc yn rhan o'r ymgyrch honno i wneud Merthyr yn dref fwy dymunol i fyw ynddi.

Ac felly, gyda chaffael y castell er mwyn darparu addysg uwchradd am ddim, fe ddechreuodd canrif o gyfle i genedlaethau o ddinasyddion ifanc Merthyr, er eu bod wedi eu cyfyngu gan yr 11+ nes i'r ysgol newid yn ysgol uwchradd gyfun.

Ni chefais gyfle, fel y cyfranwyr eraill i'r gyfrol hon, i fynychu Ysgol Cyfarthfa. Fe es i ysgol ramadeg Porth County. Ond aeth ein tri phlentyn i Gyfarthfa ac fe fwynheais i a Janice berthynas waith agos am 30 mlynedd gyda'r ddau bennaeth, Dennis Bennet ac Alan Pritchard. Daeth llawer o'r staff yn gyfeillion a chydnabod i ni.

Rwy'n cofio'n arbennig gyfraniad yr ysgol i Eisteddfod yr Urdd hynod lwyddiannus 1987. Janice oedd y cadeirydd ond roedd rhywun agos iawn at ein calonnau'n is-gadeirydd iddi, Ray Gethin.

Wrth i'r ysgol ddathlu ei chanmlwyddiant mae'n wynebu her newid unwaith eto gyda chyflwyno system drydyddol ac, am y tro cyntaf yn hanes Ysgol Uwchradd Cyfarthfa, Prifathrawes.

Rwy'n gwybod ein bod oll yn dymuno pob llwyddiant i Carolyn Meade a'i staff yn cwrdd â'r her newydd hwn ac rydym yn hyderus y byddant yn gwneud hynny'n llwyddiannus.

INTRODUCTION

JOE ENGLAND

Where there is no vision, the people perish (Proverbs ch.29, v. 18)

When, in 1913, the Cyfarthfa schools opened, the school leaving age was 12. Boys in South Wales who reached that age normally went down the pit, 'underground'; my father did, along with thousands of his generation. The girls went into 'domestic service', worked in shops, or stayed at home to help their mother bring up younger children. Yet, on 20 January 1913, two municipal secondary schools — one for girls and one for boys — opened their doors at Cyfarthfa Castle, offering the opportunity for free secondary education, beginning at the age of 11, to children from homes where 96 per cent of those in employment mined coal or made iron and steel. It seemed to many a foolish waste of money. That kind of education for working-class children was unnecessary. Their parents would not support it.

How wrong those critics were. Coalmining and steel making in Merthyr Tydfil have disappeared but the achievements of Cyfarthfa pupils over the past century in serving the borough and the wider world resonate and continue. In 1913 Merthyr Tydfil Council had a vision that was both enterprising and daring. As Alfred T. Davies, the head of the Board of Education in Wales, reminded everyone at the opening ceremony, 'the eyes of Wales will be upon the experiment you are making . . . to bring the advantages of good secondary education within reach of the poorest parent who is fortunate enough today to find himself living within the borders of your progressive municipality'. The Cyfarthfa schools were not the first to offer free secondary education, as often claimed, but they were probably the first in Wales where that was the intention from day one. Children from Merthyr's middle class were in that first intake, but so were many from working-class families.

Cyfarthfa Castle 1913

A centenary can be an occasion for celebrating survival, for remembrance of times past, for reflecting upon change. For Cyfarthfa School it is all three. One hundred years is not a long time in the life of a school, many can boast a history three or four times as long. But political, social and technological revolutions in the past century have transformed our world in startling ways. The story of Cyfarthfa School revealed in these pages is one of remarkable change and adaptation. And this hundredth anniversary comes at a poignant time. No longer after July 2014 will Merthyr children be able to say: 'I went to school in a castle'. The impact upon Cyfarthfa pupils of walking through the Park and entering, by right, that extraordinary building with its history and symbolism, shines through in more than one chapter. Already dwindling is the number of former pupils who have memories of sunlit days at the tennis courts, shove halfpenny on park benches, teenage romances in the park and growing intellectual confidence in the Grammar School's Sixth Form.

This is not, and was never intended to be, a detached formal history. On the other hand, the story of the school over the past 100 years, told in the first four chapters, reveals important changes in educational philosophy and developments in Merthyr Tydfil. The chapters vary in style, depending upon the personality of each author, their experience and the events they are portraying. But three write from intimate personal knowledge of the periods they describe and a fascinating story emerges. Those chapters are followed by *They Made Their Mark,* a chapter in which 35 former pupils are profiled for their very different achievements. It shows that although education is an engine of social mobility that takes people out of Merthyr onto a bigger stage, often never to return, there are those who do return and those who have made a mark whilst still living amongst us. Whether they return or not, there are few who forget their home town.

Next is a chapter that many will find the most interesting. *Reminiscences* is where past pupils and teachers reflect upon their schooldays, their first day at Cyfarthfa, fellow pupils, the abrupt change from primary to secondary education, and the impact upon their lives of individual teachers. Throughout the book we have used photographs that illustrate events and personalities and the changing times.

From Barry Island to Cape Canaveral

And how times have changed! The most striking is the change in the standard of living. The girls' and boy's schools that opened their doors in January 1913, just four years after the first manned flight across the English Channel, were in a County Borough still dominated by coal and steel, and with a population of 80,000. Today, the heavy industries have gone, the large factories that provided thousands of jobs until the 1980s have gone, and the population is now around 59,000, with many jobs in public services and in Merthyr's growing retail sector. Although 30 per cent of Merthyr Tydfil households of working age are without work, a century of social and technological advance has raised the level of incomes and the material expectations of ordinary people beyond anything dreamed of in 1913.

In 1913 children did their homework by gaslight or by candlelight, and that continued for some into the early 1950s. In 1913 a 'trip' for most Merthyr children meant a Sunday School outing by train to Pontsarn, clutching a bottle of pop and a packet of jam sandwiches. In the early

1950s a trip to Barry Island was still an event. My post-war generation at Cyfarthfa was taught French and German, but never saw France or Germany. Today, Cyfarthfa pupils have enjoyed life-changing school visits that include Berlin, Mt. Vesuvius, Auschwitz, Costa Rica, the Austrian Alps, and the Johnson Space Centre at Cape Canaveral, Florida. It is a fact that not all pupils who are eligible can afford the cost of such visits, poverty, relative and absolute, has always been an aspect of life in Merthyr. But money-raising events within the school, donations by charities, the work of the PTA and subsequently Friends of Cyfarthfa High School, and not least, contributions by grandparents who 'in *their* day' could never have dreamed of such visits, make them possible for a large majority.

Another great change has been increasing State intervention in the qualifications awarded by schools, the very type and nature of schools, and the curriculum to be taught in schools. The most significant change for Cyfarthfa was when the school became comprehensive. The story of Cyfarthfa High School is told in the last part of Chapter Two and in Chapters Three and Four. But for 57 years from 1913 to 1970, the Cyfarthfa schools, amalgamated into one co-educational school in 1946, were secondary grammar schools, and the story of their evolution and achievement is told in Chapter One and most of Chapter Two.

The Cyfarthfa Brand

In their time, the state funded secondary schools, after 1944 called 'grammar schools' marked an important stage in democratic public education. In an age of heavy industry employers required manual labourers whose education generally ceased at 12, craftsmen who acquired their skill through apprenticeships, and clerks with writing and calculation abilities gained through some extra years of elementary education up to 14. Education beyond that level for working-class children was not thought necessary, as the row over the founding of the Cyfarthfa |Schools illustrated.

The far-sighted Liberal and Labour councillors in Merthyr thought otherwise and provided through the Cyfarthfa schools a route into the professions for working-class girls and boys, that had not until then been available, although the Merthyr County Intermediate School, opened in 1896 as a fee-paying school, had a limited but growing number of free places. No-one knew when those Castle schools were opened in January 1913 that Europe would soon be plunged into a terrible war, followed by years of depression and bitter hardship in south Wales, followed then by another war that would ravage much of the planet. Yet it was during those 32 years, 1913-1945, that the Cyfarthfa brand of education was established. What was that brand?

Undoubtedly, 'Cyfarthfa was the school to aim for', as one former pupil remembers. Once there, it was understood that you did nothing to disgrace the school uniform. Girls, in particular, were expected to speak properly and were given lessons in deportment. The dominant ethos, however, was academic achievement, for that after all was the purpose of the school. 'Matriculation' (a term explained in Chapter One) with its subsequent entry to the sixth form and the opportunity to sit for university entry dominated the curriculum. There is some emphasis in the first two chapters upon those pupils who achieved State Scholarships, university entrance scholarships, and access to Oxford or Cambridge. This is no more than a reflection of what Cyfarthfa, and every grammar school, saw as success and how, largely, they were judged. Until the 1950s, it was 'a big thing' if children went on to university. From 1961, under the headship of Lloyd Williams, the most academically able pupils were fast-tracked through to the sixth form and then given the opportunity to spend a third year there to read more widely, digest what they had been taught and to retake and improve their A level grades, if necessary. It was a more determined drive for academic success than had gone before; but not a change of mission. Increasing affluence and the expansion of the universities in the 1960s underpinned this success.

It was, of course, the tip of the iceberg. The majority did not go to university nor did they jump all the hurdles necessary to achieve 'the matric'. What they did was achieve a perfectly solid school-leavers' certificate, leave school at 15, and enter white-collar jobs in the local steelworks, collieries, railway companies, solicitors' and auctioneers' offices, hospitals, police and the various branches of national and local

Derelict Dowlais Works, 1936

government. Girls might also become primary school teachers, nurses, and shorthand secretaries. Over the next 40 years many rose to responsible positions in the businesses, industries, services and community life of the borough and further afield. It is this unacknowledged majority that is the bedrock of the Castle school achievement in its defining years, (and still is today).

However, greater numbers fell by the wayside than should have been the case. In the 1920s and 1930s more than one in five pupils left the school before taking the school certificate examinations. Many were casualties of the depression when domestic poverty meant they had to leave school and, if possible, find work. Girls in addition suffered from low expectations on the part of their parents, and themselves. The early determination of Bryneilen and Rosentyl Griffiths to become doctors (see *Reminiscences*) was exceptional.

The *Reminiscences* chapter also provides examples of unfulfilled potentialities. It was probably during the inter-war depression that a decision was made to enable boys to sit the School Certificate examinations after just four years of schooling instead of the normal five. This was done by simply calling the entry class Form Two instead of Form One, a practice which has puzzled many. It seems the purpose was to reduce the time boys spent in school so that they would be less of a financial burden on their family, and enable boys to enter the labour market with a school certificate. For some the pressure was too demanding, and they either left school without that precious piece of paper, or stayed on for a second year in the fifth form to get it, a practice that continued until the introduction of lower and upper fourth forms in the 50s. (A consequence was that through all the classes the boys were usually a year younger than their opposites in the girls' school who had entered in Form One.)

Unjust and Wasteful

Under-achievement was not an issue confined to the depression years or to Cyfarthfa. In 1959 the Crowther Report found that 48 per cent of the children in England and Wales with an IQ over 120 had left school by 16 and that the ones who left were predominantly working class. By that time there was a growing realisation in Britain that many children were not realising their talents under the existing system of education and that the home environment and social conditions had a major effect on academic achievement. Even in Merthyr with its high percentage of grammar school places the problem was evident. Although the grammar schools had provided free quality education to many working-class children, there were still those whose talents were not developed until they entered the world of work, where many flourished and accepted heavy responsibilities. Others found their way back into education and realised their potential, after some years in work, by going to Coleg Harlech, or a technical college, or by taking correspondence courses, an external or Open University degree.

An essential requirement of the grammar school system was the 11 plus examination which labelled children as 'successes' or 'failures' at the age of 11. This too was increasingly seen as unjust and wasteful. When

Anthony Crosland became Secretary of State for Education in 1964 he was convinced that the state should do its utmost to make it possible for those without money or position or a literate family background to have equal access to decent education opportunities. He encouraged local authorities to introduce non-selective 'comprehensive' schools.

The decision was made to merge Georgetown Secondary Modern School with Cyfarthfa Grammar School. It caused a huge upheaval and Cyfarthfa in particular faced severe pressures in the process, as Chapters Two and Three tell. But it was done and Cyfarthfa High School emerged, with the Castle on the hill, a symbol of power and exclusion, finally open and accessible. The story of Cyfarthfa High School during the past 42 years is told in Chapters Three and Four and that is where most readers will find familiar names and events that reawaken memories.

Some Lessons Learned

What can we learn from this century-old story? In 1913 The Cyfarthfa schools were a major advance in the democratisation of education with Merthyr proudly among the first to offer free secondary education. Gradually, over half a century, a serious weakness in the system became evident. Many talented individuals were dropping out of both the grammar and the secondary modern schools, particularly those from a working-class background; and Merthyr is a working-class town. The answer was seen to be a more open yet more challenging form of secondary education, the comprehensive school. The challenge for these schools has been to do what the grammar school did for the brightest pupils while fostering the talents of all pupils. The evidence on this from Cyfarthfa High School is reassuring. Academic standards are externally judged to be high, while all pupils receive help and guidance on a scale that was totalling missing from the Grammar school.

This improvement in pastoral care, with greater attention given to individual pupils, became generally apparent in schools from the 1970s onwards. It arose from a variety of reasons. Among them the challenge of mixed-ability teaching, an understanding that under-privileged children need help if their abilities are to be developed to the full, and, to some extent, the abolition of corporal punishment. A former Merthyr Tydfil Director of Education once commented that until the 1970s Cyfarthfa School 'was ruled by the cane'. It was an exaggeration but not at times without foundation. After Dennis Bennett prohibited corporal punishment and ended a regime that enabled certain bullying teachers physically to assault children, new methods of positive discipline had to be introduced in Cyfarthfa and developed through experience, as elsewhere. It may seem contrary to those of an older generation ('caning never did me any harm') but the abolition of caning reduced the amount of aggressiveness in the school.

There is now an emphasis on achievement and success with stars, merit certificates, rewards (such as ten-pin bowling in Swansea), and open acknowledgement and commendation. Encouragement is given through pastoral care, learning pathways, careers advice, and contracts with the pupil and his or her parents on attendance and behaviour. This concern is evident too in the collaboration between the school and its feeder primary schools so that children are better prepared for that difficult transition from primary to secondary education. Taken together these changes add up to a significant and successful quiet revolution. They also illustrate an old truth sometimes forgotten: children respond to how they are treated.

Startling changes have taken place in how we earn a living. There has always been a tension in education between the practical demands of enabling children to compete for jobs, and Matthew Arnold's vision, 'to make the best that has been thought and known in the world . . .' available to everyone. That is a noble ambition in which schools play an essential role but it asks too much of ten or twelve years of schooling. It challenges the relations between culture and society, democracy and education, and points the need for continuing education throughout life. The best schools prepare for that by feeding imagination, arousing curiosity and teaching children how to learn.

Learning how to learn has never been more important. So rapid are the all-pervasive changes in information and communication technology and biological sciences in the 21st century that schools face the challenge of having to equip children for jobs not yet invented. To survive and thrive in such a rapidly changing world, flexibility of thought and mind-sets that welcome innovation, creativity and entrepreneurship are essential. Thankfully, as Chapter Four illustrates, Cyfarthfa High School is stimulating and encouraging these skills in all pupils.

What links with that, and achieves greater significance in today's world, is Cyfarthfa's long record of encouraging pupils in public performance, through eisteddfodau, plays and music. A recent Europe-wide study of 5,000 13-16-year-olds found that participating in school drama productions builds self-confidence and self-esteem, increases teenage capacity to communicate and to learn, and develops teamwork skills. Playing in orchestras and singing in choirs have similar effects. Whether on the curriculum or not, these activities are building skills essential for tomorrow's world. They help both the academic and the non-academic pupil and foster the blossoming of talents that may lay hidden.

Time to look to the future

Of course there are regrets about finally leaving the Castle and deep concern over the loss of a Sixth Form that provided role models for the rest of the school. It remains to be seen whether fifth formers (Year 11) can fill that role. Evidence from elsewhere suggests that they can. For Merthyr College the challenge is to achieve the same or better educational outcomes for those students who would otherwise be in the sixth form of Cyfarthfa and other Merthyr schools. A great deal rests on the response to that challenge.

But drawing upon the experience of 100 years of change and development, Cyfarthfa High School can confidently look forward to teaching on one site with modern purpose-built buildings and facilities. Its teachers know that success comes not only from setting high standards, but from expecting and encouraging achievement at whatever level. It is their fortune and privilege to teach the extraordinary stream of talented children that continues to rise within Merthyr Tydfil.

HOW THE CASTLE BECAME
A SCHOOL

JOE ENGLAND

'. . . a vigorous, happy community life has been steadily maintained within the school'.

(HMI Report 1937)

On the afternoon of 18 September 1908 five men stood on the terrace before Cyfarthfa Castle admiring, with some excitement, its grand proportions. Then, the Mayor of Merthyr, Alderman David Evans, led the way into the building which had been neglected and occupied only by rats for the past 19 years. He was followed by two local councillors, J. M. Berry and Arthur Daniel, and the Town Clerk, Aneuryn Rees. They represented the newly empowered Merthyr Tydfil County Borough Council which two months earlier had unanimously agreed to buy the Castle and its parkland from W. T. Crawshay. (The details of the sale were not actually settled until the following year when the Council paid £19,700 – agreed to be a bargain.) The fifth man was O. M. Edwards, former Fellow of Lincoln College, Oxford, author, founder and editor of periodicals through which he massively influenced Welsh sensibilities, and recently-appointed Chief Inspector of Education for Wales.

Earlier that day the five had met to discuss the future of secondary education in Merthyr. Since the granting of County Borough status in April this was now the new council's responsibility. There was much to

1

discuss for each of Merthyr's three existing post-elementary schools had problems.

The County Intermediate School, opened in 1896 for 180 pupils was overcrowded, having grown by 1908 to 296 boys and girls. It was a fee-paying school primarily providing for children of the middle class, although under the influence of the Labour members on the Council, the number of free places would steadily increase to 35 per cent of the intake by 1913. In 'temporary' premises in Zoar Chapel vestry a Pupil Teacher Centre prepared students for entry into Teacher Training Colleges. At Caedraw an Advanced Elementary School took pupils beyond the elementary stage. Most of its pupils left at 14 or sooner, but those who stayed on, and there were almost twice as many girls as boys who did so, were being prepared for apprenticeship as pupil-teachers. It had neither laboratories nor work-rooms and it too was overcrowded. A proposal to replace it with a new building that would function as a higher elementary school providing an education for working-class children that would, in the words of an official report, 'make them efficient members of the class to which they belong' had aroused considerable controversy. The local Trades Council and the Merthyr branch of the Independent Labour Party (ILP) were campaigning for a free secondary school to be built.

O. M. Edwards had been forthright but also helpful about this rather chaotic situation. The Board of Education, he said, would not allow the overcrowding at the County School to continue. Pupil Teacher Centres were old-fashioned and being phased out; the modern practice for pupils who wished to become teachers was for them to attend secondary schools. Merthyr, with its new County Borough status, could go for another secondary school which would remove the need to build an extension to the County, and would also provide opportunities for the senior pupils in Caedraw. A government grant of £5 per head was available for pupils in a municipal secondary school. Under the 1902 Education Act 'the matter', he said, 'is entirely in your own hands'.

So the five had decided to inspect Cyfarthfa Castle for, during the debate about whether to buy, more than one councillor had suggested that the Castle could be used as a school, perhaps for housing the girls in the

Owen M. Edwards

County school. During his tour of the building Edwards was highly impressed and enthusiastically suggested that, with very little alteration, it could be adapted as a new Municipal Secondary school and Technical School, with provision for an Art Gallery and a Museum, both of which would add to the school's facilities.

These were heady days for the new County Borough. Frustrated nineteenth century ambitions were at last being realised. Three years earlier, after three-quarters of a century of agitation, Merthyr had achieved a Charter of Incorporation and finally its own Borough Council. Now it had been raised to the status of a County Borough and had acquired its own police force and a Court for Quarter Sessions with a Recorder: council houses were being built, the Mardy Isolation Hospital was newly opened, work was starting on the Taff Fechan reservoir and Cyfarthfa Castle and the Park were about to be acquired. Since 1880 coal had replaced iron and steel as the dominant industry, employment was growing, and the Borough population would increase to 80,000 by 1912. From Flooks at Pontmorlais stretched an unbroken line of shops and businesses down the long high street to the Parish Church. Between 1904 and 1914, more than a quarter of million pounds was spent by tradesmen on the reconstruction of their shops. The national coal strike in March 1912 scarcely dented business confidence, for it ended in victory for the miners who would have more money to spend, and in that same year, King George V and Queen Mary passed under the Coal Arch – symbol of Merthyr's wealth – and inspected the modernised Dowlais Works.

The spirit of Edwardian self-confidence that gripped Wales could be seen in the new civic buildings in Cardiff, the prosperity of the coal and shipping companies and even in the militancy of the South Wales Miners' Federation. In Merthyr the new County Borough Council, which included a number of talented and far-sighted individuals, was grasping the new possibilities opening before it. Some were members of that middle-class group of Liberals who had fought for years for Merthyr to have its own town council. The key men included Sidney Simons, Frank Treharne James (chairman of the secondary schools sub-committee) and D. W. Jones – all three of them solicitors — and John Mathias Berry, a wealthy auctioneer. D. W. Jones, active in public life since 1894, was the local solicitor for Guest, Keen and Nettlefolds, and for Crawshay Brothers. When he became Mayor for the term 1907-8 he seized the opportunity to begin negotiations on behalf of the Council with William Thompson Crawshay for the sale of the Castle and its grounds. By July 1908 terms for the Castle had almost been agreed and the Council took the decision to buy.

Also on the Council were about a dozen Labour men, most of them miners, who had been elected to the first Borough Council in 1905 and who were determined that working-class children should be given every opportunity. Outstanding were Enoch Morrell from Troedyrhiw, Andrew Wilson from Treharris, Rowland Evans from Merthyr Vale, and David Davies a railwayman from Pant, secretary of Merthyr Trades Council. Morrell was chairman of the Education Committee.

O. M. Edwards as Chief Inspector for Wales, polished, intellectual and with a magnetic personality, carried the day. On 18 December the Education Committee decided to site a Municipal Secondary School with two departments, one for 200 boys, and the other for 300 girls, at Cyfarthfa Castle together with a Technical School 'with provision for Manual Instruction'. The Higher Grade School at Caedraw would revert to being an elementary school for the town. All the boys and girls over eleven who desired to do so would be transferred from Caedraw to Cyfarthfa. The Pupil Teacher Centre at Zoar would close and the pupil teachers would be taught at Cyfarthfa. To supplement the intakes from Caedraw and Zoar additional pupils from elementary schools would be recruited to the Castle Schools after taking an entrance examination that soon became known as 'the scholarship'. In the curriculum for boys, science would predominate. Unlike the County School no fees would be charged to pupils in the Borough, so enabling working-class children to attend. Pupils from down the valley would travel free by train; pupils from Dowlais would travel free by tram. Although many believed Merthyr to be the first authority not to charge for admission to a secondary school, in fact Rhondda Urban District Council had abolished fees at Ferndale Secondary School in 1904.

Then, after 1908, there was a four-year delay. A meeting of local Chambers of Trade in September 1909 raised a number of objections to the scheme: the site was too far from the lower end of the borough; it was too far from Dowlais; the school should not be sited in a public park; the cost of the necessary conversions would be too much; the scheme was too ambitious; working-class children would be sent out to work not to school. A deputation went to see the Council. All these objections had to be heard

Enoch Morrell

and overcome. Enoch Morrell as chairman of the Education Committee stood firm and insisted that a new secondary school at the Castle was in the best interests of the Borough. The structural conversions, greater and more expensive than first envisaged, had to be carried out, but not before the architectural plans were approved by the Welsh Department of the Board of Education, loans raised for the building work, and consent gained from the President of the Local Government Board. The conversion work together with furniture came to almost £22,000.

In May 1912 the ILP held its National Conference at the Olympia Rink, Merthyr. Its founding chairman had been Keir Hardie who, in 1912, was one of Merthyr's two MPs. Unanimously the delegates at the Rink passed the following resolution:

> That this Conference expresses its strong disapproval of the policy of the Board of Education in regard to higher, elementary and secondary education, inasmuch as that policy is directed at making the opportunities for education beyond the elementary school the monopoly of the middle classes, and [Conference] demands that ample facilities for secondary and higher education for the children of the workers shall be provided by the state.

In Merthyr they were preaching to the converted. Plans for the brand new secondary school in Cyfarthfa Castle were already coming to fruition. The two 'departments' were to be quite separate: boys on the ground floor and girls on the first floor; with different entrances, separate assembly halls and staff rooms. They shared, however, the school motto: 'Rhinwedd o Flaen Clod' (Virtue before Fame).

By the autumn of 1912 teaching staff were being recruited. The headmaster of the Caedraw school, the bearded and heavily moustached Scotsman George Fleming, was appointed Cyfarthfa's first headmaster. Born in 1856, a Master of Arts graduate of Edinburgh University who gained a Teachers' Certificate (First Class) in 1876, he had taught in Galashiels Public School before being appointed Headmaster of Dowlais Advanced Elementary School in 1882 and in 1890 head of the school at Caedraw. Tall and dignified and a firm disciplinarian — caning of course was part of daily

George Fleming

school life — he preferred to use the Scottish leather tawse rather than the cane. He was appointed in October 1912 at a salary of £275 per annum advancing to £300 after 12 months from the opening of the school.

The first headmistress was 30-year-old Miss Juan Evans, a former pupil at Merthyr's County School and a graduate of University College, Aberystwyth. She had taught English and French at Llandeilo County School and was currently senior French mistress at the County School for Girls, Norwich. Her commencing salary was £225, advancing at the end of the first year to £250. So she received £50 per annum less than Fleming although there would be one third more girls than boys in the school.

Male assistant teachers were appointed on a salary of £150 p.a. advancing by annual increments of £10 to a maximum of £180. Female assistant teachers were appointed at £120 p.a. advancing by £5 yearly to a maximum of £140.

What Kind of School?

After all the delays, the opening day finally arrived. Just after 3 pm on Thursday 16 January 1913 'in the presence', as the *Merthyr Express* put it, 'of hundreds of Merthyr's best known citizens' Frank Treharne James as chairman of the secondary schools committee opened the building with a large golden key. Within a few yards of the Castle, he said, a Roman road used to run from Penydarren Park to Brecon via Pontsarn. On the new road to the Castle, 'instead of the tramp of the Roman legions, the road will echo to the children's feet on their way to a free secondary school situated on one of the finest sites in Wales'. Other speakers included Enoch Morrell, Tudor Crawshay, a grandson of William Crawshay II who had built the Castle, and D. W. Jones. Alfred T. Davies, secretary to the Welsh Department of the Board of Education, was unable to be present but wrote:

I have taken the deepest interest in your Town Council's scheme for acquiring the Castle and devoting it and its grounds to the highest interests of the people of Merthyr. It was the labour of the latter in earlier times which helped to create the material wealth which made the erection of the Castle possible; it is surely fitting, therefore, that the present generation should now enter into possession, through their children, of what [the] industry of their forefathers brought forth.

Let [the Council] never have any doubt that they did the right thing in acquiring this fine open space, with its stately building – so bound up with the history of the industries of your town – and in dedicating both, for all time, to the service of the people.

Councillors and parents were then taken around the brand new school. The next two days, Friday and Saturday, the Headmaster and the Headmistress attended the school to interview parents and impress upon them the importance of children attending regularly. On Monday 20 January 1913 teaching commenced.

And then, after the opening there was constant rain and snow. Anyone who has walked to the boys' entrance along that open terrace in front of the school with the rain sweeping across from Aberdare will know what that means. Juan Evans, the new headmistress, remembered 'it was with a feeling of great responsibility and somewhat of awe that we entered into possession of our Castle'.

What a day was that! Who of us that were present can forget it? – three hundred pupils gathered together in the Central Hall, all waiting to be placed in classes, all ignorant of the geography of the building, each full of excitement! Who can forget having to sit in turns on the floor, as there was not enough seating accommodation! Then there was the problem of dividing seven teachers between twelve classes, and doing work without books. How it rained and snowed that week! Merrily did we improvise umbrella stands in the wash basins, and try to shut our eyes to the fact that our unwiped boots were transforming our floors to coal black hue. What ingenuity was displayed during the dinner hour, when for lack of other accommodation, we ate our lunch sitting even on the washing troughs!

Juan Evans

Altogether there were 542 pupils, 336 girls and 206 boys. Their ages in that first intake ranged from 11 to 18 so that teaching from the beginning entailed some sixth-form work. In the Girls' School 209 came from the Caedraw school, 36 were pupil-teachers, and 91 had passed 'the scholarship'. In the Boys' School there were 60 'scholarship' winners. Among the boys who entered that polished interior for the first time were 76 whose fathers were underground workers. Two future teachers at Cyfarthfa were also in that first intake of boys: Victor Bale (Woodwork) and miner's son Idris Morgan (Mathematics).

So, in January 1913 there was a building, with teachers, with girls and boys and a future as a secondary school. But what kind of school was it to be? Not as envisaged by O. M. Edwards. His original vision was that the building would also contain a technical school and both Frank Treharne James and Rhys Elias, Merthyr's Director of Education, believed there should be a strong bias towards commercial and science subjects. Merthyr after all was an industrial town. Technical instruction in engineering and metallurgy with appropriate workshops had been originally contemplated but in the event did not materialise. In the full inspection of the schools that was held in June 1913 their absence was regretted. (The reason was probably due to the cost. There were complaints in the Borough about the increases in rates as the council undertook new schemes, usually it must be said to catch up on years of neglect.) After the inspection a small committee was set up to investigate whether there were rooms suitable for conversion to engineering studies but the issue was lost sight of during the World War that came soon after.

There is a postscript. In 1917 Seymour Berry offered the council £10,000 for a technical and mining school to be called the J. M. Berry Institute in memory of his father. A site was found in the north-east corner of Cyfarthfa Park and when increased costs threatened the project Berry doubled his original offer and raised £33,000 from local firms. However, the Board of Education delayed giving approval and in time the funds were used to give scholarships to students at other technical institutes. Eventually in 1929 a technical institute was opened at Quakers' Yard for evening students and in 1937 provision was made for pupils aged 13 to15.

But overall the inspectors in 1913 were impressed by the work at Cyfarthfa especially in the girls' department, and by the magnificent park which 'would have an uplifting influence upon pupils of a town generally devoid of scenic or architectural beauty'. Their Report concluded that the youngest county borough in Wales had 'partly through its foresight and energy and partly through good fortune' made better provision for its daughters than any other place in the country. The school with its two 'departments', swiftly seen as separate schools for boys and girls, was therefore recognised by the Board of Education as a Secondary School which the 1904 Regulations defined as one that offered a four-year course of study in four groups of subjects: English language and literature, History and Geography; at least one language other than English; Mathematics and Science (theoretical and practical); and Drawing. Clearly the education envisaged was academic.

The syllabus in the Girls' School did offer some variety. After a general course in the first two years girls could choose either an academic course (for entrance to university or training college}; a commercial course introduced in September 1914 (including short-hand, typing, and book-keeping); or a domestic course (to prepare for becoming teachers of domestic subjects, or matrons, housekeepers, dressmakers, etc). Nonetheless, the emphasis was still academic, opening up university and college opportunities and avoiding the stereotyping that would have exclusively pushed girls into domestic studies, nursing and secretarial work. Furthermore, the pupils who came from Zoar and Caedraw were already launched upon the path to school teaching or the professions and when more and more pupils arrived after successfully passing 'the scholarship', there were obviously a number who were academically able.

Shortly after the Cyfarthfa Schools opened, a controversy broke out. The secondary schools committee decided that pupils should buy text-books, subject to parents' income. Two years later the policy ended following a debate in which Morrell declared: 'We want it to be the inalienable right of every child in the borough to have the opportunity to develop his (sic) faculties to the fullest extent . . . it was distinctly understood that this school was to be an absolutely free secondary school'. From 1 January 1915

Dressmaking Room

all text-books required by pupils attending Cyfarthfa were provided by the Council.

Early Successes

The combination of new laboratory facilities, quality teaching, and the entry of talented older pupils enabled Cyfarthfa to claim early academic successes, important for a school without academic traditions and whose very existence had been criticised. They also set a benchmark for future pupils. Henry Thomas, son of a collier, entered the school in 1913 from Caedraw aged 18. A year later he won an open mathematical scholarship to University College, Cardiff. Also from Caedraw came 16-year-old Francis Davies who went on to University College, Cardiff and the University College Hospital, London, before eventually becoming Professor of Anatomy at Sheffield University and a Fellow of the Royal College of Surgeons. Another entrant from Caedraw was fifteen-year-old Samuel Bloom, son of Merthyr's Rabbi Eli Bloom. Samuel and his brother Myer, who also attended Cyfarthfa, went on to University College, Cardiff, before becoming well-known local doctors. Harris Teitelbaum, who entered in 1916, became an ear, nose, and throat specialist who counted Chiang Kai-Shek, leader of nationalist China, among his clients. Another early scholarship boy was Glyn Maliphant who went straight from school into the wartime Navy but later became a Fellow of the Royal College of Surgeons.

Girls too were soon entering and graduating from universities, with Dorothy Lloyd in 1919 the first. Among the early scholarship girls were the Griffiths sisters – Rosentyl and Bryneilon – who both went on to qualify as doctors, the first girls to do so from the school. These successes in the medical profession were helped by Cyfarthfa in 1920 becoming the borough's centre for teaching Zoology and Botany. Sixth form pupils were taught in mixed classes and pupils in other schools who desired to follow this course could be transferred.

A 'scholarship boy' in the first intake was Gilbert Horton who many years later became headmaster of the County School. Reginald Freedman, the first pupil to go to Cambridge, entered Cyfarthfa in 1914 and later became a well-known local solicitor. As Merthyr Council had wished, Cyfarthfa was giving opportunities to bright boys and girls, many from working-class backgrounds. An outstanding later example was Aubrey Jones from Penydarren who went from Cyfarthfa to the London School of Economics and by the 1950s was a Tory Cabinet Minister, perhaps the first boy from a working-class background to do so (see *They Made Their Mark*). It was not an outcome the ILP had envisaged!

Encouragement to academic achievement came from the Education Committee in 1920 when, under Morrell's influence, it awarded the boys' and the girls' schools three School Leaving Scholarships valued at £30, £25 and £20 per annum, tenable at a university for three years, and awarded for academic achievement in public examinations. Further help for those going into higher education came from Seymour Berry (Lord Buckland) and, for the children of ex-servicemen, from the British Legion.

The public examination requirements were stringent. Initially Cyfarthfa pupils sat the Oxford Board Local Examinations which from 1933 were replaced by those of the Central Welsh Board (CWB). Both required a candidate to sit papers in English language, Mathematics, at least one other language than English, a science subject and one other subject and to pass in all five before a School Leaving Certificate could be awarded. The pass mark was 40 per cent. In order to 'matriculate' and gain entry into the sixth-form to undertake studies for the Higher Certificate and entry to university a candidate had to get 'credits' in all five subjects, which meant achieving 50 per cent in each one. Pupils who gained 70 per cent in any subject were awarded a 'very good' or 'distinction' in that subject. Faced with these hurdles, a number of pupils eventually repeated fifth-form work in order to re-sit the School Certificate, some to gain it and others to achieve the 'matric', which dominated the curriculum. The hurdles were made higher by an anomaly. Initially, the eleven-year-old boy entrants had been placed, as might be expected, in Form I but strangely - we know not when or why - Form I disappeared and boys began their Cyfarthfa experience in Form II. It meant that they sat the CWB examination after four years, rather than the five taken by the girls.

World War One

Hardly had the schools begun to settle down when in August 1914 the Great War erupted across Europe. Despite predictions that it would be 'over by Christmas' it stretched into the succeeding four years. The Red Cross was given permission to use the Castle as a temporary hospital 'should the occasion arise'. Fortunately, it never did. The war which seemed far away was yet always present. Boys who were old enough, left school and joined the army or navy. Concerts and plays were held in both schools to aid war charities. The girls set up knitting clubs to make gloves, socks and scarves for refugees and soldiers and sent many parcels to the trenches. The trains bringing the injured back from the Western Front thrust the horrors of war into local homes. And then it was over. Miss Davenport, newly-appointed headmistress, as one of her first acts, organised a spectacular 'Pageant of Peace'. Some boys demobilised from the forces in January 1919 actually returned to the school to refresh their studies before going on to college in September. But seven former pupils

WW1 Memorial Plaque

did not return: William Charles Redvers Dando, David Daniel Davies, Simon Haines, John Hopkins, Howell Wyndham Powell, David Howard Roderick, and Ivor Richard Thomas. Each one had entered the school on that first day.

On 20 November 1924 a memorial was unveiled in the school. It was in memory of the seven boys killed in action and in gratitude for those pupils who came back from 'the blood and mire of death-strewn battlefields'. The funds for the memorial were raised by an Old Boys' Association whose president was the former headmaster George Fleming, by then retired. He unveiled the plaque and it was dedicated by the Rev. Harry Thomas, a first-day Cyfarthfa entrant who had been severely wounded in the war. Both made deeply moving speeches. Twenty-eight years later Thomas, as Bishop of Taunton, was to dedicate a memorial to the 52 pupils and one staff member who died in World War Two.

The Early Head-Teachers

The initial head-teachers did not stay long but they laid foundations and set standards on which their successors could build. Juan Evans, the first headmistress, stayed for four years and with dignity and charm created an atmosphere and 'tone' that remained. She encouraged the acquisition of pictures by the school, believing 'that pictures are scarcely second to books as a means of education'. She introduced a system of prefects and established a lively magazine (*Baner Y Castell*) in July 1914 that appeared regularly each term until 1917 when, for unknown reasons, it ceased. In addition to printing poems and articles it reported sports events, lectures, debates and Christmas parties. The Debating Society, established in the Autumn of 1913 with Dorothy Lloyd as secretary, had a long and flourishing life that included guest speakers and debates on such issues as 'Are Expeditions worthwhile?', 'The modern girl versus her grandmother' (there were 25 votes to 13 in favour of the modern girl) and 'should girls have the same education as boys?' (the majority said 'yes'). The girls do appear to have had a livelier time than the boys. Inter-school hockey matches were played and sports days held in co-operation with the boys until the 1914-18 war caused their suspension. Juan Evans left in December 1916 to marry.

The second headmistress was Miss Cecilia Newton, a graduate in both arts and sciences of the University of London and a teacher at Tottenham

Cecilia Newton

High School for Girls. She organised the school into houses and encouraged internal competitions in sport, music and singing. Tall, straight-backed, she carried herself with dignity and expected the girls to do the same. Boys should not be spoken to when walking to and from school, not even if they were a brother! An incident remembered by Bryneilon Griffiths speaks volumes for the headmistress's influence. When pupil Harris Teitelbaum plucked some roses while walking home through the park and presented them to one of the girls, 'a girl prefect at that, she maintained strict decorum and marched ahead apparently heedless of the gallantry'. Cecilia Newton left after little more than two years to marry Merthyr businessman W.R. Williams and after her marriage remained active within the social and adult educational life of the town.

George Fleming retired in 1921 and received a special resolution of thanks from the Education Committee for guiding Cyfarthfa Boys' School through its first years. His task had been to do exactly that: to launch and steady the ship on its course. Already 56 when appointed he was unlikely to be an innovator, but he ensured that school activities were maintained despite the war, that a high proportion of candidates succeeded in meeting the certificate requirements of the University of London with 75 achieving matriculation standard, and with flexibility and common sense he enabled Rosentyl Griffiths to study Physics and Chemistry in the Boys' School. (The amusing aspects of this episode are remembered by Rosentyl in the *Reminiscences* chapter).

Apart from his reputation as a stern disciplinarian, he is remembered for introducing a prefect system within the small sixth form and for expecting its members to wear straw boater-hats with blue and yellow bands, to and from school during the summer months. This fashionable head-gear, which the girls also wore, might not have been easy to carry off in a coal and steel town. Perhaps it was in recompense that sixth-formers received an annual invitation to tea at his home in West Grove.

The Boys' School had 12 assistant masters and the Girls' School 8 assistant mistresses, a number that soon increased to 17. In both schools there was a fairly rapid turnover of staff as women teachers left to get married (at that time women who married were not allowed to teach) and masters found other jobs or enlisted in the forces. Yet, some became a core that would influence generations of pupils. J. R. Evans taught History from 1913 to 1930; Henry Evans taught Maths from 1913 to 1934; Sam Adams, remembered by many as 'a brilliant exponent of English language and literature', served from 1913 to 1936; and Arthur Beynon taught Woodwork from 1913 to 1939. Among the teachers who departed was Cyfarthfa's senior master, Thomas Jacob Thomas, the Chemistry teacher and composer of the school song 'Ienctyd y Castell' (Youth of the Castle) who as 'Sarnicol' won the chair at the National Eisteddfod in Abergavenny in August 1913. He became in 1922 the first headmaster of the newly opened Quakers' Yard Municipal Secondary School which drew its pupils from those who lived in the lower part of the Borough, including some already in the lower forms at Cyfarthfa and the County.

Another who left was Isaac J. Williams who combined teaching Art with being curator of Cyfarthfa Museum. After one year he became the first Keeper of Art at the National Museum, Cardiff. A more remarkable transition occurred when Henry Harris, who taught Geography from 1913 to 1916, left to become a medical student at University College, London and eventually became Professor of Anatomy at Cambridge.

In the Girls' School a similar core emerged. Margaret Jenkins taught Needlework from 1913 to 1942, Hettie Morris taught Welsh from 1913 to 1948, Elsie Sharpley taught Science from 1916 to 1947, Gertrude Jones taught English from 1917 to 1952, and Gladys Kenshole taught Maths from 1917 to 1954.

The Setting

The Castle, the Park, and the nearness of open country made an especially strong impression upon those early pupils, as they did to later generations. To Blodwen Davies from Troedyrhiw, a miner's daughter, one of thirteen children, and a scholarship winner in 1913, it remained a source of wonder throughout her life that she should have been chosen to go to a school in such beautiful surroundings: a park with a lake and the needlework room set in one of the round towers, like a medieval fable. She revelled in this new world. Haydn Perry, who entered the school in 1919, remembered how 'half-a-dozen of us would rush out at dinner-time and hare up Cefn and down to the river Taff where we managed to get in a short spell of swimming in one of the pools.'

> I was tremendously lucky in going to the Castle. Physically, the school was romantically-tremendous – a castle (although pseudo) standing in acres of grounds, with many lakes, the remains of an ice-house, Crawshay's original coach, a first-rate museum. Why it beggars description . . . We roamed like noble savages through the woods, around the lakes, along the gravel paths. We took part in the earliest forms of love-play, for we threw the girls' hats into trees, dropped leaves down their backs, or pushed them into the bushes. Those were halcyon days!

Miss Davenport

The retirement of Cecilia Newton in 1919 and George Fleming in 1921 opened the way for two dominant personalities to take over during the twenties and thirties and for the Castle Schools, contrary to original intentions, to consolidate as secondary schools providing a largely academic education.

In the spring of 1919 Annie Chamberlain Davenport, aged 34, science mistress at the County School, was appointed headmistress at Cyfarthfa. There she remained until her retirement in 1945. Miss Davenport was Cyfarthfa School for Girls. She was tall, elegant, decisive, compassionate, and a strict disciplinarian. Educated at Howell's Girls' School, Llandaff, and University College, Cardiff, 'the Dame' was recalled with admiration for decades after her departure. On her retirement in July 1945 a member of the education committee referred to her as 'the Queen of Cyfarthfa' and the usually undemonstrative councillors gave her 'an enthusiastic cheer'.

'The Dame', Annie Chamberlain Davenport

An idealist who agreed with Browning that a man's (and a woman's) reach should exceed their grasp she set standards to which all 'her' girls should aspire. Shortly after being appointed she spoke at the 1920 speech day.

> I venture to say that in the past it has been too easy to become a teacher in this borough, and it has not been necessary to 'strive mightily'; indeed, a lazy girl of quite average intelligence could quite easily obtain the bare academic qualifications required, and this has led her to being satisfied with a meagre qualification, and having no ambition beyond this. If the present shortage in the demand for teachers will do something to mitigate this evil and cause girls to develop to the utmost the power that is within them, then, I say, that will be a good thing for the teaching profession.

She insisted that Cyfarthfa girls should be recognisable everywhere by their deportment, good manners, and clear diction. The award of a yellow sash (known as 'a girdle') for deportment was, in her words, 'a much coveted honour'. She drew up reading-lists for each form so that girls would read something of the great authors. She saw to it that prints by old masters decorated the corridors and emphasised the importance of exercise and gymnastic training. Each year there was a physical exercise and dance display. She introduced a school orchestra and annual Shakespeare productions: involving pupils in music, scenery design, painting, and costume making, as well as acting.

She recruited mistresses who were to give long service and contribute to the school's corporate life in many ways: Gwladys Jones taught Art from 1920-49, Ellen Morgan, Maths, 1921-43, Annie Lewis (Lewi Geoger) Music and Geography, 1921-60, Nellie Jones, Domestic Science, 1922-56, Ethel Williams (Willie Hist), History 1924-63, Mary Addie, Physics 1926-1965, Mildred Jones, French 1929-64. Nancy Thomas (Tommy Lat), Latin, 1930-65. Her determination to get the best is exemplified by her writing in 1921 to Walford Davies, then professor of Music at Aberystwyth and later Master of the King's Music, asking him to recommend a person to teach

Taken on the roof of the Castle in 1945, this shows the Girls' School Staff on the occasion of Miss Davenport's retirement.

Back Row (l-r): Miss James (Maths), Mary Davies (PE), Stella Coburn (Biology), Veigan Hughes (German). Middle Row: Edith Thackery (Needlework); Mildred Jones (French), Nancy Thomas (Latin), Ethel Williams (History), Mary Adie (Physics), Elsie Sharply (Chemistry), Kathleen Harrison (Music), Glenys Evans (English). Front Row: Gwladys Jones (Art), Annie Lewis (Geography), Nellie Jones (Cookery), A. C. Davenport (Headmistress), Hettie Morris (Welsh), Gertie Jones (English), Gladys Kenshole (Maths).

Music. It was on his recommendation that Annie Lewis came on to the staff. The girls' choir she trained was 'exceptional' said Davenport, praise not lightly given. A branch of *Urdd Gobaith Cymru* flourished under the guidance of Hettie Morris.

The upstairs school hall and wooden corridors shone in a way that was never equalled downstairs. An inspection report in 1937 noted: 'The choice selection of pictures, together with the good taste displayed in the arrangement of flowers and plants, set up a high standard of cleanliness and beauty for the pupils'. The classics and science departments assumed greater importance as did modern languages with the addition of German in 1934; the teaching of commercial subjects was encouraged. The academic standards of the school rose, girls began to win scholarships to a range of universities. And the good relationship she had established with George Fleming continued with his successor, D. J. Davies.

D. J. Davies

David John Davies followed George Fleming as headmaster in 1922 and remained so until his premature death in 1941. When appointed he came from Llanelli County School but he had also taught at Queen's College, Taunton, and Cirencester Grammar School. His path to the headmastership had not been conventional. Born in New Tredegar, he had worked underground aged 12, assisted in his father's bakery, attended night classes in science and art, and eventually won a Glamorgan County Scholarship to University College, Cardiff, where he gained an honours degree in science. After brief periods of teaching in Beaumaris and Carlisle he entered Sidney Sussex College, Cambridge, where he took a first-class honours degree in History. His combination of intellectual ability, practical experience and sound commonsense brought innovations to Cyfarthfa that soon became accepted as 'traditional'.

He introduced Welsh language into the curriculum in 1924, thereby redressing an omission criticised by Glyn Jones, a Cyfarthfa pupil 1917-23, in his *The Dragon Has Two Tongues* (published in 1968). It also increased pupil numbers by about 40. He gave greater responsibilities to sixth form prefects; in 1926 he established the House system with sporting competition between the houses; in 1927 he replaced the St. David's Day concert with a school *eisteddfod* where houses competed against each other

D. J. Davies

for a house trophy; sporting activities were given extra time. A major annual event from 1922 was the prize-giving day held in the Miners' Hall, attended by the boys and girls, senior councillors and education officials, with well-known speakers to present the prizes. It was the occasion too when both heads reviewed the academic, social and sporting achievements of the past year.

The prize-days deliberately focussed attention on academic achievement as increasing numbers entered training colleges and universities. There were high-flyers with Lilian Morris becoming the first girl to win a State Scholarship in 1924, followed by Lydia Williams (1925), and Eunice Rees (1928). The first boy to do so was Bleddyn Thomas (1930) followed the next year by A. J. Francis, by T. V. Davies (1934), Ralph Twomey (1936), and Gareth Davies and Glanmor Williams (1937). (State Scholarships founded in 1920 and awarded for academic merit, paid university tuition fees. They were means tested.) In addition to these awards there were each year pupils who gained Open Scholarships to universities, Aberystwyth being a frequent destination. The range of subjects at Higher Certificate level was widened through the heads arranging that sixth-form boys and girls would be taught in mixed classes using both men and women teachers. By 1937 boys were studying Latin, Welsh, Botany and Zoology in the Girls' School whilst girls attended the Boys' School for Modern History, Geography, Mathematics and French. Clearly, the segregation of boys and girls, although often reported, was far from universal, probably occupying the thoughts of juniors more than their seniors.

Sport

From the beginning sporting facilities at both schools were rudimentary – there was no gym and very poor playing fields. The Pandy field was slag and ash. The girls had to play hockey on what Miss Davenport referred to as 'the hill' where the school canteen was later built and where the Park visitors' centre and splash pool are now sited. Until Gwaunfarren baths were opened in 1924 swimming took place in the lake, dependent upon wind and weather. After the baths were opened, however, the school

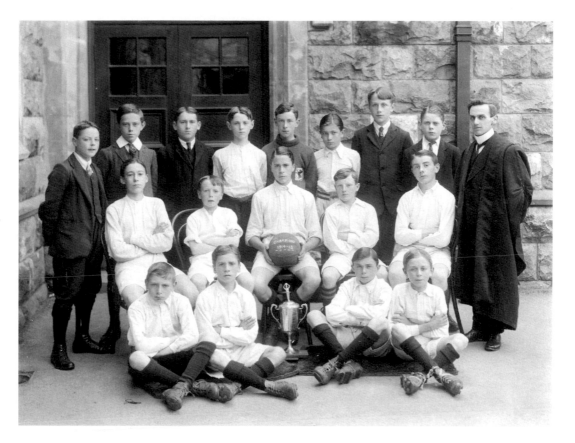

*The Cyfarthfa team that won the Merthyr Schools' League Championship Cup in
1914-15.*

*Back row (l-r): G. A. Horner, G. Horton, H. Davies, E. Jones, D. T. Jones, W. C.
Webber, R. Davies, A. Jones, Sam Adams (master). Middle row: J. R. Thomas, J. B.
Parry, R. Owen (Capt), W. Williams, D. G. Lewis. Front row: J. Bow, R. K. James, R.
E. Lewis, A. Powell.*

developed a tradition of producing excellent swimmers, early examples
including Frank Hawkins and Peter Phillips. In 1933 John H. Thomas won
the Welsh Diving Championship. The swimming gala, held every year
since 1924 and open to the public, was always an exciting occasion. So too
were the annual sports days held at Penydarren Park. Merthyr's traditional
enthusiasm for and prowess at boxing found occasional expression

through Cyfarthfa boys: in 1925 T. Barnes won British and Welsh boxing championships at 7 stone 7lb; in 1933 Stan Thomas won a Welsh schoolboy boxing championship (the same Stan Thomas who later became a Freeman of the Borough); and in 1938 P. Toomey won the British 6 stone 7lb schoolboy title.

Merthyr has always been known as a soccer town and for its first fifteen years Cyfarthfa was a soccer school with very successful junior and senior teams. Eddie Jones, Aneurin Jenkins, Lewis Owen and Eddie Rowlands all

First XV 1933-1934

won Welsh Schoolboy Caps, with Rowlands captaining the Welsh team in 1920-21. Three former pupils, W. J. Evans, D.J. Gilbert and Clifford George went on to play for Wales in amateur internationals. The change to rugby came in 1928, although former pupil Bryn Phillips had been capped by the

Welsh Schools in 1925 and 1926. The team made steady progress and in 1931-2 no opposing team crossed its try line and in 1933-4 it lost only one match. As the photo show, Elwyn Thomas gained a Wales schoolboys 'cap'. In cricket, despite not having a suitable field, the team blossomed in 1933 reaching the final of the Schofield Shield, a competition open to all secondary schools in Glamorgan. The next year, under the captaincy of Colin Howatson, the team went one better and won the Shield, for the first and only time, beating Quakers' Yard School in the final by five wickets.

New Blood

In these social, sporting and academic achievements, the Boys' School was helped by an infusion of new blood when, just as in the Girls' School, young graduate teachers joined the staff, most of them remaining for the next 30 years and longer – Evan Davies (Dai Bump) taught Physics from 1919 to 1950; Tom Whitney, English (1920-51) ; Idris Morgan, Maths, who also trained the boys' choir (1924-62); Lewis Lewis, French (1929-62), Arthur (Gus) Harris, Geography (1929-65) who encouraged drama; Dan Jones, P.E. (1930-72); Havard Walters, Welsh (1930-72) who nurtured the eisteddfod; and Gwilym Williams (Nero), History (1930-65). In November 1923 the opening of the oak-lined reference library and reading room, situated where the Crawshay's former harness and saddle room had been, provided the boys with a valuable resource.

By 1929 an inspection report could reflect: 'The school is building up for itself sound traditions of culture, scholarship and athletics; the boys are cheerful, alert and well-behaved, and should develop into worthy, thoughtful citizens'.

The Ashes of Vesuvius

Yet these achievements took place in the grimmest years South Wales has experienced. 'Unemployment' reported *The Times* in 1928 'descended like the ashes of Vesuvius and overwhelmed whole towns': Merthyr was among the worst hit. Well over 12,000 jobs disappeared between 1921 and 1931. By 1934 62 per cent of the Borough's insured population was unemployed, in Dowlais the figure was 80 per cent; by 1938 unemployment assistance – 'the dole' – was costing half-a-million pounds a year in Merthyr. A hundred years of industrial development and painful advance towards a civilised society had culminated in the Means Test and Protest marches, mass emigration, widespread misery and malnutrition, and an undermining of local government. Between 1921 and 1939 almost 27,000 people left Merthyr: an average of 1,500 people every year.

Education could not escape the consequences. Merthyr Council was proud of its no-fee policy and of the fact that it provided a higher proportion of scholarship secondary school places than any other urban area in Wales. But in 1933 the government imposed an annual fee of £9 for entry to secondary schools. The Council strongly protested having to abandon its no fee policy, especially in the prevailing circumstances; but a deal struck with the Board of Education considerably mitigated the effects. No fees were payable where the parental income was £3. 10s. 0d, or less, and only when the weekly income was more than £6 was the full fee liable.

More significant was the tide of emigration that took children away from the school — 'It is clear that we are providing higher education for pupils who will serve other areas' reported headmaster D. J. Davies in 1936. Most significant was deep and wide-spread poverty. Forty per cent of secondary pupils in the borough in 1932 had parents who were unemployed or widowed. No wonder that in the mid-thirties almost half of Cyfarthfa boys left at the statutory school leaving age of 14 without even sitting for a School Certificate, while in the Girls' School the proportion approached 70 per cent. Their parents could not afford to keep them there, particularly if there was a chance of some kind of job, and there was indeed a market for cheap juvenile labour. Even those with the 'matric' could not afford to enter university unless they won state or open scholarships in nation-wide competition. The full inspection of the schools in 1937 revealed that only 15.6 per cent of those who left the Boys' School in 1933-36 went on to higher education, the percentage in the Girls' School being 27.6 (with 16.5 per cent of the girls entering training colleges).

Boys' School Staff 1936. Back Row (l-r): Lewis Lewis (French), Idris Morgan (Maths), Gwilym Williams (History), W.C. Bickley (Chemistry) Arthur Gus Harris (Geography), Tom Whitney (English), Dan Jones (PE). Seated: Evan Davies (Physics), ?, ?, J. R. Davies (Headmaster), ?, ?, J.R. Williams. In Front: Havard Walters, Ben Roy Jones.

Many who might have entered the professions were shunted into dead-end jobs with much talent wasted.

Would the situation have been different if the original intention of teaching technical subjects at the Boys' School had been carried out? From 1924 to 1941 the headmaster frequently returned to this in his annual reports, believing that technical instruction should be given in a secondary school 'where theory and practice may be properly combined'. In 1939 he regretted his lack of success in bringing a metal workshop to the school in order to equip pupils for the openings that might come if new factories were established locally. Yet, throughout the twenties and thirties, with local industries outdated and depressed, it is more than likely that technically trained boys would have joined the exodus to the engineering works in Oxford, Slough and Coventry, the destinations of so many Merthyr people.

Despite all the disappointments and difficulties, it was during these depression years that both schools established themselves. Influenced, as all municipal secondary schools were by the public school model of uniforms, 'houses', 'house colours', 'prefects', and teachers in gowns, the schools through the yearly rituals of prize days, sports days, swimming galas, *eisteddfodau*, plays and concerts, became living institutions in the fabric of the Borough and in the minds of their pupils. The 1937 inspection of the Girls' School summed up what was also true of the Boys': 'Throughout the many years of industrial depression from which the district has suffered it is pleasing to note that a vigorous, happy community life has been steadily maintained within the school'.

War Again

At 11.00 am on Sunday 3 September 1939 Neville Chamberlain announced that Britain was now at war with Germany. As so often before, war brought work to Merthyr. The coal and steel industries revived, unemployment fell as men and women joined the armed forces and, because Merthyr was thought to be an unlikely target for bombing raids, new factories moved in. At the height of the war some 5,600 workers in the Borough, half of them women, were employed in factories making chemicals, explosives and electrical components for aircraft. Merthyr was also seen, along with other valley towns, as a safe reception area for children evacuated from the English towns most in danger from bombing and invasion.

In the Dunkirk summer of 1940 invasion seemed a stark reality. On 4 June Churchill rallied the nation in one of the twentieth century's great speeches: 'we shall fight on the beaches, we shall fight on the landing grounds, we shall fight in the fields and in the streets, we shall fight in the hills; we shall never surrender . . .' Two days before this speech, 3,200 children carrying gas masks, ration cards and identity cards departed from Folkestone Central Station for the safety of south Wales. At 9 am the first train left for Merthyr Tydfil over 250 miles away. It carried 350 evacuees from Harvey Grammar School, 216 from Folkestone Girls' County School, 135 from the Grange (Folkestone Junior Technical School), and 91 from Stella Maris (Roman Catholic school) together with teachers and helpers. There were also 716 children from various Deal junior and infant schools among the evacuees. Not until around 5.30 that afternoon did the passengers finally reach Merthyr, tired, dispirited and apprehensive about what awaited them.

They need not have worried. As the train ran into Merthyr station a banner over the platform read 'Welcome', there was a line of flags and a poster 'Folkestone gets a Deal at Merthyr'. In the High Street people five or six deep assured the boys and girls that they would be happy in Merthyr. At the Miners' Hall there was a meal followed by a medical; there was much sorting out and checking to be done but by 10 pm all were in their new homes.

When it came to allocating pupils to schools, those from Folkestone Junior Technical School went to Quakers' Yard Junior Technical and to Quakers' Yard Secondary Schools, and those from Stella Maris went to Dowlais R. C. Schools. The evacuees from Deal, some of primary and infant school age, went to appropriate local schools throughout the Borough. Altogether, in the autumn of 1940 1,686 evacuees were being taught in the Borough's infant and junior schools.

Harvey Grammar School and the Folkestone Girls' County School found a home in the Castle but retained their separate identities, the Cyfarthfa boys and girls using the Castle from 8 am to 12.45 pm and the Folkestone schools from 1 pm to 5.45 pm. There was nonetheless some interchanging of staff with Cyfarthfa masters teaching Maths and Physics to the Folkestone boys and a mistress from Cyfarthfa Girls' School teaching the Folkestone boys French. The Cyfarthfa gym and art mistresses taught the Folkestone girls. These time-tabling arrangements were too tiring and disruptive to continue for long. At the end of the first term the fifth and sixth forms from Folkestone remained in the Castle but from September

1940 their forms 1-3 were housed in Georgetown school with the fourth form following in 1941. One of the Harvey masters, Arthur Giardelli, who taught French and English, was dismissed when he registered as a conscientious objector; but in 1942 Merthyr council employed him to teach violin at the Cyfarthfa and County schools. 'Jelly-Belly' was a familiar figure in war-time Merthyr and later became a distinguished adult education lecturer and innovative artist.

In time, the number of evacuees fell as some failed to return from holidays, or parents found work elsewhere and their children joined them, or older pupils joined the armed forces. While Merthyr largely escaped enemy attacks, Folkestone was in the front line of bombing and cross-channel long-range shelling from German occupied France. In 1940 the 'Battle of Britain' was fought in the summer skies above the town as Spitfires and Hurricanes attacked incoming German bombers and their Messerschmitt fighter escorts. As late as 25 September 1944 a long-range shell hit the Harvey Grammar School building, destroying the headmaster's study and the library. Soon afterwards those guns were captured by Allied forces and it was considered safe for the evacuees to return. On 23 December 1944, just in time for Christmas, 550 boys and girls returned to Folkestone, of whom 140 were Harvey Grammar School pupils.

Those who served

Just how many ex-Cyfarthfa boys and girls served in the armed forces during 1939-45 we do not know; four of the younger masters served – Spencer Jones, R. D. Owen, Ben Roy Jones, and Havard Walters (who volunteered in 1940). One master, R. D. Owen (a pilot officer), one girl (Valmai Anderson) and 52 boys were killed in action and they were commemorated by a plaque in the downstairs hall in the Castle. Ten decorations for bravery went to those in the Royal Air Force: six receiving the Distinguished Flying Cross, squadron leaders Ken Francis and D. W. Griffiths showing exceptional courage by winning it twice. Four gained the Distinguished Flying Medal – Flight Sergeants E. Sullivan, A. Driver, J. V. Bevan and T. Watts. Chief Petty Officer Peter Phillips of the Royal

Navy (surely the boy who excelled at swimming) was awarded the Distinguished Service Medal. Among those in the Army, Captain D. G. Rees received the Military Cross and Sergeant E. G. Berryman the Military Medal.

A New Headmaster

Two years into the war on 3 November 1941 D. J. Davies died. His end after a long illness was not unexpected but the sense of loss was tangible.

J. R. Williams

Many tributes were paid to the unsparing work he had done for the school and to the considerable contribution he had made to town life. After a brief interregnum, John Rhys Williams succeeded him as headmaster in February 1942. 'JR' had been French master at Cyfarthfa since 1921 and a major personality within the Boys' School. Known as 'JR', or 'Froggy', he had been born in Cefn Coed, educated at Brynmawr County School and then University College, Bangor. A strong disciplinarian, he projected an aura of firm (for many, fearful) authority and soon became known as 'The Boss'. Thoroughly familiar with all aspects of school life and an efficient administrator, he had no difficulty in maintaining the school's traditions and academic standards, while encouraging its social and cultural activities. His immediate task was to ensure that relations with the Harvey Grammar School continued on a friendly and even path, which they did. He was the last headmaster of the separate Boys' School and during the immediate post-war years the dominant personality in ensuring that the amalgamation of the Boys' and Girls' Schools in 1946 was smoothly achieved.

Despite wartime pressures and the use of temporary staff in place of those on active service, academic standards remained high in the Folkestone schools and at Cyfarthfa. State scholarships were won by Eryl O. Davies (1940), J. Desmond Price (1941), Sybil Rees and Gareth Rogers (1942) and Joseph Evans (1943). Open scholarships continued to be won to a range of Universities including Aberystwyth, Oxford and Imperial College, London. Many boys, of course, had to enter the armed forces upon leaving school as did, for example, Gwyn A. Williams who won an Open Scholarship to Aberystwyth in the summer of 1943 but by November was in the army. (For his later career see *They Made Their Mark*.) Not all the highflyers returned; among those who fell were Desmond Price and Joseph Evans.

The Flagships

The war also brought a determination to build a better world, expressed most clearly in the Beveridge Report of 1942 and the Education Act of

1944. The 'Butler Education Act' abolished all fees for state schools, the 'scholarship' examination became known as 'the eleven plus'; 'senior' elementary schools became secondary modern schools and municipal secondary schools were to be designated 'grammar schools'. The school leaving age was raised to 15 as from 1945 (subsequently postponed to 1947). In truth, viewed from Merthyr it was a cautious Act, for Merthyr Council with its high intake into secondary education and no-fee policy had anticipated it by 31 years. In 1938 the proportion of secondary school places in Merthyr was 23 per thousand of the local population compared with an average of 17.8 for all Welsh county boroughs.

When in 1908 Merthyr councillors had enacted their vision of giving working-class children the benefits of a secondary school education, the Castle Schools had been the flagships of that policy. The two young comparatively small schools at Cyfarthfa had produced from the most working-class town in Wales, teachers and lawyers, university professors and doctors, surgeons and ministers of religion, engineers and pharmacists, dentists, vets, and high level civil servants. It was a record of which the schools and local councillors were proud. There was, however, growing and justifiable concern about those who had not, for various reasons, entered higher education or fulfilled their promise in other ways. In the affluent fifties and sixties a much higher proportion of pupils was enabled to follow that path. But those were years of unprecedented change.

YEARS OF GROWTH AND CHANGE:
1945-1972

MANSELL RICHARDS

Wales ... an old stronghold of grammar schools ... so that they could surpass the public schools by example and academic excellence.

(Labour in Power 1945-1951, Kenneth O. Morgan)

On Thursday, 19 July 1945, only ten weeks after the surrender of Hitler's Germany, an excited Cyfarthfa Boys' cricket team left Merthyr for the 200-mile rail journey to Folkestone. They were responding to an invitation from the grateful staff and pupils of Harvey Boys' Grammar School who had recently returned to their homes from the safety of Merthyr Tydfil. That weekend in Kent was a great success. The Cyfarthfa boys, thanks to Glyn Evans of Jones Terrace, Dowlais, gained a notable victory in a traditional heartland of English cricket. Glyn, a tall athletic sixth-former, was the 'hero of the hour' for in a remarkable spell of fast left arm bowling, he took seven wickets for 20 runs.

This apparent return to normality after the turmoil of the war was swiftly shattered. A heated debate broke out in Merthyr over a proposal to amalgamate the separate girls' and boys' schools, a change that took place in the next school year 1946-47. A generation later, the change to

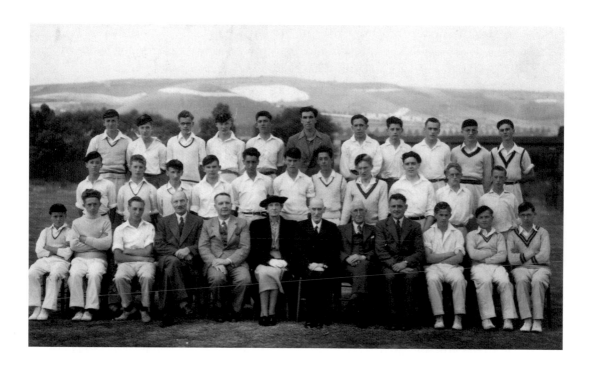

The Cyfarthfa and Harvey Grammar School cricket teams. Not all the Harvey boys can be named. Back Row (l-r): Mick Bowler, Clem Agonbar, ?, Tommy Walsh, ?, Frank Harris-Jones, Willie Charles Evans, Humphrey Prothero, ?, Graham Lewis, John Cynog Price. Middle Row: B. Ayling, Len Spicer, ?, Randall Watkins, Bernard Bridgland, Gus Griffiths, Glyn Evans, Graham Gossage, John Ellis, JC 'Jayce' Evans, Mick Allan. Front Row: Alan Chamberlain, John Whiting, John Berville (Capt.), Mr. Redhouse, J.R. Williams (Cyfarthfa Headmaster), Lady Mayoress, A.B.Downing (Harvey Headmaster), Cllr Rule, Dan Jones, Gareth Hughes (Capt.), Gordon 'Tucker' Thomas, Gerwyn Watkins.

comprehensive education during the years 1970–72 would be even more 'revolutionary'.

How Two Schools Became One

The retirement of Miss Davenport, headmistress of the Girls' School, in July 1945 marked the end of an era in more ways than one. W. T. Owen, Merthyr Tydfil's visionary Director of Education seized the occasion to advise the Education Committee of the advantages of merging the two schools of 355 girls and 301 boys, into one co-educational Cyfarthfa School. This startling recommendation sent shock waves through the female staff room. A petition against amalgamation was organised, while strongly worded letters of opposition from both Miss Davenport and the lady teachers appeared in the *Merthyr Express* (the male teachers appear to have offered no objection). The proposal also produced disquiet among many parents. The schools, located on separate floors since their opening in 1913, had remained distinct entities, with their own proud traditions, separate entrances at the front and rear of the school, assembly halls, staff rooms and classrooms. Apart from some co-operation in sixth-form work, they could have been located in different parts of the town!

W. T. Owen put forward three main arguments in favour of his proposal. First, the boys' school with a two-form entry of 60 pupils each year was too small to provide for an effective sixth form. The girls' school being larger, offered a wider range of subjects denied to the boys, including Greek, Latin, German, Botany and Zoology, although he argued, the girls too, would benefit from a wider range of subject choices, including the emphasis on higher Mathematics and Physics in the boys' school. Second, staffing a single school inside the Castle would be more cost-effective, with fewer teachers required in the future. Finally, he envisaged 'a richer corporate life', with improved extra-curricular activities, including 'expanded school societies, instrumental music-making and drama'. Adding power to his argument, he pointed out that the average pupil numbers in Welsh secondary schools were increasing (the two Cyfarthfa schools were relatively small), while Merthyr Tydfil's other selective schools, Merthyr Intermediate (County), and Quakers' Yard Municipal Secondary School had been 'co-educational' from their foundation.

The anti-amalgamation campaign quickly gained ground. Two well attended meetings in the autumn of 1945 were held in Merthyr's Town Hall. The first chaired by Captain William James, the borough coroner and son of Frank Treharne James, (chairman of the schools' original foundation committee); the second by Longville Bowen, managing-director and editor of the *Merthyr Express*. Both men had daughters at the girls' school. The paper reported arguments ranging from the disservice to girls' careers, the possible disappearance of headmistresses and the proposed reduction in the numbers of female teachers, to the views of one man who commented:

> I am the father of girls and I want to pay tribute for what is being done for them. I may be old-fashioned but I don't agree with boys and girls in mixed classes, they should be separated between the ages of 12 and 16.

A sixth form boy agreed totally with amalgamation but a girl argued that both schools should be merged for extra-curricular activities only.

Not the future of a nunnery

At a meeting of the Education committee, the Director urged members to keep an open mind:

> We are discussing neither the *Merthyr Express* ... nor the future of a nunnery, nor that of a school for the refined daughters of rich gentlemen ... we are concerned with the future, with long term policy affecting two schools. We are concerned with principles rather than priorities; with the future of 600 children and not with the views of 20 employees (female), however estimable ... In my view, good as the Cyfarthfa schools are at present, they are not as good as the combined school should be.

Despite this strongly-held belief, a resolution opposing the merger of the two schools was carried by 81 votes to three at one of the public meetings.

However, the *Merthyr Express* reminded its readers that the great majority of Cyfarthfa's pupils (including the girls) came from ordinary working-class homes where money was tight. The newspaper commented sympathetically, 'Parents send their children, often at great personal expense'.

The firmly focused Director of Education persevered with his 'one school' campaign, eventually winning the argument within the Education Committee, where his proposal was adopted with only two votes against. Both sides now lobbied the newly elected Labour Government in London. Ellen Wilkinson, the Minister of Education, sent inspectors to report on the situation and in early May 1946 she wrote to say that she accepted the proposed amalgamation.

The influence of the boys' school headmaster, John Rhys Williams (1942–53) in effecting a smooth and successful transition for both staff and pupils cannot be over-estimated. He led the 'new Cyfarthfa' with the help of two senior mistresses, initially Hettie Morris (Welsh) and later Gladys Kenshole (Mathematics) until his retirement in July 1953. A strong disciplinarian, the appearance in corridor or classroom of his stern countenance produced an immediate effect. But senior pupils saw a more relaxed side. His sense of humour, allied to firmness of purpose is well illustrated by the occasion when J. R. stumbled across three card-playing boys in an empty classroom. Unaware at first of his presence at their shoulders, their anguish was not eased by his vividly remembered advice, 'I would play the Jack first if I were you' followed by the ominous instruction 'afterwards all three of you get to my room'!

The newly amalgamated Cyfarthfa Municipal Secondary School almost immediately acquired a change of title. In 1947 as a result of the 1944 Education Act, it was designated a 'grammar school' as were Merthyr's other selective schools, the 'County' and Quakers' Yard.

The Great Freeze

But it was the extreme winter of early 1947 which made a greater impact. From late January to early March children and teachers were forced to grapple with the 'Great Freeze'; the arctic blizzard conditions and deep bedroom height snow drifts, preventing many children from emerging from their streets, let alone attend school. For several weeks, to the delight of many, schools remained closed that winter. At Cyfarthfa (in parts of the Park snow lay over five feet deep), every effort was made by the Park's employees and the school caretaker to open the school at the earliest opportunity, especially to pupils in their examination years.

A New Economic Base

The snow and ice of 1947 almost brought industry to a standstill, threatening Merthyr's fragile economy. The closure of local ordnance factories at the end of the war had created 5,000 unemployed in October 1945, 7,000 by the summer of 1946 and a return to pre-war depression seemed imminent. But from 1946 the Attlee government began directing firms away from overcrowded English regions, providing Merthyr with the manufacturing base it sorely needed. Hoover Washing Machines, Teddington Aircraft Controls, Lines Brothers, Thorns' Atlas Lamps, BSA, and Export Packing, now appeared alongside the flourishing pre-war Kayser Bondor and OP Chocolates factories and wartime ICI plant in Pant. The historic GKN Dowlais Steel Foundry to the north and the newly nationalised deep coal mines to the south completed a scenario of relatively full employment across the County Borough.

Despite continuing post-war austerity, with a wage freeze in 1948 and most major foodstuffs rationed until 1954, the families of pupils attending Cyfarthfa and other Merthyr schools were now better off than at any time since the end of World War I. In addition to regular pay packets there were the benefits of the newly created National Health Service and the early Welfare State. Nonetheless, some of Merthyr's early and mid-Victorian housing remained unfit for human habitation. Indeed, more than one Cyfarthfa pupil completed his or her homework in the shadow of a gas lamp or in a bedroom lit by flickering candlelight.

New momentum

But a release of new energies and a quickening of pace at Cyfarthfa followed the difficult war years. Returning to the school were servicemen, keen to resume their teaching careers. These included Havard Walters (Welsh), Ben Roy Jones (Mathematics) and Spencer Jones (English). They were soon joined by new enthusiastic teachers such as Jane Owens (Mathematics), Claudia James (Instrumental Music), May Treharne (Latin) and Ann Thomas (Art). Among the new male arrivals were Mervyn Powell (Maths), Lionel Fisher (Chemistry) and Bernard Jenkins (English).

An acceleration of cultural, sporting and social developments followed. In 1948 keen anticipation pervaded the school following an invitation to participate in 'Top of the Form', a popular BBC Radio, inter-school quiz. The nationally known broadcaster Richard Dimbleby chaired the programme from the downstairs hall; but Newport High School proved too strong for Cyfarthfa's team of sixth-former Vincent Lee (a later head of the school's English Department), future college principals Joe England and Alyn S. Davies, and third year pupil Michael Allan. (Perhaps a representative from Cyfarthfa's girls would have brought richer rewards!).

The Sporting Scene
The war's end brought some reflected glory to Cyfarthfa with the news that former pupil Hywel Davies of Tai Mawr Farm, Gellideg, a Welsh Schools' rugby cap and Open Exhibitioner to Brasenose College, Oxford, had gained his 'Blue' in the Pole Vault. Despite the school's relatively poor facilities, the hockey, cricket, athletics and rugby teams more than held their own against other South Wales schools. Among the creditable achievements in the summer of 1945 were those of sprinter Colin Williams and the Senior Boys' Relay Team who won their events in the 220 yards and relay respectively at the Welsh Schools Championships. Among the sporting highlights of the late 1940s was the 1947 success of Eric Baker in winning the Welsh Junior 100 yards Breast Stroke title in record time. Similarly, several of the girls contributed to Cyfarthfa's and the Merthyr Swimming Club's reputations, the grace and style of the contemporary Hollywood star, Esther Williams, finding local expression in the success of Pauline Prosser, Pat Wade and Carole James as Welsh Schools' Champions. Meanwhile, soccer success returned to the school in 1949 following a 20-year concentration on rugby only, with a talented team, captained by Mansil Morgan (a future three-times Mayor of Hungerford) winning the coveted Keir Hardie Shield.

First XI Girls' Hockey Team 1945/46. Back row (l-r): Cynthia Jenkins, Betty Smith, Sheila Reed, Miss Mary Davies (PE teacher, daughter of S.O. Davies MP), Pat Wade (Head Girl), Nansi Ellis, Pearl Barsi. Front row: Dorothy Drew, Zoë Richards, Nona Wilks (Captain), Edna Rees, Mair Owen.

Some High Achievers

Major contributors to the school's post-war music reputation were Glynne Jones, future flamboyant conductor of the Pendyrus Choir; Harold Nash, later principal trombonist at the Royal Opera House, Covent Garden (see *They Made Their Mark* for both); Peter Hill, who became chief clarinettist in the Band of the Royal Scots Guards and John Newman and Terry Strachan, talented viola players. Nesta Lewis, a fine piano accompanist, shared many concert platforms across the U.K with her tenor-soloist husband, David Leyshon Williams. Other accomplished piano players in those years were Carol Hickey, Val Price, and Ann Lindsay.

Some prospered later in the world of science and industry. Terry Jenkins and John Spackman, are both noted in the chapter *They Made Their Mark*. Peter Harris Jones and Vernon Lewis respectively became directors of

Rolls-Royce and Pirelli. Their contemporary, Gareth Daniel, popular concert compere and brilliant after-dinner speaker, later became a governor of the newly formed Cyfarthfa Comprehensive School and first chairman of its PTA.

There were also academic achievements. Gareth Hughes, later to be awarded a golfing 'Blue' and Frank Harris Jones, head prefect, both won admission to the University of Cambridge in 1945. Basil Arthur (1947), Howard Williams (1947), and Geoffrey Leonard (1948) all won State Scholarships and Graham Lewis in 1948 won an open scholarship to Aberystwyth. The achievement of a State Scholarship was regarded as an honour both for the individual and for the School and its announcement in school assembly was followed by the declaration of a day's holiday, much to the delight of pupils and staff!

The Early Co-educational Years

The school year 1946–47 was different from any previous year. It opened with the ground floor echoing to the sound of some 300 girls' voices; while the highly polished corridors, classrooms and upstairs hall, became part of an everyday experience for all boys, not just a few sixth-formers. No longer would images linger such as those recalled by early war-years sixth-form pupil, Gwyn Alfred Williams: 'Boys at the bottom of the staircase, girls at the top, and a form of frustrated social tension occasionally present, half-way up'. Nor is there evidence that the new co-educational Cyfarthfa improved or reduced educational standards. Possibly the more conscientious female approach to school studies encouraged some Cyfarthfa boys to work harder, despite undoubted distractions. Certainly, the arrival of the fairer sex in the rather gloomy classrooms and corridors on the ground floor did much to brighten the lives of the boys. Recalling the change, former cricket captain, Gilbert Williams, over 60 years later, likened the presence of Cyfarthfa's girls to 'the pleasing sound of the first cuckoo in spring'.

Inevitably, a period of adjustment followed: some of the Cyfarthfa staff discovered the need for new teaching skills. One or two male teachers who had taught in a firm, authoritarian manner, more suited perhaps to boys, were quickly jolted into awareness that loud and high-pitched commands and voluble criticism contributed little to the motivation of girls. Similarly, a few lady teachers, encountering teenage boys for the first time in their careers, soon realized they had been untested to deal with the sometimes disruptive tendencies of mischievous male adolescents. But overall, the transition passed smoothly.

For the pupils the most exciting change was the mixed Christmas parties. These soon became eagerly anticipated occasions and a popular lead-up to the wider Christmas festivities. Several weeks of dancing classes temporarily replaced rugby and hockey lessons, the initial disappointment felt by some rugby stalwarts, soon evaporating with the arrival of the girls in the upstairs gymnasium. Former male pupils (and more than one suffering female partner!) will recall nervous, sometimes clumsy attempts at the St Bernard's Waltz, the Fox-Trot, the Gay Gordons and the Conga on party night, the latter forming an energetic finale around the Castle's corridors. Many a serious sixth- form courtship commenced at Cyfarthfa's Christmas Dance, while other teenage couples held regular Saturday night trysts at Merthyr's YWCA, the Kirkhouse, the Miners Hall and the Dowlais Catholic Hall.

There was too the annual trip to Stratford-upon-Avon. From 1948 this excursion organised by the English Department became a popular event. The riverside Memorial Theatre echoed to performances from some of the country's most celebrated actors and actresses. But if truth be known, a number of Cyfarthfa's apparently studious male students derived greater enjoyment from the hiring of one of the many boats in which to row the girls along the tree-lined Avon. Polite conversation, between those senior male and female pupils fortunate enough to share a back seat on the long return journey to Merthyr, was another source of pleasure forever associated with the occasion.

With the end of the 40s in sight, it was clear that the foresight and perseverance of W. T. Owen, Merthyr Tydfil's Director of Education, allied to the firm leadership of Headmaster, J. R. Williams, supported in turn by good quality teachers, had laid firm foundations for the new co-ed school.

Into the 1950s

The 1950s opened with Merthyr Tydfil basking in sporting success. The town's football team were recent winners of the Welsh Cup and acknowledged leaders of national non-league soccer. Eddie Thomas had recently become British, Empire and European Welterweight Boxing Champion. Cyfarthfa's contribution to this sense of wellbeing was mainly

Cast of Macbeth *1951. Back row (l-r): John Williams, Marcel Pulman, John Lewis, Gilbert Crook, Geoff Hosgood, Brian Duke, ?, Geoff Rose, Michael Allen.*
Middle row: ?, Gwyneth Williams, Joyce Chappel, Alyn S. Davies, Bella Jacobs, Glyn Llewellyn, Bernard Jenkins, Gwyneth Burley, Philip Jones (Madoc), David Leyshon Williams, John Knott, Marie Bracchi, Connie Ulyett, Elizabeth Atkins, Gareth Davies, Gareth Williams.
Front row: Brian Bell, Peter Smith, Glyn Evans, Bryn Powell, David Hosgood, Windsor Lewis, Keith Oates, Peter Murray, Colin Mulcahy, Anthony Johnson

cultural. Under the direction of Bernard Jenkins, senior English Master and survivor of World War II Arctic convoys to Russia, a talented cast in the downstairs hall gave long-remembered performances in Shakespeare's *Macbeth* during the dark, cold winter evenings of December 1951. The title role was played by sixth-former Philip Jones of Bryn Street, Twynyrodyn, who displayed the skills that, as Philip Madoc, later made him a highly successful actor (see *They Made Their Mark*). But there were admired performances also from Gwyneth Burley (as Lady Macbeth), David Leyshon Williams, Michael Allen, Marcel Pullman and Geoff Hosgood.

Within two or three years, *The Tempest, A Midsummer Night's Dream* and Marlowe's *Dr. Faustus* had been performed before an appreciative Merthyr public. Then in 1954, an exciting departure from tradition occurred, with a production of Gilbert and Sullivan's *Pirates of Penzance* under the direction of music master, D. Gwerfyl Davies with former pupils Ira James and Pamela Evans in the lead roles.

In 1959–60 came splendid repeat performances of *A Midsummer Night's Dream* to mark the official opening of an impressive purpose-built school hall-gymnasium (that replaced the former downstairs hall now converted to classrooms). For the first time in 80 years, the ruined stables and coach-house at the northern end of the Crawshay mansion had been given modern purpose.

A thriving Old Students' Association

Many former Cyfarthfa students had returned to the town following war service, eager to renew school friendships. Thus a new Association was formed. Its success owed much to the drive and enthusiasm of the hard-working secretary, Ron Gethin, an old boy of the school but now geography and geology teacher at Merthyr County Grammar School. Ron and his committee implemented well-supported activities, including square dances on Friday nights in a Dowlais building purchased by the Association. The long remembered formal dances, held in the upstairs school hall at Easter, Mid-Summer and Christmas always created an overwhelming demand for tickets.

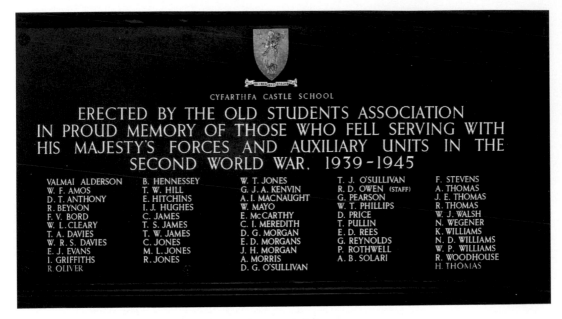

CYFARTHFA CASTLE SCHOOL

ERECTED BY THE OLD STUDENTS ASSOCIATION IN PROUD MEMORY OF THOSE WHO FELL SERVING WITH HIS MAJESTY'S FORCES AND AUXILIARY UNITS IN THE SECOND WORLD WAR, 1939-1945

VALMAI ALDERSON	B. HENNESSEY	W. T. JONES	T. J. O'SULLIVAN	F. STEVENS
W. F. AMOS	T. W. HILL	G. J. A. KENVIN	R. D. OWEN (STAFF)	A. THOMAS
D. T. ANTHONY	E. HITCHINS	A. I. MACNAUGHT	G. PEARSON	J. E. THOMAS
R. BEYNON	I. J. HUGHES	W. MAYO	W. T. PHILLIPS	R. THOMAS
F. V. BORD	C. JAMES	E. McCARTHY	D. PRICE	W. J. WALSH
W. L. CLEARY	T. S. JAMES	C. I. MEREDITH	T. PULLIN	N. WEGENER
T. A. DAVIES	T. W. JAMES	D. G. MORGAN	E. D. REES	K. WILLIAMS
W. R. S. DAVIES	C. JONES	E. D. MORGANS	G. REYNOLDS	N. D. WILLIAMS
E. J. EVANS	M. L. JONES	J. H. MORGAN	P. ROTHWELL	W. P. WILLIAMS
I. GRIFFITHS	R. JONES	A. MORRIS	A. B. SOLARI	R. WOODHOUSE
R. OLIVER		D. G. O'SULLIVAN		H. THOMAS

WWII memorial plaque

But soon the Association was turning its energies to a more worthy project. In April 1952, an impressive memorial was unveiled at the school to the fallen of World War II. The dedication service was conducted by the Bishop of Taunton, the Right Reverend Harry Thomas another Cyfarthfa old boy who, in 1924, had dedicated the school's memorial to the young victims of World War I.

Two years later, another memorial-plaque was presented by Mr and Mrs Ecclestone of Twynyrodyn, the parents of Squadron Leader Ronald V. Ecclestone DFC, AFC, a former pupil of the school who died while flight-testing a Handley Page Victor. His story is told in the chapter *They Made Their Mark.*

Concerts and the Eisteddfod

By the early 1950s, the annual school *eisteddfod* held on or near Saint David's Day, and presided over by Havard Walters, the committed Welsh teacher, had become a major event in the school calendar. Neither school

Havard Walters presides over the chairing of the bard, Diane Wilce 1961.
Pupils include Sally Davies, Catherine Duggan,
Lynda Powell and Sandra Samuel.

hall was large enough to accommodate Cyfarthfa's 600 plus pupils and so the venue moved first to Tabernacle Chapel, then to Park Chapel and later to the Miners' Hall.

From mid-January, most lunch hours were taken up with rehearsals by the various house choirs, both junior and senior, with the appointed senior pupil conductor and accompanist determined to gain 'a first' on the day. Perhaps the most dramatic moment came with the appearance of the house captains, dressed in white bardic robes, supporting the proud, sometimes self-conscious 'chair-poet' to the accompaniment of harp or piano and trumpet. Flanked on stage by an external adjudicator and by Mr Walters, the latter then uttered the three times questioning declamation, 'a oes heddwch?' (is there peace?) as the heavy, silver-mounted eisteddfod sword was simultaneously inserted into its sheath. By the 50s, moreover, the names of the school 'houses' had been changed from the unimaginative North, East, South and West to Caradog, Hywel Dda, Llewelyn and Owain Glyndwr, titles more appropriate for the Saint David's Day celebration of Wales' Patron Saint.

The girls' choir had long established an excellent reputation. Now a mixed choir brought variety under the baton of Idris Morgan. Indeed, following male requests, an initially reluctant Annie Lewis (Lewie Geoger) was persuaded to start a mixed madrigal group, with great success. The end of summer term concert, with the school orchestra making its full contribution, became an eagerly awaited occasion, with hardly a seat unoccupied in the upstairs hall.

Cyfarthfa pupils regularly brought honour to themselves and the school with as many as six or seven in some years being members of the National Youth Orchestra of Wales. In 1959 the school's strong reputation for choral singing was recognized when Cyfarthfa Girls and Neath Girls Grammar School were the first to be selected by Her Majesty's Inspectorate of Schools to inaugurate exchange visits 'between those schools, which have a long and acknowledged tradition of choral singing in Wales'.

Examination Reforms

In 1948 the Central Welsh Board had been replaced by the Welsh Joint Education Committee (WJEC) which put in place a number of reforms. In the school year 1950–51 the General Certificate of Education (GCE) was introduced at Ordinary (O) Level, and for sixth form pupils the Advanced (A) Level replaced the former 'Higher' examination. These changes were generally welcomed, particularly as they also ended the rigorous regulations associated with the 'matriculation' requirements of the Central Welsh Board. These had often been an obstacle to pupils wishing to enter the sixth form and the subsequent pathway to university or college (see Chapter 1). Many who did not gain 'matric' then left to embark on a successful career in local government, or nursing, commerce or local industry, with a sound but non-matric school leavers' certificate.

But the WJEC also introduced a regulation that briefly caused uproar in all Welsh secondary schools: no pupil could sit the O level examination who was under 16 in the preceding December. (For a brief period the eligibility date became the preceding September.) The regulation meant that the brightest pupils not yet 16 were held back a year, and pupils whose parents could not afford to keep them in school beyond the leaving age of 15, had to leave before gaining O levels. The regulation was short-lived. From 1953 heads of schools were given full discretion over the age of examination candidates.

Despite these radical changes to the examinations structure no great change was introduced to Cyfarthfa's curriculum. Only one or two new subjects appeared on the school timetable. Human Biology (particularly useful for those entering the nursing profession) and Scripture became available to pupils studying for the new GCE (O) Level qualification, while in the sixth form Geology answered a need for many Geography A Level candidates. Economics was added in the 1960s.

Discipline

Discipline remained strict. Corporal punishment for boys was accepted though not over-used at Cyfarthfa. But for girls and boys the ubiquitous 'order mark' and more seriously, the 'conduct mark' for a variety of misdemeanours, was, whenever possible, not divulged to parents. Detention at lunch-time and occasionally after school hours, was available to staff, as was ordering the writing of two or three hundred repetitious 'lines', usually of meaningless educational value. Cyfarthfa, in common with most schools had its share of naughty pupils but there was little awareness of the need for a more positive and encouraging form of discipline. Few Welsh grammar schools in the 1950s saw this as part of their remit.

A New Headmaster

In July 1953, J.R. Williams retired after 34 years service to the school, first as French master in the former boys' school and latterly as Headmaster. In his final boys' assembly, those senior boys who were members of the school orchestra's brass section, quietly and unnoticed, brought their

W. Lloyd Williams

instruments into the back row of the hall and at the assembly's conclusion, after head boy Joe England's call for 'Three Cheers for the Headmaster', they struck up 'For He's a Jolly Good Fellow'. It was picked up by some 300 boys and provided a fitting and emotional end to the Boss's career.

His successor, 45-year-old W. Lloyd Williams from the mining community of Treharris brought a contrast in style of leadership. Silver haired, quietly spoken, a reserved man of neat, well-groomed appearance, he was a graduate of the University College of Bangor, where he had gained a Master's Degree. He possessed a scholarly and independent mind and under his direction, the record of the school in work, sport and cultural pursuits was enhanced. A year later in 1954, the senior mistress, Gladys Kenshole, retired, having started in the girls' school during the World War I as a teacher of mathematics. She was succeeded as senior mistress by Annie Lewis.

Widening Opportunities

In the late 50s and the 60s more and more families could afford their children to stay on at school and realise their potential. Merthyr Council, emerging from the cash-strapped 1930s and 40s, was able to finance more clothing grants and school meals. And from 1956 the Ministry of Education enabled the Council to increase the grants for those entering higher education and provide, for the first time, travelling expenses, allowances for courses during the vacation and grants for instruments. These changes, combined with the 'Bulge' in school population (caused by the increase in the birth-rate immediately after the war) resulted in an increasing number staying on at school, with a dramatic leap from 574 pupils in 1957 to 658 in 1958, then the largest recorded number. School-leavers entered a wider range of universities, teacher training colleges, colleges of further education, art, horticultural and agricultural colleges while Lloyd Williams in his annual report for 1958–59 lauded the school's achievements in science. He noted that 14 out of 19 who entered university that year pursued science degrees, and also that 75 per cent of the boys who qualified for university from Cyfarthfa did so in science. By contrast the average from the Public Schools was 50 per cent, while from the grammar schools of Glamorgan it was 60 per cent. But Lloyd Williams also expressed disappointment with the continuing trend for girls to leave school early:

Some girls who have done particularly well at the General Certificate of Education left school early to work in offices, although they had the intelligence and character qualities which would have enabled them to take a degree ... although opportunities of higher education for girls have increased immeasurably in recent years, girls are almost as reluctant today to take advantage of their opportunities as they were thirty years ago.

State Scholarships in the 50s went to John Thomas (1951), Gwyneth Williams (1952), Geoffrey Rose (1953), Carol Edmunds (1954), Graham Rees (1955), Philip Wyn Jones and David Knapp (both 1957). Other highflyers were David Tongue (1953) and David J. Parry (1959) who won Open Scholarships, as did Graham Rees and David Knapp. Among the well-known pupils who attended Cyfarthfa in the 50s were Mansel Aylward, Stanley Thomas, (both featuring in *They Made Their Mark*), and Mario Basini, who became literary editor of the *Western Mail*.

Sport

The mid-50s brought soccer success, with the school winning the coveted Keir Hardie Shield in consecutive years, while the girls' hockey team of 1958–59 had an unbeaten season. David Jones and David Cornwall gained County representative honours at cricket with Roland Jones being selected for the Welsh schools team. Meanwhile, Gareth 'Gatz' Jones (1956) and Mansell Richards at Twickenham (1957) represented Glamorgan Schools at rugby, the latter also appearing in the Welsh Secondary Schools' 'final trial' match, while the school's powerfully built head boy, Arnold Garbett, won a 'cap' in 1959, against England Schools at Cardiff Arms Park. Stanley Thomas became a Welsh School's Boxing Champion, while several Welsh national awards were secured in athletics and swimming. Donald Griffiths won the 100 yards breaststroke at the Welsh Schools' Championships in successive years, John 'Moffin' Morris became a record-breaking javelin thrower, while Clive Ward and Arthur Williams achieved Welsh national success in the discus and 220 yards respectively. Meanwhile the school's newly formed chess club, the brain child of Maths teacher Graham Roblin, produced success for Derry Prothero (a future Head of Music at the

Senior Cricket Team 1950–51. Back row (l-r): Howard Rees, Degwel Jones, Clem Roberts, John Young Lewis, Glyn Llewellyn. Middle row: Geoff Hosgood, Mansil Morgan, Philip Jones (Madoc), J.R. Williams (Headmaster), Noel Davies (captain), Dan Jones (PE Master), Terry Jenkins, John Hywel Williams, Tom James. Front row: Johnnie Harris (scorer).

school), Harry Davies and Herbert Mueller in the Welsh Schools' Chess Championships.

Senior XV 1955–56. Back row (l-r): David Knapp, Gwyn Pearce, Clive Pugh, Howard Brougham, Geoffrey Webb, Victor Ellis, John Gillespie, Brian Stonehewer, Leonard Lee, John Kinsey. Front row: David Evans, Mansell Richards, W. Lloyd Williams (Headmaster), Wilfred Roberts, Dan Jones (PE Master), Arnold Garbutt, John Crimmins, Leslie James.

Into the 1960s

The ending of compulsory military service in the early 60s signalled the end of the disciplined society of the war and immediate post-war period. The waning influence of church and chapel combined with rising incomes resulted in a decline in deference, a rise in consumerism and the creation of a youth culture that Cyfarthfa along with other schools would have to come to terms with.

Merthyr's landscape too changed. In 1962 Isambard K. Brunel's central railway station disappeared while the Heads of the Valleys Road in 1966 brought fast (sometime dangerous) links to east and west. A modern police station and health centre at Caedraw replaced the nearby Victorian police station and market hall. No longer, after 1966, would Cyfarthfa pupils view the Iron Bridge, which had spanned the Taff since the 1790s, nor the nearby Ynysgau Chapel originally dating from 1749. New council housing estates appeared around the borough.

At Cyfarthfa the 50s had been years of solid and in some cases, outstanding achievement, under the leadership first of J. R. Williams and later W. Lloyd Williams. In the final years of the 1960s a major challenge lay in wait, but first there were years of all-round achievement in music and the arts, academic and sporting accomplishment, extra-curricular activities, charity work and increased international representative honours.

Music and the Arts

There was a flowering of musical achievement by some of the most talented musicians in the history of the school. David Chappell, leader of the Welsh National Youth Orchestra, won an Open Scholarship in 1960 to the Royal Academy of Music (see *They Made Their Mark*). He was joined in 1963 by fellow Scholarship winner and outstanding contralto Alethea Davies. Twynyrodyn's Keith Jones, also entered the Academy and later sang tenor roles at the Royal Opera House, Covent Garden. Anthony Baldwin was another who sang professionally on the British and European opera stages. By the end of the decade, Ann Hooley's violin solos marked her as a future member of some of Britain's finest orchestras. Wendy Roynen, Annette Gwynn, Ann Lewis and later Darya Brill were all accomplished piano players, several becoming accompanists to local choirs including the Dowlais Male Choir.

The school, meanwhile, had broken away from its Shakespearean productions of the 50s, a tradition stretching back to the years immediately succeeding World War I. Fresh, contemporary material was sought. Thus, the 1962 production of Dylan Thomas' *Under Milk Wood* received critical acclaim. Its director, Bernard Jenkins, was the first to acknowledge the contribution of colleagues, Trevor Jones, Vincent Lee,

Staff 1963. Back row (l-r): John Warrender, John Cynon Jones, Vincent Lee, Len Richards, Dan Jones. Third row: Alan Hill, Cliff Bale, Bernard Jenkins, Robert Thomas, Terry Strachan, Dewi Bowen, Roy James, Frank Evans, Trevor Jones, John Barberini. Second row: Chrissie Goodall, Gloria Griffiths, Jean Williams, May Treharne, Mrs Clough, Barbara Watkins, Shirley Thomas, Shirley Vowles, Edith Thackaray, Maude Davies, Nan Thomas, Mair Jones, Jane Owens, Clare Crowley. Front row: John H. Davies, Lionel Fisher, Havard Walters, Gwilym Williams, Lloyd Williams (Headmaster), Ethel Williams Mary Addie, Mildred Jones, Nan Thomas. (Missing from the photograph: Arthur Harris)

(English) and John Cynan Jones (Music) with the difficult stage-sets expertly designed and erected by specialist teachers Victor Bale, Frank Evans and with Dewi Bowen's inventiveness.

Dewi, a Cefn Coed man of considerable artistic skill, had his own distinctive style as an illustrator. He displayed widely over the years in several important exhibitions, including the annual National Eisteddfod of Wales. Conscripted as a war-time Bevin Boy, he qualified at Cardiff College of Art and taught in Cardiff's dockland before arriving at Cyfarthfa in the autumn of 1955. Over the next 30 years, he was to become one of the school's most stimulating teachers and a character who brought laughter into lessons, corridors and staff-room!

Senior Girls with Lewie Geoger, 1960. Back row (l-r): Joyce Broderick, Maureen Barbara, Pat Hughes. Middle row: Janice Jones, Margaret Newman, Janis England, Kathleen Burley, Annette Gwynne, Anne Richardson, Hilary Jones and Margaret Hughes-Jones. Front row: Naomi Bloom, Judith Wilson, Ann Richards, Jennifer Price, Jacqueline Evans, Miss Lewis, Wendy Roynan, Christine Gough, Anne Hennessy, Enid Rachel Williams and Jane Wilding.

Golden Jubilee 1963

The production of *Under Milk Wood* was a preliminary to marking the Golden Jubilee of the school in 1963. On 16 May that year a thanksgiving service in Zoar Chapel was packed to capacity as the school orchestra and choir performed Bach's 'Jesu Joy of Man's Desiring' before pupils, staff and local dignitaries. The guest speaker was the Reverend Ithel Jones, Moderator of the Free Church Council of England and Wales, and a

Orchestra with Claudia James. David Chappell is the leader

former pupil (see *They Made Their Mark*). Later, in August, the School produced a celebratory booklet largely written by deputy headmaster Gwilym Williams (Nero) and with a cover designed by Dewi Bowen.

But the early 60s also witnessed the departure of three inspirational teachers of music. Annie Lewis (Lewi Geoger) had undertaken her work at Cyfarthfa with what the headmaster described as 'religious intensity', winning the devotion of generations of girls. Idris Morgan, long-serving maths teacher and organist at Market Square Chapel, had contributed generously to the musical life of the former Boys' School and latterly as conductor of mixed choral groups. But for orchestral work and the teaching of instrumental music, one name shines through, that of petite, silver-haired Claudia James, affectionately known as 'Fannie Fiddle'. She left to take a post at Monmouth School for Girls, but whilst at Cyfarthfa had produced orchestras of the highest calibre. Her contribution was graphically summed up by the Headmaster who pointed out that since the foundation of the National Youth Orchestra of Wales in 1947, the school had contributed nearly a hundred instrumentalists, a larger number than any other school in the county.

Academic successes

The 1960s were years of high academic achievement at Cyfarthfa that owed much to a decision taken in 1961 by Lloyd Williams. He introduced a 'fast-track' for a group of able pupils who would sit O levels in four years and A levels in six. On the face of it this change was no more than a return to the situation in the former boys' grammar school (pre-1946) whose CWB 'Matric' candidates had traditionally sat the exam in their fourth year (see Chapter 1). But in the more explicitly academic atmosphere that Lloyd Williams now fostered, and in much more affluent circumstances, clever hard-working pupils after 1961 were encouraged to stay on for a *third* year in form six to prepare for Oxbridge and other University Open Scholarships. Undoubtedly this curiously named 'D Stream' (a feature in many Public and Direct Grant Schools), accelerated Cyfarthfa's academic achievements towards the end of the 60s.

Even before this innovation, and underlining the emphasis upon academic standards in the school, Gareth Griffiths, Mansel Aylward, Peter Phillips and Brendon Thomas all won State Scholarships in 1961. In 1962 David Washington won a State Scholarship, Brendon Thomas gained an Open Scholarship to New College, Oxford, while Huw D. Vaughan won an Open Scholarship to Imperial College, London. State Scholarships were discontinued in 1962 but academic successes continued. In 1963 Jeffrey O'Leary gained an Open Scholarship to Imperial College, London, and in 1965 Robert Lynn Williams entered Jesus College, Oxford. (Later, as a Fellow of Downing College, Cambridge, he was tutor to Rowan Williams and Barry Morgan, future Archbishops of Canterbury and Wales respectively. This gifted scholar died in 2002 whilst still a young man.) In

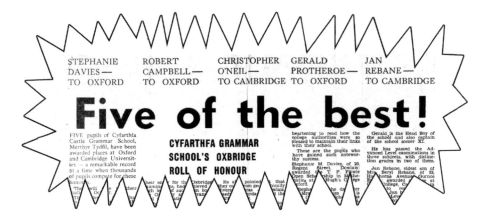

Five of the best

1966 Philip Edge went to Sidney Sussex College, Cambridge, and in 1967 David Walters entered Clare College, Cambridge while also in 1967 Rhodri Walters won a Meyricke Exhibition to Jesus College, Oxford. (His later career appears in *They Made Their Mark*).

But 1969 was Cyfarthfa's academic *annus mirabilis*. Stephanie Davies won an Open Scholarship in Mathematics to St. Hughes College, Oxford, Robert Campbell, a Meyricke Exhibition to read Medicine at Jesus College, Oxford, Christopher O' Neill, gained an Open Exhibition in English at Clare College, Cambridge, Ian Rebane joined him there to read Natural Sciences, and Gerald Protheroe, a future soccer 'blue' went to study Modern History at Jesus College, Oxford. The *Merthyr Express* referred to these successes as 'Cyfarthfa's Roll of Honour' and published a photograph of the five students. However, by the beginning of the 70s, this 'fast track' system had been discontinued, for the change to the comprehensive system in a much larger school added new pressures and priorities to an increasingly complex school timetable.

Some of these sixth-formers entered the European Essay Competition, organised by the Council of Europe in which, year after year schools from 15 different countries submitted essays on a 'European' theme. Cyfarthfa prize-winners included Ann Richards, Gareth Griffiths, Brendon Thomas,

Richard Tinsley and Robert Lynn Williams. In 1966 and again in 1967 Rhodri Walters was a prize winner. This success was continued the following year by Neil Jones, while later, in 1972, head girl, Carole Strachan also figured among top European prize-winners. Cyfarthfa's record of success during the 60s was impressive, some would say remarkable.

But these were by no means the only high-flyers in the School. Alun Morgan became a Schools Inspector, Alan David (Davies) a well-known actor, Jeremy Donne later became a Queen's Counsel, and Huw Williams took first-class honours and flourishes as a well-known local historian. Six from those years feature in the chapter *They Made Their Mark*: Randall Baker, Des Barry, Howard Denner, Ursula Masson (née O'Connor), Peter Thomas and Rhodri Walters.

By 1964–65 post baby-boom pupil numbers were peaking at 776 (426 girls and 350 boys) and a greater proportion was entering the sixth form, universities and colleges than at the beginning of the decade. Cyfarthfa was replicating a clear national trend. Not for the first time, however, Lloyd Williams made a plea for girls, many achieving very good A Level results, to apply to universities rather than teacher training colleges. He was particularly critical of medical colleges for not granting 'equality of opportunity' to girls with a 'special aptitude' and who, 'wished to dedicate themselves to medicine'. Subsequently, John Beale, Merthyr's Tydfil's new and progressive Director of Education, supported by the Education Committee, sent a letter to all the schools of medicine urging the admission of girls.

Sporting Triumphs

As early as 1958–59 the Headmaster had reported the 'best-ever' results for the hockey team. The girls built on this success under the guidance of two motivating teachers of physical education, initially Clare Crowley who left in 1964, and subsequently for nearly 30 years by her former pupil, Jane Type, (née Wilding). Games facilities remained a stumbling block however. Lloyd Williams reported to his Governing Body 'there are few schools with less satisfactory facilities for sport'. Although the boys, under the

Girls' Athletics Team 1965, Glamorgan champions. Back row (l-r): Cerys Morgan, Julia Hobby, Lynda Powell, Ann Hooley, Nesta Evans, Vanessa Brewer, ? , Jacqueline Evans, Lynda James. Seated: Linda Bowen Davies, Lloyd Williams (Headmaster), Tanya Alcock, Jane Wilding (PE teacher), Judy Alcock.

redoubtable Dan Jones kept the Cyfarthfa flag flying proudly, it was the girls who captured the headlines. There were a number of outstanding performances with Angela Hopkins (Shot-Put), Mary Meaney (Long Jump), Judith Alcock (Hurdles), Lynda Bowen Davies (100 yards), and Linda James (Javelin and Shot-Put) becoming Welsh Schools' Champions. Earlier, in 1962, the Girls' Relay Team stylishly won their event at the Women's Welsh AAA Championships, while in 1964–65 the girls remained unbeaten in hockey, winning also every age-group competition at the Glamorgan County Sports. The *Merthyr Express* headline read: 'Cyfarthfa girls smash seven records'.

Senior XV 1967–68. Back row (l-r): Granville Thomas, Phillip A. Davies, Robert Campbell, Kevin Horrigan. Middle row: Tudno Jenkins, Lyndon Jones, Godfrey Lewis, John McCarthy, Hywel Richards, Brent Miles, Peter Thomas, Dan Jones (PE Master), Colin Sayers, James Bryant (captain), John Davies (Headmaster), David Owen, Mansell Richards, John Lloyd, Michael Jones. Front row: Raymond Griffiths, Gareth Hitchens, John Owen, Roger Williams.

But it was Tania Alcock's all-round achievements that stand out: her honours included Welsh Schools 880 yards and Welsh Women's Long-Jump Champion (even though Cyfarthfa did not possess a long jump pit) and captain of the Welsh Girls' team which faced England at Brighton. She also represented South Wales at hockey (there being no Welsh Girls' Team at that time).

Among the boys, Welsh AAA long-jump champion William Jones represented Welsh Schools in 1962 against England and Scotland, while John Williams and John Davies ran for Glamorgan Schools in the Welsh Schools' Cross Country Championships. Mansel Thomas, Roland Jones, Brian Goodwin, Gerald Cavanagh, Elwyn Kinsey and Hywel Richards became final trialists for the Welsh Secondary Schools' Rugby Team, with Beverley Price gaining selection for a Welsh Schools XV versus a Welsh Youth XV. But the outstanding rugby achievement was that of Robert Pugh, a big, powerful prop-forward, who, in 1962, represented the Welsh Schools against England Schools at Twickenham. He became a double schools' international also representing Welsh Schools at cricket.

Soccer too, should not be discounted: in 1965, Cyfarthfa shared the Keir Hardie Shield with Queens Road Secondary Modern School, thereby repeating the triumphs of 1949, 1954 and 1955. The chess club brought further honours. By the 60s, Derry Prothero, Harry Davies, Howard Denner, Allan Beynon, Martin Wilce, I Powell, John S. Davies, Herbert Mueller, David Owen Jones and Paul Williams were making a mark at the Welsh Schools' National Championships. Brenda Blake and Francesca Brookes were selected for the Welsh Schools Team. In 1962, the school won the Victor Freed Trophy as the champion chess-playing school in Wales initially under the supervision of English master Vincent Lee and later, Maths teacher Ian Hopkins, a major contributor to sport, music and pupil welfare at Cyfarthfa for almost 40 years.

The Head proudly noted in 1964–5 that 'The number of international honours gained in hockey, athletics, rugby, cricket and chess, together with Welsh National Youth Orchestra representation, made the year, a record one in the history of the school'.

Outside the Classroom

The value of a school cannot be measured by examination results alone. Extra-curricular activities offer an enrichment of experience at an important stage of pupils' personal development. During the 60s,

Cyfarthfa developed a particularly vibrant sixth form, which provided energetic leadership of the school's clubs, societies and charity work. Many pupils, of all ages, benefited from membership of the Debating, Economics, History and Science Societies, while the Christian Union and *Urdd Gobaith Cymru* flourished. New clubs catered for fly-fishing, judo, jazz and classical music. Cyfarthfa's work for charity (as with other schools) was often commented upon in the local press. Regular sums were collected for the Blind, World Refugees, Dr Barnardo's, Oxfam and other charities, under the supervision of senior mistresses, Mary Adie and later, Edith Thackaray. But it was the 'Save the Children Campaign' under the guidance of Mildred Jones (French), which remained the main annual fund-raising project. Some senior pupils even opened a pre-Christmas charity shop in the town which prompted the regional organiser to comment, 'This is quite remarkable. Cyfarthfa is one of the few schools in the county that helps year after year'.

Change at the Top

In April 1967 the terminally-ill Lloyd Williams died. A man of dignified bearing and considerable scholarship, he had, in earlier years when teaching French, earned the unlikely nickname, 'Flash'. To a later generation, when he was Head, he too was known as 'the Boss'. Not a forceful disciplinarian, he had, nevertheless, during his headship years (1953–67), raised the academic tone of the school, and led the development of a rich and broad-based curricular and extra-curricular experience for many of his pupils. He was succeeded temporarily by the no-nonsense 59-year-old Acting-Head, Havard Walters, who for many years had given committed service to the school. The appointment of John Davies took into account the fast-approaching transformation of Cyfarthfa into a comprehensive school. A former Rhondda Valley Deputy-Head and latterly an education lecturer at Cardiff College of Education, the new Head proved to be a leader of impressive energy and enthusiasm. In his brief headship (1968–72), he made a forceful impact on the school. With cheerfulness and firmness he presided over the debates and turmoil that preceded and ushered in the early years of comprehensive reorganisation.

31 John Davies

The Castle Goes Comprehensive

In 1965 Directive 10/65 had landed on the desks of Directors of Education throughout the country. Later described as 'the most famous circular in the history of the Education Ministry' it requested education authorities to introduce comprehensive education. But the 'request' carried a sting in the tail: government money for all new school buildings was conditional on 'going comprehensive'. Local councils were expected to prepare immediate plans for the creation of large secondary schools, containing 'all-ability' pupils. Merthyr's Labour Council, although proud of the achievements of its schools, embraced Directive 10/ 65 with enthusiasm.

D. Andrew Davies, the recently-departed Director of Education from 1947–64, had pointed the way ahead in a lecture to the Fellowship of Zoar Chapel, in January 1960, entitled 'The Advantages of Comprehensive Education'. Before leaving his post he had added, 'In Merthyr (Secondary) Schools, only about half the pupils pass the GCE, while four out of ten do not sit the examination at all', a fact common at the time in most of the country's local authorities. Despite the academic successes achieved by grammar schools there were pupils in those schools who for a variety of reasons had not fulfilled their potential. Cyfarthfa was no exception. As for those who had failed the eleven-plus it was increasingly recognised nationally that social background was a major influence upon attainment and that not all children developed intellectually at the same pace.

The introduction of comprehensive education was now the task of the newly- appointed Director, John Beale. By September 1967 new purpose-built, schools, Afon Taf at Troedyrhiw and Bishop Hedley (Roman Catholic) at Penydarren had been completed. But for children at the northern end of the borough Penydre High School would not be ready until 1970, and then for partial occupation only and, until government permission for a 'fourth' comprehensive school was received, there would be a 'short- term' plan for pupils going to Cyfarthfa.

This entailed a split-site arrangement after a merger of Cyfarthfa with Georgetown Secondary Modern School (built in 1906). There would be a

Lower School of 460 all-ability pupils, aged 11 to 13, based in Georgetown and an Upper school of 720 pupils, aged 13 to 18, housed in Cyfarthfa Castle. (It would take 12 years before a new Upper School at Cae Mari Dwn appeared, with the Castle then becoming the Lower School following the demolition of the Georgetown School buildings). Behind the Castle, on the site of the former canteen, temporary classrooms had been placed to house the Engineering Drawing, Metalwork and Woodwork Departments.

A Castle Under Siege?
In September 1969 came a truly symbolic moment. In order that the Georgetown School could be prepared for the first intake of comprehensive school pupils in 1970, some 40 fifteen-year-olds from Georgetown Secondary Modern School were transferred to the Castle. Into the expansive parkland of the 19th century iron-master's mansion came many of the descendants of the radical iron-workers' community that had grown up in the shadow of cinder and iron slag tips. They were the first of the many that followed. But in 1969, although now less than twelve months away from going fully comprehensive, Cyfarthfa was still a grammar school in the throes of all the detailed processes and preparation entailed by the fast approaching change.

To those stresses came another. Because the new Penydre High School could at that time accommodate only the younger County Grammar year groups and the pupils of the 'feeder' secondary modern schools, Cyfarthfa was called upon by the Education Department to be home for the next three years (1969–72) to most of the sixth-form students of the County who were preparing for their A levels.

Pupils from three different schools were now in the Castle building. During this brief but complex period in Cyfarthfa's history a variety of different school colours mingled in classrooms and corridors, with traditional ties worn proudly: the red and green of Merthyr County, the blue and yellow of Cyfarthfa and (at first) the maroon, yellow and blue of Georgetown School; and all this the year *before* Cyfarthfa went fully comprehensive! New messages and strange male nicknames began appearing on Cyfarthfa's toilet walls, adding to those that had remained inviolate for decades. Such mysterious noms de plume as Tashy, Abu, Cass, Weegie and Soup, soon became identified with some of Georgetown School's more lively characters.

More seriously these arrangements imposed a significant extra work load and responsibility on the staff. One department, over this three-year period had a combined Cyfarthfa–Merthyr County sixth form of over 90 students, sitting two separate A Level examinations! Happily, the A level results were gratifying for the staffs and students of both schools. In retrospect, it certainly was hectic – but Cyfarthfa coped admirably.

New name, new colours, new uniform

The creation of Cyfarthfa High School meant breaking away from the uniforms and colours of both Cyfarthfa Grammar and Georgetown Secondary Modern Schools. John Lewis, the strong head of Georgetown, with his deputy Islwyn Rees, chaired a committee that with the expertise of Merryl Jones, head of design and dress/ textiles, produced new uniforms and colour schemes for pupils of both the Lower and Upper Schools. Pupil representatives co-opted on to the committee surprised some adult members by requesting that a tie should form part of the new school uniform. The badge and motto for the new school became subjects of much debate. Strong feeling was expressed that the distinctive Cyfarthfa Castle School badge should be retained. After all, the arms of Saint Tydfil possessed strong historical and community associations while it was a visual reminder of Cyfarthfa School's foundation soon after Merthyr Tydfil's incorporation as a county borough in 1908.

Eventually it was agreed that one of Dewi Bowen's designs, symbolic of the Cyfarthfa district, should be represented on the new badge. The name 'Cyfarthfa' is translated as 'Barking Place', a reference probably to a hunting district in by-gone days. The design of a barking hound, with the flames of an iron furnace to represent the Cyfarthfa Iron Works, etched in yellow and red on a black background, was recommended for the new comprehensive school.

The Education Committee agreed to the new name 'Cyfarthfa High School', new uniforms for the Lower and Upper Schools and the new badge and motto, *Cadarn Pob Cyfiawn* (Strength though Justice). There was agreement also that the new school's catchment area would include the feeder junior schools of Abermorlais, Caedraw, Gellideg, Heolgerrig and Twynyrodyn. But Cyfarthfa lost the northern communities of Pant, Dowlais and Penydarren, from which, decade after decade, had come many of its most able pupils.

In September 1970, some 230 first year, all-ability 11-year-olds nervously entered the Georgetown building, now designated Cyfarthfa's Lower School. Both boys and girls wore the new uniforms, predominantly primrose-yellow and grey. Senior pupils in forms V and VI were allowed a distinctive uniform, mainly pale-blue and grey, with a tie sporting the new dog-furnace emblem. A banding system was introduced for the newcomers. There were four classes for those of higher and roughly equal ability, and another four classes for those perceived to be of lesser but again of roughly equal ability. Each of these classes had between 25–30 pupils. There was also a special needs class. The pupils followed a broad and balanced curriculum of nine or ten subjects. At the end of the first year, and in succeeding years, some pupils transferred between groups, after careful assessment by Cyfarthfa's teachers. So began a new era.

Sporting Highlights
By 1972, Cyfarthfa's girls, under the continuing tuition of Jane Type, had won the Glamorgan County Shield (Middle Section), for the third consecutive year. Their regular training and sprinting track was the gravel-surfaced, public path around the park lake. On this 'make-do' track national and county champions were made, despite having to compete with walkers enjoying the park's scenic facilities. More than one member of the public stood aside as girls leapt the hurdles at speed. Nevertheless, Susan Hamer and Lynne Davies became Welsh Girls' Hurdles Champions, while Diane McCarthy and Laurie Williams gained Glamorgan county representation in hockey, with many girls attaining county status in athletics. Meanwhile, twin sisters, Vivienne and Venissa Head (by now

members of Cardiff Athletic Club) achieved Welsh national success in the Shot and Discuss respectively, with Venissa going on to represent Great Britain at the 1984 Los Angeles Olympic Games. Linda Jones became the Welsh Girls table-tennis champion.

The boys, under the teaching of Bernard Evans, Bill Watkins and Roger Law, also enjoyed success. Playing their matches on the dirt-surfaced Pandy Field (as had generations of Cyfarthfa boys before them), the strong and skilful senior soccer team reached the semi-final of the All-Wales Schools' competition, losing to Dynevor School, Swansea 2–1, in a replay. The younger boys meanwhile, shared the local Keir Hardie Shield in 1972, with a 2–2 draw against Afon Taf. Three pupils especially deserve mention: Philip T. Lewis represented Wales in soccer at under-19 level, while Stuart Meek and Gordon Davies gained under-15 caps. (Gordon's later professional career is recorded in *They Made Their Mark*.)

Head boy Ian Kelly became a member of the Welsh Schools Cricket Team, while Steven Jenkins represented Welsh Schools at chess. Two members of the rugby XV who in later years achieved outstanding success in a very different arena were Philip Joll, who also gained a place in the Glamorgan Schools' Rugby Squad, and Jason Jones, later known as Jason Howard (see *They Made Their Mark)*.

Other Achievements

The increased number of pupils helped the school's senior choir to secure the first prize at the Urdd National Eisteddfod in consecutive years, at Bala (1970) and Swansea (1971). Headmaster, John Davies paid particular tribute to Brian Evans (Head of Music) and the totally dedicated Raymond Gethin (Head of Welsh) 'whose organisational powers behind the school's success is quite exemplary'. Meanwhile, a 'second' for Paul Thomas in the pianoforte competition, and third place 'on stage' for the recitation group, trained by Welsh teacher, Linda Jones, were fine achievements.

Despite all the far-reaching changes within the school, academic successes continued with Ann Thomas in 1970 winning a scholarship in Welsh and History to Aberystwyth, and Philip Morgan (Economics) in the same year gaining entry to Clare College, Cambridge. In 1972 Richard Powell (Mathematics) also entered Clare College. In 1973 Lindsay Brown won a scholarship to Lincoln College, Oxford and Carole Strachan entered St. Hugh's, Oxford. Both were History students.

Farewell and Welcome

The story of Cyfarthfa Castle as a 'selective secondary school' within the County Borough of Merthyr Tydfil had now come to an end. The retirement in July 1972 of Havard Walters and Dan Jones, who had begun their careers at Cyfarthfa in 1930, symbolised the change as little else could. Headmaster, John Davies, who was departing to become the Head of Upper Rhondda Comprehensive School in his home town of Treorchy, graciously paid tribute to his two colleagues: 'Both these long-serving masters will be deeply missed at such a crucial stage in the history of this school, and its distinguished tradition owes a great deal to men of this calibre.' Although Headmaster for only four and a half years, a similar tribute by Director of Education, John Beale was accorded John Davies, who had led the school through challenging times and helped shape the early years of Cyfarthfa as a comprehensive school.

With these retirements the School had lost almost its entire senior leadership team on the same day. It was with eagerness and some apprehension that the staff awaited the appointment of a new Headmaster to consolidate the foundation work of those highly experienced, departing members of staff.

The new head was Dennis Bennett, a Senghenydd-born product of Caerphilly Grammar School and University College, Aberystwyth, with a Master's degree in Geography. He had had a varied and successful teaching career and was now returning to Wales. He brought to Cyfarthfa those qualities of sustained diligence, far-sightedness and administrative skills, which enabled him, with the help and support of his staff and governors, to bring to fruition the transformation of Cyfarthfa into a well-regarded comprehensive school containing over 1,100 pupils, almost double the number educated within the Castle at the end of World War II.

A HEADMASTER REPORTS:

1972–1990

DENNIS BENNETT

Images and precious thoughts that shall not die

(Wordsworth)

In September 1972, just two years after the amalgamation of Cyfarthfa Castle Grammar School and Georgetown Secondary Modern School, I entered Cyfarthfa High School as headteacher. To many, the grammar school stood for success, the secondary modern for failure, and the comprehensive that had emerged stood for an unacceptable compromise. Fusing these schools into a successful single educational body, and persuading a reluctant community of its merit, would not be easy; but it was a task well worth tackling. My aims, policies and actions were driven by a Christian conscience and educational convictions. The central task was to release the potential of pupils and staff. The context was the monumental changes brought about by the technological revolution and by government intervention in the education process without heeding Edmund Burke's warning 'against a blind and furious spirit of innovation, under the name of reform'. Patience and dogged persistence would be essential to avoid turmoil and secure a modicum of tranquillity and precious harmony!

Buildings Ancient and Modern

Every new head faces a series of challenges and opportunities. An early task was to improve the interior of the Castle building where damp, cold classrooms and corridors gave an air of neglect. Buckets and bins placed in strategic locations caught rain-water dripping from the ceilings. Classrooms were painted a dull grey, and many on the sunless side had

Dennis Bennett

heavy plaster blistering and breaking off the walls. There were over 100 broken windows. Graffiti, the scourge of that generation, was widespread, especially in the toilets. An occasional swastika was visible alongside the word 'Colditz'!

Temporary classrooms extending up the hillside behind the Castle were reached by a flight of stone steps which, from the ground floor of the Castle to the topmost classroom, numbered approximately 100. Staff using the steps requested that wellington boots be provided for the inevitable wet weather.

In April 1974 Merthyr Tydfil County Borough was abolished and Merthyr became part of the new Mid-Glamorgan authority. That same year Cyfarthfa was designated a Social Priority School on the grounds that more than 25 per cent of the pupils were on free meals and that the school was disadvantaged by the age and state of the buildings. The most serious concern was inadequate heating. Classrooms in both the Castle and Georgetown buildings endured temperatures between 7°C and 11°C for long periods. By the early 1970s more homes had some form of central heating than in previous decades, and children and teachers were leaving a warm house to attend a cold school. Pupils and staff complained yet carried on their work with remarkable resilience until, on the morning of Thursday 18 January 1973, a strike threat by the Castle staff precipitated rapid action. John Beale, the Director of Education, promised that the boilers would be checked, the windows glazed, outside doors fitted with closure springs, and fire doors repaired. The strike was averted.

Cyfarthfa High School was then given a face-lift. Brighter colour schemes were selected by the classroom teachers themselves. Graffiti removal signalled a determined effort to keep it under control. By late 1973, pastoral rooms and a combined male/female staffroom, suitably furnished, had been completed; the sixth form had been moved to ground floor rooms near the Head of Sixth Form's Office, and provided with carpeted flooring, easy chairs and coffee-making facilities. Even the ladies' toilets were renovated – but not without the ladies describing the new provision, scathingly, as 'open plan'!

By the autumn of 1975 the Castle interior was much improved. New work included the refurbishment of the Chemistry and General Science laboratories, the renovation of the Canteen, the upgrading of the overloaded electrical wiring for the first time, and heavy ink-welled old oak desks replaced with more manoeuvrable Formica-topped tables and light chairs. Just after half term 1979, the bay window of the Round Library (Music Room), was found faulty and the room was vacated. The single male staff toilet on the first floor, suspended on iron girders over the courtyard, was discovered by vigilant workmen to be in imminent danger of collapsing, and was demolished. Its destruction was seen as a great 'inconvenience'. In the Castle, it was not until 1984, when a new heating system was fitted, that the staffroom's coal fire, lit each morning by the caretaker, was dispensed with, and the bodies huddled around it dispersed themselves throughout the room. Whisper it quietly, the only other room warmed by a coal fire was the headmaster's study!

A major change came with an agreement to accommodate disabled pupils. Ramps were provided for wheelchair accessibility, and lessons were programmed on the ground floor wherever possible as there was no lift. Two who benefited were Mark Beadle, wonderfully supported each day by his mother, and Lynne Downes, whose older brother Steven was already attending Cyfarthfa when she applied for entrance. Both were a credit to the school and to their families, and won the hearts of pupils and staff.

There were unexpected setbacks. One weekend, Ron Davies was shocked to learn that the roof of his well-appointed Technical Drawing Office had been badly damaged by fire. The *Merthyr Express* reported on Friday 18 January 1974:

> A twelve year old boy who ... had caused damage by fire to a Cyfarthfa High School mobile classroom amounting to £1,295.60, was placed in the care of the local authority and ordered to pay £200 in compensation ...The father of the boy said it was the pursuit by two boys after wasps' eggs for ... fishing.

For some staff at County Hall, Merthyr Tydfil seemed to be a foreign land and Cyfarthfa High School an enigma. A response to a report submitted to the Education Department describing how a pupil had sustained an injury by stumbling over an obstacle in Cyfarthfa Park was in the form of two questions: 'How far is the Park from the school?' and 'Has the offending obstacle been removed?'

A New Upper School Building

In January 1979, the local authority announced that a new Upper School would be constructed at Cae Mari Dwn at a cost of £1,689,761.40. It was a privilege and pleasure for staff and pupils to enter the fine red brick, pitched roof, purpose-built Upper School premises in September 1981, although the official opening did not take place until Monday 9 July 1984. The consequent virtual absence of vandalism and graffiti reflected the pride and respect pupils had for their new surroundings.

The provision for the Upper School at Cae Mari Dwn meant that the Georgetown premises were vacated in 1981, and the Lower School transferred to the Castle. The Georgetown school had seen the best of its days. It consisted of two older buildings, a two-storey wooden structure housing practical and science rooms, and two mobile classrooms. Occasionally, a rat or two would be killed in classrooms before school started! The main building was heated by two almost inaccessible coal-fired boilers in a boiler room heavily polluted by sulphurous fumes. Room temperatures in the winter months were frequently as low as those in the Castle, and one very cold Christmas holiday in the mid 1970s, the double-decker annex building was flooded when the radiators burst. It was with little heartache that the move was made.

Staff Matters

Another immediate challenge in 1972 was how to replace a number of senior staff who, either through promotion or retirement, had left in the

Georgetown School, Cyfarthfa Lower School, overlooked by tip

summer. As the school had a full complement of 66 teachers, 15 of them ex-Cyfarthfa pupils, the first senior appointments were mainly by internal promotion, which was good for the morale of the staff and for the health of the Head! From the outset John Lewis, the deputy headmaster, and I found that in educational principle and practice we had much in common and worked well together until his retirement in 1976. Continuity of staffing provided a stability and dedication many schools would envy; over 20 of them were still there in 1990. Gwyn Rees, Head of Science, retired in 2002 after 36 years in the School.

Another issue was to create a framework through which, by integrating academic and pastoral duties, the objectives of the school could be achieved. Planning teams, with the full engagement of members of staff, produced an appropriate management system. (See the Appendix to this chapter.)

Commuting between the Castle and Georgetown was reduced to a minimum to ensure that there was a core of teachers in the Lower School to provide academic and pastoral stability. Some subjects such as French, which functioned best on single period lessons, were more affected than others. Mary Owen, who commuted most, complained pleasantly about her lot!

There was a staunch camaraderie among both the men and women staff, with many social, sporting and cultural events where relaxation and enjoyment was the intention – and the product! The male staff played soccer and cricket against local schools and made sporting competitions an excuse for travelling wider afield, even travelling 'on tour' to destinations as far afield as Ireland. Memorable staff functions were capped by an occasion at a Blackwood nightspot which I described as '*savage amusement*'– no-one else agreed with me!

The loss of seven members of staff in July 1984, tempted by a generous early retirement offer, was a severe blow to the school. They had given many years of faithful and dedicated service to Cyfarthfa, with huge credit. They were: Betty Roberts, Senior Mistress and motherly matron of Lower School; Cliff O'Shea, Head of and patient shepherd of the difficult Middle School; Dewi Bowen, Head of Art and Design and willing patron and patriarch of the whole school; Glanville Jones, Head of Technical Subjects and a meticulous and excellent teacher of metalwork; and three other able members Margaret Jones (Art), Shirley Rees (Geography) and John Battenbo (Mathematics).

Some, of course, left for promotion, mainly within the teaching profession: David Young became Director of Education for Monmouthshire; Tony Whiley, David Painter, Phillip Atkinson, Huw Morris and Gary Brame became headteachers; and Bernard Evans, Steve Barnes, Mansell Richards, Trevor Jones, Robert Butcher and Carolyn Meade, became deputy headteachers. Quite a record!

From October 1984 to June 1985, while I was on leave of absence carrying out a research project for Her Majesty's Inspectorate, the senior staff of Ray Gethin, David Young, Janice Williams and Ron Williams more than held the fort despite an exasperating period of coal shortage and winter flooding at Cae Mari Dwn.

Happy and sad memories dot the years. Highly respected members of staff were lost, beginning with the much loved Head of the Remedial Department, Margaret Roderick, who passed away on Christmas Day 1975 after a heroic and protracted battle with ill-health. Vincent Lee, a fine Head of English, died of cancer in November 1979 when his children, Mark and Vanessa, were pupils at Cyfarthfa, and in 2004 Marilyn Bassett, a most conscientious mild-natured member of the Welsh Department, lost her long fight against a rare illness. The affection of her colleagues was shown by a remarkably large number attending her funeral in the summer vacation. Some staff lost their husbands or wives, namely, Islwyn Rees, Head of Lower School, Liz Leese, Head of German, and Sandra Jones, Year Tutor, whose husband Digby was a Councillor and much valued member of the Governing Body. 'Babs' Bowen, Bob Thomas, Vic. Davies, Anne Aldred, and Ron Davies retired with ill-heath. By contrast, there were marriages between members of staff – Islwyn Rees to Shirley Vowles, Ray Iverson to Meriel Thomas, Jeff Meade to Carolyn Coakley, Alun Hughes to Susan Lewis, and David Powell to Helen Mochan.

The First Computers
Dramatic advances in technology between 1970 and 1990 affected both administration and teaching. At the beginning of that period duplicating equipment, of fundamental importance for administration and as a teaching resource, consisted of the Gestetner stencil duplicating machine and the Banda colour carbon spirit duplicator. The introduction of photocopying machines revolutionised the time spent by teachers and secretaries on producing documents. In 1990 there were 62 clerical staff – 58 of whom were teachers!

Converting the curriculum into an efficient timetable remained a paper, pencil and rubber exercise, relished if not loved by David Young. In the early 1980s BBC computers were introduced with staff receiving training in their use. As the decade reached its end, computer technology was racing forward and the school was provided with much more sophisticated equipment, housed in specialist computer rooms and in subject classrooms. The Upper and Lower School staff rooms had designated information technology areas. By 1990, a satellite dish provided the foreign language department with access to Europe and further afield, and the first phase of cable networking, the establishment of a Media Resources Centre and the fitting out of a large room as an Education Technological Resources Centre were all imminent. Undoubtedly, Cyfarthfa was moving with the times!

Teachers v The Government

Turbulent relationships between the teachers' unions and the Government were common in the years 1972–1990. The two major unions, the National Union of Teachers and the National Association of Schoolmasters/Union of Women Teachers, had almost equal numbers in Cyfarthfa so action by either union seriously disrupted teaching. When one banned the use of teachers' cars for commuting between sites, teaching was prevented from grinding to a halt by the prompt action of the District Education Officer who engaged taxis for the purpose! There were various occasions in the 1970s when 'overtime duties' were banned, or 'goodwill' withdrawn. When teachers withdrew from voluntary lunch hour supervision in 1979 the shortened lunch period was detrimental to many extra-curricular activities that used that break. Later, the situation eased as teachers willing to supervise, received payment for the duty.

Much more damaging was the protracted and bitter action by teachers in support of their pay claim, which reached a crisis level in 1985, when the government had just bullied the miners into submission. Activities outside school hours, including staff and parental meetings ended, teaching was disrupted, children were sent home, and corporate government made virtually impossible. In October 1985, on one afternoon session, almost 700 children were excluded from school out of a total school population of 1107. Nevertheless, every effort was made by the staff to provide continuity of education for the fifth and sixth form examination classes.

Staff Photograph 1977

(Compiled from 1977 panoramic photographs of Upper and Lower School)

1st D. Young, R. Gethin, J. Lewis, D. Bennett, M. Treharne, I. Rees, B. Phillips, G. Owen, W.T.A. .Jones, M. Sims

2nd I. Hopkins, D. Leigh, A.C. Davies, G. Jones, C. Browning, P.Weslake-Hill, M. Morgan, F. Watkins,
H. Young, S. Lewis

3rd P. Deeks, J. Battenbo, A. Whiley, V. Lee, L. Fisher, V. Davies, R. Roberts, R. Butcher, P. Atkinson

4th J. Blunsdon, M. Jenkins, R. Iverson, C. Davies, R, Walker, H. Morris, M. Wood, D. Prothero , S. Barnes,

5th G. Rees, B. Evans, M. Richards, D. Bowen, R. Davies, C. O'Shea, O. Caudle, G. Jones

6th R. Shipton, S. Vowles, J. Bowen, M.M. Jones, M. Bowns, R. Evans, A. Aldred, M.K. Jones, E. Leese

7th S.S. Jones, _G. Hughes–Evans, M. Owen, M. Adams, A. Jones, J. Cressey, P. Whiley, H. Rees, D. Pearce

8th Secretaries: N. Sharp, G. Williams, E. Evans, E. Smith. Lab Technician: A. Callaghan

P.E. Staff at County Athletics Championships: Mrs J. Type, Mrs A. Lewis, Mr R. Coombs, Mr R .Lane

Other Staff: Mr R. Burgum, Mr R. Walker, Mrs J. Howells, Mrs M. Iverson, Miss A. James, Miss L. Jones,
Mrs E. Meyrick, Mrs A. Thomas

Staff 1977

Teachers had no wish to see pupils suffer, or see destroyed what they had built over years of painstaking and conscientious labour. Their action therefore was all the more poignant.

Relations between teacher unions and the government were finally settled by the Teachers Pay and Conditions of Service Act in 1987. With the unions now much weakened, the Government relentlessly pursued its autocratic policies which included the introduction of the National Curriculum and the distasteful testing processes which went with it.

Pupil Numbers

It is, of course, the pupils who give life and meaning to a school. In the following pages many individual pupils are mentioned, but here I want to look at the overall picture. When I took up the headship there were 1115 pupils drawn from the 'feeder' primary schools of Heolgerrig, Gellideg, Cyfarthfa, Caedraw and Twynyrodyn, with some pupils from Gwaunfarren. But over the years considerable changes took place. Between September 1972 and September 1974 the school population expanded from 1115 to 1244, stabilising at around that figure and reaching a maximum of 1248 in 1978, before falling to under 1000 by 1990. (*See Graph 1*) This drop in numbers could have had serious implications for staffing, but it was countered by two factors. First was the intake from schools outside the catchment area (19 in 1985), and second was a surge in sixth form numbers from under 100 to over 150 by 1983, equalling the first year pupil intake in both 1987 and 1990!

The sixth form at 150 remained the largest in the Borough, a size quite exceptional even in Mid-Glamorgan. It reflected success at GCSE level, and the introduction of more appropriate courses for non A level students. The 1982 Inspection Report noted that the number of pupils entering the lower sixth had steadily increased over the previous five years from 28.6 per cent of the year 5 cohort to 48.4 per cent.

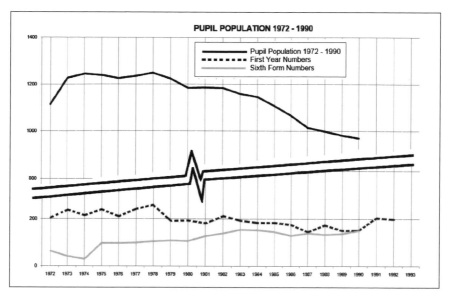

An important reason for the increase in sixth formers was the high level of unemployment in the 1980s, as local mines and factories closed. Jobs had the scarcity value of gold. The 'new' sixth formers believed it was better to pursue education to a higher level than to stagnate on street corners, or even to be swept up by the Youth Training Scheme. Several new courses fulfilled their need.

The Curriculum Cake Conundrum

In their first three years, and eventually in mixed ability classes strongly advocated by Ron Williams, Head of Lower School, Cyfarthfa pupils followed a broad and balanced curriculum. For the following two years the demands of external examinations dictated a reduction in the number of subjects. In 1972 the maximum number taken at O level was seven, but by 1990 educational changes had gradually increased them to ten or eleven. Coping with the large number of subject options without reducing the curriculum cake into valueless crumbs was a major headache. The core subjects were English, Mathematics, Religious Education and Physical

Education, with other subjects being chosen from option boxes that included Physics, Chemistry and Biology and other traditional subjects. In time new courses were introduced across the school, including Personal, Social and Health Education, Drama, Business Studies, Commerce, Computing and Information Technology.

The massive expansion of higher education places and the flurry of new and innovative courses diminished the traditional science/arts division and Latin, no longer a requirement for university entrance, became an optional subject at O level. Takers dwindled until, regrettably, it was removed from the curriculum.

At A level, pupils chose three or four subjects from up to 18 on offer. The inspectors' report in 1982 (the first exposed to public scrutiny) commended the school on showing 'considerable flexibility in the way it accommodates relatively unusual subject combinations'. The needs of the growing number in the sixth form who were looking for routes into further education and work other than by A level, posed a further challenge. One-year courses for non A level pupils, begun in 1983, were expanded in September 1984 with the introduction of the Business and Technical Education Council's General Certificate (BTEC). Two other non A level courses were also offered – Catering, and Child Care. There was 100 per cent success in Catering and Child Care and over 90 per cent in the BTEC General Certificate.

Other radical changes came in 1988. The General Certificate of Secondary Education, with new subject syllabuses, replaced the GCE O level and the Certificate of Secondary Education. This welcome change simplified the examination system and ended an academic divide within the school. Less welcome was the Government's imposition of the National Curriculum in 1988 which took decisions about what subjects to teach, away from teachers. It also introduced a totally new nomenclature. Four 'Key Stages' in a child's education were identified with Key Stages 3 and 4 applying to the secondary years of compulsory schooling. To match the stages, each year in school was numbered, with the first three years in secondary school being years 7, 8 and 9 (KS3), and the final years of compulsory education, 10 and 11 (KS4).

Work-Related Courses

With the country suffering from rising unemployment and the decimation
of large sectors of the economy, courses with a work-related bias, aimed at
responding to the demands of a fast changing and technical society, were
promoted and financed by the Government under the auspices of the
Manpower Services Commission. The Technical and Vocational Education
Initiative (TVEI), piloted by a consortium of Cyfarthfa, Penydre and
Vaynor and Penderyn High schools with the Technical College, was
introduced for the fourth year in autumn 1984, led by Owen Caudle. A
one-year 17+ Certificate course of Pre-Vocational Education (CPVE),
under Maisie Prosser, followed in 1985. To these, before the end of the
decade, was added the less arduous Mid-Glamorgan Certificate of
Education, run by Jon Allen, which proved attractive even to special
education needs pupils and very few left school without an externally
validated certificate. These courses, especially the TVEI with its
substantial financial input, had a major impact on the curriculum, staffing
and resources, and propelled the school forward in promoting work
experience, school-industry links, careers programmes and pupil profiling.
Academic progress and personal development were now to be documented
in a Record of Achievement compiled for each pupil.

Examination Results

Examinations and examination results are far from being everything, but
no school can afford to ignore them. In the 1970s the GCE O Level was
seen to be for the most able 20 per cent of pupils, the Certificate of
Secondary Education for the next 40 per cent, with the final 40 per cent
of pupils regarded as non-examinable. Government, examining bodies and
others encouraged this three-fold division. Our policy was to gradually
widen the A and B bands and to eliminate the C band altogether, giving the
opportunity to sit external certificated examinations that could motivate
more pupils and give them a sense of purpose, self-respect and fulfilment.
In 1979 26 per cent left Welsh schools without a single GCE/CSE subject
success: at Cyfarthfa in 1982, it was around 19 per cent. The external
examination system also underwent a series of changes in the 1980s with

GCSE syllabuses placing greater emphasis on oral, practical, course and field work, each of which received a varying percentage of the total examination mark depending on the subject.

Throughout the 1980s Cyfarthfa made steady progress, examination results at least matching those of the former Grammar School. The 1982 Inspectors' Report noted: 'The pass rate at A-level for all subjects in 1982 was 76.3 per cent; A grades were achieved in eight subjects. These results reflect well on the preparation for A level examinations in most subjects.' Progress continued gradually, but there was a surge in better results towards the 1990s, as the government pressed for improvement and examination systems changed. At A level the pass rate reached 82 per cent and in 1991 Alun Hughes, Head of Upper School and the School's Examinations Officer, wrote to the *Sunday Times* to point out that Cyfarthfa, a true comprehensive, achieved 23.8 per cent A and B grades at A level which was well within the top 250 schools in Britain as recorded in that paper, and that recognition should be given to the many candidates with D and E grades who went on to higher education.

The number of pupils going to university increased proportionately, and Cyfarthfa students achieved first-class honours at a widening range of universities. Exceptional successes, however, were achieved by the chemistry department. In 1988 Richard Bennett entered Churchill College, Cambridge, to study Biochemistry and graduated with first-class honours. In 1991 Matthew Davies gained entry to the same College to study Chemical Engineering and he too achieved first-class honours. To round off a hat-trick, in 1993 Peter Bezant entered Churchill College and also graduated with first-class honours in Chemical Engineering.

Behaviour, Discipline and the School Day

The guiding principle was 'Courtesy and consideration for others at all times'. Behaviour and discipline were covered by rules ranging from simple verbal reprimands to more stringent sanctions and ultimately exclusion. At first there were natural tensions arising from the merger of two distinctive schools, but the vast majority of pupils accepted the fairness of the rules, understood the benefits of them, and for the most part, obeyed them. Corporal punishment was abandoned in 1983–1984, three years before it was abolished by law in September 1987. In Lower School, rewards proved more productive than sanctions, with the results of behaviour and attendance competitions recorded monthly, displayed prominently on wall charts, and announced in assemblies. New crazes were monitored very carefully, especially solvent sniffing and later, drug taking. Fortunately, these occasions were intermittent, small in number, never out of control, and hence caused little disruption within the school. Her Majesty's Inspectors wrote in 1981 of an orderly and happy community. Later in the 1980s, two separate groups of inspectors gave unsolicited and fulsome praise of the relaxed atmosphere and positive ethos they experienced on their visits.

In the 1960s–1970s the revolt against many of the traditions of previous generations created a reaction against school uniform. The comprehensive school name, uniform, badge and motto had been agreed by a staff working party, as described in the last chapter. One parent fiercely opposed the boys' grey shirt on the grounds that it resembled 'prison grey'! A realistic reform, in the cold school conditions, and at the request of the girl pupils, was to allow navy-blue trousers to be worn as an alternative to skirts.

Occasional and memorable confrontations with irate parents occurred, and there were always interesting interviews with Mr David Young the conscientious 6ft 4in and 15-stone Park-keeper in his police-styled uniform and peaked cap. This affable giant with the large boots and splayed feet would tramp through the school to the head's office to deliver an oral or written complaint against a pupil or a gaggle of the same. The written messages would be carefully and beautifully phrased in 'court' language, often in blue and red ink to distinguish between his words and those of the culprits. The first letter of any pupil expletive would be followed by the appropriate number of dots. A fitting punishment was imparted to the miscreants! The collection of conkers in the autumn, a time-honoured activity, was frowned upon by Park officials, but never encouraged or discouraged by the school – nor did thoughts of danger in that activity ever cross our minds or be threatened by Health and Safety regulations!

There were encounters with pupils too, when a spontaneous gesture could give rise to difficulties. Early one autumn morning, having apprehended a young girl smoking, I offered to purchase a box of chocolates for her if she stopped smoking for the rest of the term. On the very last day of that term, the young lady claimed her box of chocolates! A dash into town saved my embarrassment but had I neutralised the possible growth of an addiction to smoking only to encourage the road to obesity?

Issues of disciplinary control over the lunch hour and the provision of school buses resulted in a number of changes to the school day over the years, the most dramatic and innovative of which occurred from September 1987 when school buses were rescheduled for a 8.30 am start and a 3.00 pm finish. Cyfarthfa was the first state school in Wales to make the change, but many copied the pattern in the following years.

The Governing Body

Few areas within secondary education remained unaffected by government policy in the 1980s, including the governing body. The 1944 Education Act required all secondary schools to have governors and, as they were appointed by the local education authorities, the majority were councillors. They therefore exercised considerable power in the functioning of the school and especially over the appointment of teachers. Fortunately, disagreement and conflict with the governors was rare.

The composition of the governing body gradually changed. By 1976 there were four co-opted governors, and in 1979 a pupil governor was added, who left meetings when new staff were appointed. A greater shift in emphasis occurred with the 1980 Education Act when the influence of non-LEA representatives became more marked. Even so, LEA representatives remained in the majority at Cyfarthfa.

The big change came with the 1986 Education (No2) Act. That was deliberately designed to switch power from local councillors to parents and co-opted members, and to direct attention to the massively increased and quite onerous responsibilities now delegated to them as governors.

Despite there being no legal hindrance to one being co-opted, the new governing body did not include a pupil governor.

In December 1988, at the request of the governors, I agreed to produce a paper suggesting means by which the vital School–Governing Body partnership could be made more effective. This paper, "Managing the Future', recommended devolving responsibility for key matters to sub-committees, and in 1989 the governors resolved to establish the following working groups which would report their recommendations to the full governing body for consideration: (i) Staff and Personnel, (ii) Finance and Resources, (iii) Curriculum, (iv) Building and Maintenance, (v) Welfare. A totally new form of school government began tentatively, with the leadership of the Head still very significant.

Sporting Achievements

Generations of boys and girls remember toiling up through the woods from the Castle to reach the sloping and uneven 'top field' to play rugby and hockey. Things were no different in 1972 except that as other schools acquired modern sports amenities, both indoors and out, Cyfarthfa's deprivation was accentuated. The downstairs hall doubled as a gym; changing rooms remained spartan. Strong pleas from the school for Mid-Glamorgan Education Authority to finance the use of the new Rhydycar Leisure Centre and its outdoor facilities by the school were rewarded, and between 1975 and 1981, form groups travelled to the centre by buses provided for that purpose. It was a timely decision, as in 1976 the local Council designated the Pandy Field for use by circuses and fairs which churned up the surface and prevented its use for months on end. Ironically, there was a period in 1976 when Mid-Glamorgan, 'strapped for cash', withdrew its financial support and Rhydycar's use was sustained by the School Fund and the PTA.

When in 1978 the prospects of a new Upper School became a reality, one of the first concerns was that the new building and its sports fields should become available in tandem. Open-cast coal mining dashed that prospect! It would be seven years after the Cae Mari Dwn building was opened in

First XV 1973-74. Back Row (l-r): H. Daniel, A. Foley, L. James, S. Meek, J. Pittick, S. Wilde, I. Price, M. Davies, S. Brown. Front Row: H. Jenkins, D. Hughes, W. Allman, I. Kelly (Captain), W. Astley, G. Murphy, M. Cable.

1988 that the fields became available, although a much needed hockey/netball pitch adjacent to the premises was ready earlier. The boys' rugby matches were played mainly on the Mountain Hare pitch approximately a quarter of a mile from the new school building. It was now the turn of Lower School to use the 'Castle' facilities and the infamous top field.

Despite these difficulties, the school continued to compete in all the traditional games of rugby, soccer, hockey and netball and, in addition, new sporting activities became popular. These included badminton, squash, golf, and outdoor pursuits such as caving, sailing, canoeing, mountaineering and orienteering. This expansion was under the heads of the Boys and Girls P.E. departments in the years in question – Bernard Evans, 'Bob' Coombs and Gareth Francis, and Jane Type – was supplemented by other teachers steeped in sporting traditions, who gave hours of their own time to coach and run teams at each age group level in the school. Unfortunately, inter-school sport competitions practically ceased during the teacher unions" industrial action between 1984 and 1986, and were slow to recover afterwards.

Time and time again reports reaching Cyfarthfa from other schools spoke of the high standards of sportsmanlike and dignified behaviour shown by the school's pupils whether matches were won or lost. Accolades of this nature were gratefully received and acknowledged. Good manners and courtesy were prized – almost as much as regular victories. Here are a few of the individual and team achievements over the years.

Rugby

The 1st rugby XV had its best season in 1981–1982 winning 15 out of 17 matches, before losing momentum, with the ebb tide continuing into 1983–1984 and with results best not recorded! Nevertheless, there were hopeful signs, many games being closely fought with the spirit of the side never – or hardly ever – flagging! Simon Davies won a place in the Welsh Schoolboys B side against Italy, and a year later, Dale Ford played for the Boys Clubs of Wales, followed by matches for the Welsh ATC team.

A prized annual rugby event, played alternately home and away, was a match against Stoneham Boys' School, Reading, arranged by Mansell Richards who had taught history there before returning to teach at Cyfarthfa. The journey was made by minibus and the team members stayed overnight with the families of the opposing team, adding a valuable cultural and social flavour to the trip.

Soccer

But it was in Association Football that the school sparkled in the 1972–1990 period. The selection of Stuart Meek as Under-19 goalkeeper for the Welsh Schoolboys against England, following on Gordon Davies' international achievements, was a precursor of a string of phenomenal

Under 15 Soccer XI 1979. Back Row (l-r): *Tony Rees, *Jonathan Jones, Steven Peters, Gideon Gratton-Smith, Robert Davies, Sean Murphy. Front Row: Paul Davies, *David Owen, Dennis Bennett, *Kevin Rogers, David Leigh (PE), *Martin Williams, Robert Thomas. (*Denotes international.)

Association Football successes, building up to the 1976–1977 season when the Under-13 side swept the board, winning the Merthyr Schools League, the David Beynon Cup and the Jubilee Competition at Rhydycar. Outstanding successes continued at town, county and national level. In the 1978–1979 season the Under-14 Five-a-side team became Merthyr Schools Champions, Mid-Glamorgan Champions, and then the National Champions. Tony Rees played in ten internationals, Kevin Rogers in seven, and Jonathan Jones in one, and only injury limited Jonathan from further appearances.

Six boys were members of the Under-15 team which became joint holders (with Afon Nedd) of the Welsh Shield in 1980, and four boys were members of the Merthyr Tydfil Under-15 side which lost by the narrowest of margins in the semi-finals of the Welsh Under-15 competition.

A baker's dozen of pupils won schoolboy caps, many playing numerous times at international level. Kevin Rogers and Tony Rees (who captained the Under-15 side) went on to play professionally for Aston Villa and Birmingham, respectively. Martyn Williams won the remarkable total of 39 caps during his time at school, and captained both the Welsh Under-15 and Under-18 sides. It was a golden period, particularly between 1976 and 1986, when teams and individuals flourished.

Cricket

Despite the absence of a decent cricket pitch, the heavy annual rainfall, and the precedence given to external examinations in the summer term, the cricket teams tended to win more matches than they lost. The first team won 13 of the 19 matches played in 1980, with Martin Williams, Neil Jenkins, Dean Cadwallader and Simon Davies representing the County in their respective age groups. Another Simon Davies, an extremely talented first year pupil, played for the Welsh Schools Cricket Association against Middlesex, and with Neil Jenkins, joined the Welsh Schools Cricket side at Under-15 level. Simon played with distinction against Scotland, Northern Ireland and England, and proceeded as the sole Mid-Glamorgan player, to tour Barbados with the Welsh Under-15 side in November 1984.

Swimming

Cyfarthfa's long established swimming traditions continued at Gwaunfarren Baths where the coaching team of Mr and Mrs Orville Jones held sway. In 1973, Julian Stamp and Lawrence James gained third place in the semi-final of the National Schools Life Saving Championships as well as in the semi-finals of the WSASA Championships, and Alan Powell became Welsh Champion at the 100m front crawl and was one of the winning Medley and Front Crawl teams in the Welsh Championships in 1980- 1981.

Hockey and Netball

Jane Type rightly described the school's sports facilities as 'the worst of any school played against'.

As a result, until the benefits of the all-purpose pitch and tennis courts at Cae Mari Dwn became increasingly apparent after 1981, many matches were played away from home, and the availability of a school minibus was crucial in maintaining inter-school competition. In fact, the hockey and netball teams achieved extraordinary success, some seasons winning all their matches! Gail Hopkins represented Mid-Glamorgan in both hockey and netball. A highlight of the 1988–1989 season was Janine Power obtaining Cyfarthfa's first international hockey cap, playing in eight matches and being the star in an international tournament in Holland at Easter 1988. The Junior Team did extremely well to reach the Urdd National hockey finals in May 1990.

Athletics and Gymnastics

Until 1988 athletics was severely handicapped by the absence of a suitable running track and adequate field event facilities, yet teams competed annually in the Mid-Glamorgan Championships with a reasonable degree of success across all events. The leadership qualities of Gail Hopkins, a fine hurdler and long jumper, were recognised when she was honoured with the captaincy of the Mid-Glamorgan Athletics team in 1978. In 1980 Lynne Davies became Welsh Open Champion in the hurdles, going on to run in Ireland for the Welsh Ladies Team where she was presented with a plaque for outstanding achievement.

A new day dawned in 1988 when the grass running track and field facilities at Cae Mari Dwn became available and sports days became a reality. The school, at last, was ready to move forward on the athletics front!

Gymnastic skills flourished under the guiding hand of Jane Type, with the most spectacular successes occurring in the later 1980s. The girls were overall winners of the Mid-Glamorgan Gymnastic Championships in 1979; two pupils went forward to the AAA National finals of the Urdd Superstars Competition at Aberystwyth; the Girls Gymnastic team won

Hockey Team 1979. Back Row (l-r): Andrea Samuel, Carolyn Donaghue, Delyth Williams, Deborah Evans, Ceri Williams, Lorraine Preece. Front Row: Claire Davies, Zoe Treharne, Dennis Bennett, Carolyn Mahoney, Jane Type, Ruth Goodman, Melanie Jones.

the Urdd title in 1987; the Over-13 and Under-13 teams won the gold medals in the Glamorgan Schools Vault and Tumble Championships in both 1988 and 1989, and the senior team completed a hat-trick in 1990 when Kelly Sullivan won the individual title.

New and Expanding Sports

Rapid success came to the badminton team under the coaching of enthusiast 'Pat' Weslake Hill. The mixed badminton team in 1978–1979 won the Mid-Glamorgan Under-16 Championships. Gideon Smith won the Under-16 title and with Kevin Rogers won the Doubles title. The next season Jane Perkins and Cheryl Daley won the Welsh Girls Doubles title Under-18, Martin Coffey and Peter Williams the Boys Doubles title Under-18.

A school squash team was fielded for the first time in 1987–1988. Debbie Newton won a full Welsh cap in Squash at Under-16 level and in 1990 Debbie, as Welsh Under-18 Squash Champion, travelled to the European Squash Championships at Zurich in May as reserve to the Welsh Ladies Team. In addition, Reba Dunn and Richard Barrell earned national honours the following season.

The Merthyr Tydfil Schools Bowls Championships was well supported by Cyfarthfa pupils over the years, with singles, pairs and fours being won. Ian Bishop actually reached the last eight in the Welsh Open Indoors Bowls Championship, an excellent achievement, and in 1987 Martin Thomas was a member of the bowls team which became Welsh Schools Fours Champions.

In 1983–1984 Brian Newman (5th year) represented Wales in the British Boxing Championships and Stephen Phillips (3rd year) was runner up in the Welsh Boxing Championships. National honours in boxing were gained in 1986–1987 by Stephen Sutton, who became British Army of the Rhine champion, and by Ashley Evans, who won the British Karate title for the second year running in his age group, travelling to Germany to represent Wales in the European Championships.

The Dolygaer Outdoor Pursuits Centre and the Merthyr Tydfil Sailing Club gave pupils the opportunity to learn to sail and enjoy the sport. After some success in 1973, The Enterprise Class was won at the Welsh Schools National Sailing Championships in both 1975 and in 1976, first by Keith Dowling and Gary Thornley and then by Gareth Morgan and Delyth Jones. Robert Wookey won the overall Mid-Glamorgan Schools Sailing Championships as well as the laser class in 1979–1980, and was the 1981–1982 Mid-Glamorgan Regatta laser and overall champion.

Jane Type, who was the Secretary of the Mid-Glamorgan Schools Association in the 1980s, encouraged golf as a pastime and took a boys golf team to a number of championships from 1988 onwards, with the boys, still novices, acquitting themselves well. In 1989–1990, Richard Morgan became the Welsh Under-15 Open Golf Champion.

Eisteddfodau Successes

Music and drama have always been strengths at Cyfarthfa, the school eisteddfod an annual high point. Competition between the four Houses on Eisteddfod day, was passionate and fierce, as becomes the Welsh language and culture, and would end with the winners of the House shield being announced, to the deafening cheers of the winning House members and a subdued but amicable booing from the rest!

Urdd eisteddfodau were a regular target. The input of the Welsh Department led by Ann Jones, and then by Bethan Jenkins ably supported by Marilyn Basset before her terminal illness, was critical to the many successful Urdd competitions, supplemented by Ray Gethin's energetic influence. Pupils and staff will recall pleasant (and perhaps some less pleasant!) memories of journeys to North and West

Yr Helgwn Pop Group 1976. With teacher Huw Morris are Vivienne Jenkins, Deborah Edwards, Carolyn Owen, Jayne Cordle, Ian Jones, and David Butler.

Mixed choir 1982, winners of First Prize at Urdd National Eisteddfod

Wales by hired coach, school minibus and staff cars; the various fund-raising events to cover costs; and the hospitality of the families who hosted the school's competitors. At the Urdd National Eisteddfodau, Cyfarthfa was recognised by other schools as a force to be reckoned with, and regularly came away with results in the top three places across an impressive array of activities.

Wins at National Urdd Eisteddfodau between 1972 and 1990, included

the Senior Girls Choir, conducted by Rosalind Pulman, taking the School Cup in 1973
the exhibition of pottery by Alison Couch, David Beynon, and Ian Evans in North Wales in 1976 when Sally Perman won the Under 15 Girls' solo, and Huw Morris' Pop Group 'Yr Helgwn' the Pop competition
the Senior Creative Dance Team and Cathy Druce in the recitation

for Welsh learners, gained first places at Abergele in 1980
the exciting successes at Rhymney in 1981 when the Pop Group and
the Mixed Choir won first prizes, and Ceri Williams, Cathy Druce and
Bhanu Ramaswamy gained places in their individual events. The Mixed
Choir won again in 1982
the tradition of success at was upheld at Aberavon in June, 1983, when
first places were gained by Susan Thomas (Woodwind Under-15 – flute)
and by the Creative Dance Team trained by Huw Morris.

1987 was a very special year, when the Urdd National Eisteddfod was held
in Merthyr. The only stage success that week was the magnificent win of
our Girls' Gymnastic Team, but there were considerable achievements in
other fields. Owain Rowlands won the BBC competition for the
composition of a signature tune to be used for its cover of the Urdd week;
Cyfarthfa pupils won the Science 'Homework' Competition; Stuart
Hinton and Geraint Hughes won first and second prizes in their respective
photography sections, and the first three prizes were won in the painting
sections for the fifth and sixth years. The school textile department under
Merryl Jones entered 21 items, all of which went through to the National
where they recorded a remarkable eight firsts (one jointly), five seconds
and two thirds, with 20 of their entries being kept for exhibition. Julie
Druce, Head Girl 1986–1987, gained a first and a joint second, and Carol
Wilding's collage won the overall prize in the textile competition. It was
an extremely proud textile department that then displayed its work in the
Newport National Eisteddfod, August 1987, at the behest of the WJEC
examiners!

Over the three years preparatory period for the Urdd National Eisteddfod
in Merthyr Tydfil, a significant proportion of the Cyfarthfa staff were
heavily involved. The Vice-Chairman was the School's Senior Deputy, Ray
Gethin, who, with Janice Rowlands, wife of the Merthyr Tydfil MP, helped
guarantee the exceptional quality of the Eisteddfod that year. Bethan
Jenkins, Head of Welsh, was one of the two Executive Secretaries.

Success continued in the years following, with outstanding wins at Cwm Gwendraith in 1989 for Kellie Sullivan in the individual Gymnastics Competition and for the Cyd-Adrodd (Choral Recitation for Learners) 15–19 Group.

Musical Highlights

Certain annual events stand out: none more than the Christmas service of carols and readings held in St David''s Church with the kind permission and wholehearted support of the rector, the Rev. David Lee. The inclusion of a candle-lit procession in the darkened Church was most memorable. Under the batons of Derry Prothero, Ian Hopkins and Gwilym Jones, and accompanied on the pipe organ by Maureen Prothero, the music was inspiring. Staff and pupils from each year group read the sequence of Bible lessons. After the teachers' industrial action ended, the service recommenced in December 1987.

The reputation of the school as a musical force grew once more. Over 40 enthusiastic pupils from the school appeared on the live showing of the 'Pop' programme *Disc a Dawn* on Saturday 2 December 1972. Apart from the thrill of being on television, they found the experience of seeing how a television programme was put together quite fascinating! The local newspaper, on 25 July 1975, reported the production of an LP by the school's choirs, and complimented the Girls' Choir's rendering of Benjamin Britten's 'Ceremony of Carols' stating that it 'makes singing sound fun ... the tone is light and lithe throughout ... a magnificent sound'.

On two occasions in June 1975, the Senior Girls' Choir featured in the BBC TV programme *Dechrau Canu, Dechrau Canmol*. During 1975–1976 fine concerts were staged by Derry Prothero, Head of Music, supported by a young orchestra conducted by Terry Strachan. In 1979 the Senior Girls' Choir received acclaim, when it made a significant contribution to an evening's entertainment by the well-known Cardiff Polyphonic Choir at Soar Chapel. This performance led to an invitation to participate in the prestigious Cardiff Festival of Choirs Welsh Night on 8 April 1981 at the

Girls' Choir 1976. 'A magnificent sound'

Ely Leisure Centre. That event was recorded and televised by HTV on the night of 11 August. One success led on to another and HTV invited the Girls' Choir to make a second recording on Saturday 26 September, this time for the *Sing to the Lord* programmes.

Choir members came and went, entering as young recruits and some years later leaving with a treasure house of good music and life-lasting memories. In fact, the first concert at Cae Mari Dwn was staged in response to a request from members of the Senior Girls' Choir who had left in the previous June and who felt a strong desire to take part in one last concert together. Since then, they have re-formed as an adult choir conducted by Derry Prothero, and given many concerts for charity. The Girls' Choir then had a remarkable year, following its autumn concert on Tuesday 22 September 1981, by contributing to the popular annual Carol Concert at St David's Church on Tuesday 22 December, taking part in the Dowlais Male Voice Choir's St David's Day concert at Rhydycar Leisure Centre on Saturday 27 February, appearing on HTV in *Sing to the Lord* on Sunday 2 May and Sunday 18 July 1982, and singing at the Royal Welsh

Show, Builth Wells, at the invitation of the Mid-Glamorgan Education Authority, on Tuesday 20 July 1982.

In 1983 the Girls' Choir participated in the Alun Williams' *On the Road Show* and in repeats of *Sing to the Lord*, took part the following year in the Salvation Army Band Centennial Salute, in the Boys' Brigade Centenary Concert at Cwmbran, in a joint venture with Heolgerrrig Primary School and for the second time in Alun Williams' BBC Road Show. Not to be completely outdone, the Mixed Choir joined with the Treorchy Male Voice Choir on 10 May 1984 to raise funds for the St. David's Church Restoration Appeal. Lastly, in 1985 the Girls' Choir was chosen to represent the County at the highly esteemed Severnside Prom in a concert televised from St David's Hall, Cardiff.

More Musical Achievements

In 1987 the Owain Rowlands' Pop Group won the Welsh heat of BBC TVs *Saturday Superstore* Talent Competition. Susan Thomas, whose flute playing has delighted many audiences, won the D. T. Davies Music Prize and the individual Round Table award of the Tydfil Prize Competition. She was a member of the Welsh Youth Orchestra. (Susan's sister, Julia, also a former pupil, was awarded the Final Year Prize at the Cardiff School of Music.) The Girls' Choir sang at a musical evening jointly organised with Heolgerrig Primary School in 1988 and the first school concert following industrial action was held on Thursday 4 May 1989, when pupils from both Upper and Lower School took part, adding lustre to the school year.

Cyfarthfa pupils were well represented in the Mid-Glamorgan Youth Orchestra and Choir between 1972 and 1990. In 1982 22 pupils, believed at the time to be a record attendance from any one school, were accepted on the Mid-Glamorgan Summer Choral Course. Steven Downes became a member of the Welsh National Youth Choir and two outstandingly talented instrumentalists, Alun Thomas (violin) and Susan Thomas (flautist), were members of the Welsh National Youth Orchestra. Alan Thomas later became its leader. Richard Bennett also played the violin for that orchestra and later for the Cambridge University Orchestra. A

Susan Thomas, a gifted flautist

number of pupils were members of the Mid-Glamorgan Orchestra and Choir.

Drama and Musicals

The untimely death of Vincent Lee, Head of English, the absence of a qualified drama teacher, and poor stage and lighting facilities, meant it was 1976 before the school staged its first dramatic production as a comprehensive. Then, in April, Emlyn Williams' play *The Corn is Green*, directed by Helena Rees, was put on in the main hall of the Castle building. Further excellent drama productions followed: *Witness for the Prosecution* by Agatha Christie (September 1977), *A Christmas Carol* adapted by Shaun Sutton from Dickens' novel (December 1983), *The Drunkard* by Brian J. Burton (April 1984) and *All Fair* by Frank Vickery (July 1988). Interspersed with these were two superb musical productions of Rogers and Hammerstein's *The King and I* (March 1978) and *South Pacific* (1980).

Reminiscing on the early productions, Helena, who became Mrs Mobley in 1978, comments on the accomplished and mature performances of Caroline Owen as Miss Moffat and of Andrew Strachan as Morgan Evans in *The Corn is Green*, and observed that the whole production, for which the audience paid the princely sum of 25p each, was 'worthy of the professional stage'. Glanville Jones and Vic Davies constructed the set; Dewi Bowen devised the frontispiece of the programmes and painted the set, a task he revelled in for every production. Lighting was in the hands of Ron Davies and costumes bore Merryl Jones' masterly touch. Meriol Iverson took charge of make-up with the assurance of an expert, and with results that matched!

The King and I was an ambitious production with complex sets and 'a cast of thousands' including Gwilym Jones as King, Sandra Jones as his wife and Huw Morris as Lun Tha. Sixteen-year-old Sian Davies was Anna and Andrea Samuel was Yumkin. Derry Prothero ensured that the music was of the highest standard, and once again Dewi Bowen did not miss a trick! To cap it all, Eira Smith, a school secretary, returned from viewing the same musical at the Palladium to proclaim that the school's production was much better!

Cast of The King and I March 1978

That first musical was magical. It was to be followed in 1980 by *South Pacific* and another stunning production. Gwilym Jones, Sandra Jones and Huw Morris re-appeared and Andrea Samuel took a lead role as Nelly Forbush. Phil Atkinson stood in for Rod Walker whose father had died in Northern Ireland, cleverly reading his lines from a clip-board, and cutting a dash in his American Officer's uniform! Wonderful songs and performances were many – such as Sandra Jones' *Bali H'ai*, and Andrea Samuel and Gwilym Jones' duet *Some Enchanted Evening*. Andrea as Nelly sang *A hundred and one pounds of fun* as Michael Treharne danced in a grass skirt, wearing a bra made of coconuts from which he threw sweets at me sitting in the front row, causing some hilarity.

Two years later, in the first production at the new Cae Mari Dwn Upper School, fresh faces appeared in *A Christmas Carol* with Robert Purdy playing Scrooge, Robert Evans as Bob Cratchit and Arfon Rees as Tiny

Tim. Ever faithful Huw Morris took the part of Marley. Helena Mobley presented her final production, *The Drunkard*, in 1984. Soon after, the teachers' industrial action began and sadly, productions ceased for a number of years.

In their first year in the Castle (June 1982), the Lower School pupils and staff showed what they could do. They produced a fine concert/musical involving half the Lower School pupils, virtually all the staff based in Georgetown and the peripatetic instrumental teachers. Gwilym Jones and Allison Lewis deserved particular praise, and the event was the precursor of major productions led by the inexhaustible Allison and a stalwart team of staff.

The Joseph Parry Project

The raising of the school leaving age to 16 in 1971 was an opportunity for teachers to design courses which would attract and hold the interest of young people compelled to remain at school when they had hoped to leave. So was born the Joseph Parry project, centred on the almost derelict iron-workers' cottages in Chapel Row where the famous Welsh musician was born. John Hindley, science teacher, and some 20–30 pupils surveyed the empty and decaying properties of Chapel Row, together with the uneven waste ground in front of it where the Glamorganshire Canal was hidden. A trench dug roughly at right angles to Chapel Row revealed the line of the canal, and a small section with its stone walls was exposed to view. Excitingly, the remains of an old barge were discovered in the process. After John Hindley left the school, Mansell Richards, head of History, who had also been involved in the project, took over as co-ordinator.

Work involving the history, geography, biology, art and craft departments continued throughout the 1970s on this exemplary project involving in all over 120 pupils. A brochure compiled by Mansell Richards and pupils, with splendid drawings by Dewi Bowen, was printed in the summer of 1977 by Merthyr Council. In that year the project gained the Prince of Wales

Alison Kinsey unveils the plaque, made by Dewi Bowen,
at Joseph Parry's birthplace

Award, which was received by Mansell Richards on behalf of the school at a ceremony in Llanelli. That year, too, the project received the Shell 'Better Britain' Award.

On Friday 22 September 1978, well over 1000 people from near and far celebrated on that bright sunny evening the foresight and ingenuity of Cyfarthfa High School staff and pupils who, together with a grant of some thousands of pounds from the Borough Council, had brought the Dr Joseph Parry Birthplace Project to completion. A plaque designed by Dewi Bowen was unveiled by Alison Kinsey, a sixth-form pupil, and the official opening of the birthplace at number 4 Chapel Row was performed by Elizabeth Parry, great grand-daughter of Joseph Parry. Gareth Daniel officiated at the ceremony and music was provided by the Senior Girls' Choir, the Dowlais Male Voice Choir, and the Salvation Army Band.

Two years later on Tuesday 14 July 1980, Prince Charles came to see the restored cottages when the School was represented by the Head Girl, Sharon Rogers. The cottage contains mementos of Dr Joseph Parry"s life and the site remains an important historical attraction.

Beyond the Classroom

By the 1970s–80s the increased affluence of Merthyr families, despite economic difficulties, was reflected in a wide range of out-of-school activities. In February 1975, the mathematics department took a trip to London to hear the London Symphony Orchestra conducted by Andre Previn, a trip repeated annually for some years. A popular summer holiday in the 1970s was a cruise organised by the Local Education Authority, well supported by Cyfarthfa staff and pupils. In 1980 Huw Morris and Jane Type co-led a group of 28 pupils aged between 13 and 15 years on a cruise from Southampton to ports in northern Europe. In 1983, Ron Roberts, Head of Geography, planned a flight to view South Wales from the air, a unique experience for those taking part.

During 1988 a link with a school from Merthyr Tydfil's twin town of Clichy-la-Garenne involved a combined outdoor course at Dolygaer

Centre and cultural visits within South Wales. Jon Allen, who organised the link, arranged a reciprocal visit to France in 1989. In 1988–1989 alone, first year pupils visited Blaenavon Big Pit, soon an annual event; the Home Economics Department visited the Ideal Home Exhibition; sixth formers in the French Department made an exchange visit to Normandy; Bill Dines, Head of Science, led a ski trip to Austria; and Gareth Francis led a combined Cyfarthfa/Cathays High School ski trip to Switzerland at Easter 1989. Ron Williams, Head of Lower School, took regular summer trips to various destinations on the continent. All these are examples of a rich variety of opportunities offered to Cyfarthfa's pupils, and not unknown to be occasions when the staff 'let their hair down'!

Community Service

Another aspect of activities beyond the classroom was the range of voluntary and charitable activities undertaken by pupils – activities that gave much pleasure to those who planned and executed their ideas, and which provided valuable support to the beneficiaries. Food parcels were distributed at Christmas, older pupils helped with selling flags for different charities over week-ends, and regular visits to and parties held in three hospitals, Sandbrook Old People's Home, the Adult Training Centre and the Hollies Day Centre. The work of the pupils was recognised in 1978–1979 when the school was presented with the National Westminster Bank 'Project Respond Award'.

Many charitable activities were held within the boundary of Cyfarthfa Park, from barrel rolling to sponsored fun runs. Credit has to go to the pupils, who appeared to be able to persuade the public to dig into bottomless pockets and purses! Between Upper and Lower School something in the region of £5000 was raised in the single academic year 1988–1989; £922 was raised by massed ranks of Lower School pupils taking part in the Mayor's Fun Run. Incidentally, Allison Lewis, who organised the pupils, not only had the uncanny knack of persuading them to take part, but had an insatiable appetite for collecting the proceeds! Non-uniform days became a popular, safe and easily organised means of raising monies.

Upper Sixth Form 1990

Proceeds were distributed to various good causes such as the Mayor's Appeal, Shelter and Make Children Happy at Christmas Time. Across the country children were gripped by powerful media appeals which portrayed the desperate plight of families and children suffering from earthquake, drought, famine, tsunami, flooding, poverty, and endemic illnesses such as poliomyelitis. Great support was given to the Blue Peter Kampuchea Appeal, Comic Relief, Children in Need, the Blind, and the staggering sum of over £2000 was raised in 1988 towards the Rotary Polio Plus Campaign which aimed at immunising the whole of the world's children against poliomyelitis.

Farewell

In 1990 I accepted an invitation to become Senior Adviser for Assessment with Mid-Glamorgan Education Authority and left Cyfarthfa High School.

When, at farewell assemblies in both Upper and Lower Schools, I expressed a wish to shake each of the pupils present by the hand, to my great delight the response was warm and unanimous. The occasional spontaneous peck on the cheek by the girls was at first embarrassing and then very pleasing! It was an occasion not to be forgotten. Within the limits of this chapter it has been impossible sufficiently to express my grateful thanks to my teacher colleagues, the secretaries, technicians, caretakers and canteen staff for their loyal support in serving the pupils of Cyfarthfa High School during my time there. I thank them all.

Some Welsh schools, in more socially and economically privileged locations, may have had better academic, sporting, and cultural success, but Cyfarthfa High School has displayed the professional capacity, the tenacity and the resourcefulness to stand the test of time and rise to considerable heights. This locality has often featured in the press and mass media for unfortunate reasons, but Cyfarthfa High School is one example of an institution which in its resilience and determination has every reason to be proud of its achievements – and so does Merthyr Tydfil.

A quotation from Wordsworth's poem *Excursion* sums up my feelings for Cyfarthfa High School:

And when the stream
Which overflowed the soul was passed away,
A consciousness remained that it had left,
Deposited upon the silent shores of memory,
Images and precious thoughts that shall not die,
And cannot be destroyed.

Appendix to Chapter Four

MANAGEMENT STRUCTURE 1972 –1990

HEAD
Mr D. Bennett

DEPUTY (Pastoral)	DEPUTY (Academic)	THIRD DEPUTY (General)
Mr J. Lewis (1970–1975)	Mr D. Young (1976–1987)	Miss M. Treharne (1972–1977)
Mr R. Gethin (1974–1990)	Mr P. Atkinson (1987–1990)	Mrs J. Williams (1977–1990)

HEAD OF LOWER SCH.	HEAD OF MIDDLE SCH.	HEAD OF UPPER SCH.	HEADS FACULTIES/DEPTS
Years 1 and 2	**Years 3 and 4**	**Years 5 and 6**	**Not listed**
Mr I Rees (1972–1981)	Mr R. Gethin (1972–1974)	Mr T. Strachan (1972–1978)	
Mr R. Williams (1981–1990)	Mr M. Richards (1974–1977)	Mr A. Whiley (1977–1978–Acting)	
Mrs M. Iverson (1988–1990	Mr C. O'Shea (1977–1984)	Mr D. Painter (1978 –1982)	
–Acting)	Mr R. Butcher (1984–1990)	Mr P. Atkinson (1982–!987)	
		Dr C. Ferguson (1987–1989)	
		Mr A. Hughes (1989–1990)	

YEAR TUTORS	YEAR TUTORS	YEAR TUTORS	SUBJECT TEACHERS
Mrs B. Roberts (1972-1984)	Mr G. Rees (1973-1981)	As for Middle School	Not listed
Mrs G. Owens (1972-1978)	Mr C. O'Shea (1973-1977)	(in rotation)	
Mrs M. Iverson (1978-1988)	Mrs S. Jones (1973-1990)		
Mrs A. Lewis (1988-1990)	Mr B. Evans (1977-1980)		
	Mr R. Butcher (1979-1984)		
	Mrs H. Mobley (1981-1990)		
	Mrs J. Type (1984-1990)		
	Mr G. Brame (1990)		

FORM TUTORS	FORM TUTORS	FORM TUTORS
Not listed	Not listed	Not listed

SUPPORT STAFF

SECRETARIAL	LABORATORY TECHNICIANS	WORKSHOP TECHNICIAN
Mrs N. Sharp	Mrs S. Jones	Mr L. Griffiths
Mrs G. Williams	Mrs A. Weller	
Mrs E. Smith	Miss P. Nicholls	
Mrs E. Evans	Mr P. Davies	
Mrs S. Coombs		

Note: Year Tutors attended Head of Department meetings to help Pastoral/ Academic cohesion
A House System encouraged vertical integration

CHANGE, CONSTANT CHANGE:
1990-2013

TREVOR JONES

We should provide . . . for all the nation's sons and daughters, an education generous, inspiring and humane.

(R. H. Tawney)

That change is the only constant may be true of life in general, but of education during the past two decades, it is particularly apposite. At the commencement of the 1990s, Cyfarthfa High School was confronted by, and had to adapt to, changes that came from both inside and outside its walls. First were changes at the top.

The resignation, after his lengthy and distinguished tenure, of Dennis Bennett in 1990, and the decision of Raymond Gethin, senior Deputy at the school, not to stand for the acting headship because of his imminent retirement, meant that Janice Williams was appointed acting head, a role she performed with distinction until the appointment of Trevor Church as Headteacher in the Autumn of 1991.

With his background in the English educational system, Trevor Church brought a marked shift in perspective together with considerable energy

Alan Pritchard

and a desire to embrace whole-heartedly the agenda for change. Intelligent and extremely articulate, Trevor Church also exhibited a certain restlessness, and it was no great surprise when, in December 1995, it was announced that he had become Headteacher of Olchfa Comprehensive School in Swansea. (He later became Principal of the Sir James Henderson British School in Milan and sadly died, when still quite young, in Italy in 2009.)

After these years of interregnum, Alan Pritchard, deputy at the school since 1992 and previously Geography adviser for South Glamorgan, was appointed to the headship in January 1996. A first-class honours graduate in Geography from Swansea University, the new head brought a wealth of educational experience, a clear vision for the school and personal skills that enabled him to take the staff, with a shared sense of purpose and direction, on a momentous journey.

The Political Environment

The external changes came from political and educational developments. First, the progressive implementation of the 1988 Education Reform Act created a dynamic for change through the publication of examination results and league tables. Then the Local Government (Wales) Act 1994 led on 1 April 1996 to Merthyr Tydfil once again becoming a County Borough, complete with its own Director of Education, just as at the beginning of this story in 1913. Although the benefits of scale enjoyed within the old Mid Glamorgan Authority were no longer available, greater proximity enabled the school to develop close working relationships with the Merthyr Authority, and make a major positive contribution to educational standards within the Borough.

More significant was the Government of Wales Act 1998, which brought into being the Welsh Assembly Government, with its determination to impose a distinctively Welsh dimension upon Education. In 2001 it ended the publication of school league tables in Wales (but from 2011 began to publish secondary school banding tables). Its approach to funding education was also distinctive. UK Treasury funding, earmarked specifically for schools in England, has in Wales been filtered, first through the Assembly Government's own network of priorities, and secondly through those of the local authorities, before, in diminished form, reaching the schools. Consequently, funding for schools for much of the past decade has been at a consistently lower level than that for their English counterparts. In 2011 it was more than £600 per pupil less. The Assembly Government also pursued a distinctive vision of post-16 education and training. That vision, with its huge impact upon Cyfarthfa School, is discussed later in this chapter.

Another consequence of the political developments of the 1980s was the new-look Governing Body whose structure and nature were moulded, first by the 1986 Education Act, and secondly, by the Education Reform Act of 1988 which devolved responsibility for the budget and strategic oversight of the school into the hands of Governors, as mentioned in the previous chapter.

Since the 1990s, Cyfarthfa's Governing Body has played a major role, together with the Headteacher, himself a Governor, in ensuring good quality education. Its work has been overseen by three Chairs of Governors of exceptional ability, dedication and integrity: Peter Bezant, David Lewis and Gareth Morgan, under whose chairmanship, the Governing Body has truly become the critical friend of the school, staunchly defensive of its interests and extremely supportive of the staff. The Board currently comprises 20 members: 5 LEA representatives, 5 co-opted members, 6 parent representatives, 3 staff representatives and the Headteacher.

Inspection and School Improvement

Benjamin Franklin stated that there are only two certainties in life: death and taxes. Contemporary Welsh schools can add a third: Estyn Inspection! Regular inspections, added to the publication of examination results and banding tables, mean that the pressure to raise standards is continuous.

Cae Mari Dwn school building

Cyfarthfa High School enjoyed – if this is the appropriate term – a period of fifteen years without a full school inspection, from 1982 until 1997. Then it experienced the new breed of inspections, carried out on that occasion by the Salford Business School inspection team. The verdict was that Cyfarthfa was a good school with many signs of improvement in place. One highly significant action point to emerge was the need to increase the range of teaching and learning strategies. This led directly to the adoption of a radically new approach to staff development, based initially on the Improving the Quality of Education for All (IQEA) model. It incorporated a refreshingly new approach.

For many years, schools had been subject to the 'top-down' model of school improvement, involving centrally identified priorities expounded to teachers by outside advisers. Teachers dutifully absorbed and fed back to their colleagues and undoubtedly much good practice was disseminated in this way. IQEA was different. First, the staff themselves identified important areas for improvement within the school; secondly, staff expertise in specific areas was recognised and further developed by action-research projects undertaken voluntarily by staff who received appropriate training; thirdly, the focus was exclusively on Teaching and Learning, the core school function; fourthly, and very significantly, teachers themselves became the 'experts', who, after researching their topic thoroughly and producing and trialling the teaching techniques and resources which resulted, delivered training to their colleagues at events in the school, often including staff from Cyfarthfa's associate primary schools.

Practical Relevance

No longer was staff development delivered by outside 'experts' but by respected colleagues, at the 'chalk-face' every day of their working lives, and whose 'street cred' was consequently far greater. Furthermore, improvements were presented whose practical relevance to teaching was clear, having grown out of the recognised needs of Cyfarthfa, and been thoroughly evaluated by groups of staff - and pupils. Numerous surveys have enabled pupils to identify both positive and negative aspects of the teaching at Cyfarthfa. Such surveys are completely anonymous, with no opportunity for improper or negative comments regarding members of staff, with the results fed into school improvement processes.

In this highly significant departure the role of Alan Pritchard cannot be overstated. A prominent figure among a like-minded group of headteachers in south Wales, he was instrumental in moulding what had been an informal association of comprehensive schools, dipping their collective toe into shared training and development, into a fully-fledged south-east Wales branch of IQEA, incorporating at its peak some thirteen schools, anticipating by several years (and arguably, prompting) the Welsh Assembly Government's recognition of the importance of school collaboration and action-research-based training.

Prior to the 1990s, an experienced teacher's classroom was more or less sacrosanct, with the notion of lesson observation by other staff within the school viewed with unease, misgivings and even resistance by the teacher concerned. From the mid 1990s, however, the observation of lessons by colleagues gradually became the accepted norm at the school, and a pattern of constructive professional review of teachers' performance was established. While educational improvement was a prominent characteristic of Dennis Bennett's headship, with its enlightened and effective focus on curriculum development and the holistic needs of all pupils, the 1990s and 2000s witnessed intensification in the focus and methodology of school improvement.

Cyfarthfa's success in meeting the 1997 inspection recommendations was confirmed by the findings of subsequent inspections. The 2003 inspection described Cyfarthfa as very good in terms of its ethos, standards of achievement and quality of teaching. Standards achieved by pupils were deemed good or better in 89 per cent of classes observed (95 per cent in the sixth form), and at least satisfactory in 100 per cent of lessons, while in a major vindication of six years of IQEA inspired staff training, the quality of teaching was considered a major strength of the school, being good or better in 91 per cent of lessons. The ethos and general climate of the school was very impressive, attention to student welfare and well-being outstanding. The quality of leadership was considered very good. The overall judgement of the 2009 inspection was: 'A very good school with many outstanding qualities'.

Public perception of these qualities was reflected by the increase in pupil numbers throughout the late 90's and into the 2000's, reaching a peak in 2010, with 1537 pupils on roll.

Collaboration

A key feature of IQEA was collaboration among groups of schools experiencing similar problems or identifying similar needs. Cyfarthfa, together with its associate primary schools, shared school improvement activities with a range of schools in Nottinghamshire, Derbyshire and Bedfordshire.

Today, Cyfarthfa and its primary feeder schools collaborate in order to minimise any disruption to pupils' education as they take the leap from primary to secondary school. Headteachers and subject coordinators meet regularly to plan joint curriculum developments and assessment strategies. Joint training sessions on teaching and learning are held for Cyfarthfa and primary schools' staff. Cyfarthfa members particularly prominent in achieving this include Meriel Iverson, Christine Hamer, Allison Lewis, Helen Canney and Suzanne Mulcahy, though they would be the first to acknowledge the tremendous support of staff from across the school.

Another development over the past decade, singularly different from the competitive environment of previous years, has been increasing collaboration with other high schools, training agencies and Merthyr College (a constituent of the University of Glamorgan since May 2006). . This has been closely linked with the expansion of vocational education and the greatly increased curriculum choice available. Pupils from ages 14 – 19 receive tuition in subjects as diverse as hairdressing, motor mechanics, engineering and law at a range of off-site venues. In 2012 all four secondary schools in the Borough had a common sixth-form timetable offering over 30 academic and vocational subject choices and since September 2010, all pupils in secondary schools in Merthyr have been entitled to access all courses on offer across the entire county borough. This quantum leap in provision has been achieved only through the excellent relationships developed between Cyfarthfa and its partner providers over many years.

The Staff

School staffs evolve in line with curriculum developments and fluctuations in pupil numbers. At Cyfarthfa throughout the 90s and the first decade of the new millennium the number of teachers steadily increased, reaching 68 by 1997, 76 in 2000, 83 in 2005, and 84 by 2009. Pupil intake also increased rapidly, numbers peaking at 1,518 in 2006/07. Since then demographic trends have reduced pupil numbers in all Merthyr's schools, and despite its relative popularity, Cyfarthfa is not immune. This,

High School staff relaxing, November 2012

combined with a squeeze on school budgets, resulted in some early retirements and, very regrettably, a small number of compulsory redundancies.

This period also saw the introduction of Learning Support Assistants who provide in-class support for pupils experiencing learning difficulties or physical disability, and carry out a range of ancillary functions, from photocopying and physical production of learning resources to putting up classroom displays.

A marked feature of Cyfarthfa has always been the dedication and loyalty to the school displayed by its teaching and non-teaching staff. This is typified by the following members who all happen to have left the school since 2000, having each contributed on average well in excess of thirty years' service: Christine Hamer (Maths/Year Head), Sandra Jones (Biology/Assistant Head), Alison Lewis (RE/Assistant Head), Helena Mobley (English/Year Head), David Leigh (Maths), Ian Hopkins (Head of Maths/Senior Management Team Member)), Gwyn Rees (Head of Science), Trevor Jones (English/Deputy Head), Robert Butcher

(Geography/Deputy Head) and Desna Pearce (Food Technology/ Head of Year). And finally, though she might not be entirely grateful for this revelation, it should be noted here that Cyfarthfa's senior laboratory technician, Anne Weller, continues to serve loyally after more than forty years at the school.

In Memoriam

It rapidly becomes clear to all associated with the school that a great sense of family pervades Cyfarthfa High, its pupils, staff and governors; and sadly, experience teaches each of us in time that there is nothing more painful or distressing than losing a family member. Consequently, it has been with great collective sadness as well as individual grief that the school has faced bereavements.

Nothing can be more harrowing for a school than to lose a pupil to untimely death. The sense of personal loss and consciousness of unlived years and unfulfilled potential haunt the classrooms and corridors, casting a tangible pall over all the school's activities. There have been four occasions since 1990 when Cyfarthfa has experienced such loss.

In March 2001, the death occurred in a motorcycle accident of Michael Crompton, a gifted, humorous and well-liked sixth-form student, on the verge of achieving high academic success at school and progressing to a top British university. In June 2006, Reuben Morgan, a much respected year 10 pupil with a strong sporting background and hugely popular throughout school and community, was lost in a dreadful swimming accident. And in September 2008, the school as a whole, but Lower School in particular, was deeply saddened by the death from illness of Jessica Bentley. The silent respect of Jessica's fellow pupils, assembled on the Castle Terrace as Jessica's cortege passed through Cyfarthfa Park, was extremely moving.

No less keenly felt, although occurring shortly after he left the school, was the death in a tragic accident in February 1998 of Matthew Jones, a memorable character and son of Clive Jones, staunch supporter and governor of Cyfarthfa.

Most recently, Caitlin Edwards of Year 8 died in June 2012 following a tragic motorcycle accident. A vibrant, fresh-faced and extremely likeable young lady, Caitlin is sadly missed by all who knew her.

The period under review has also witnessed the passing of several much-loved and respected former staff members. At Christmas 1998 past colleagues were shocked by the sudden death of Robert Coombs, previously teacher in charge of boys' PE at the school, talented cricketer and gymnast, and staunch upholder of the highest standards of sportsmanship. In 1997, Raymond Gethin, renowned Deputy Headteacher, warmly remembered for his loyalty, humour and immense dedication to Cyfarthfa and to all things Welsh, died after a tragically brief retirement. The loss occurred in 2002 of another of Cyfarthfa's larger-than-life characters, the irrepressible Meriel Iverson, whose warmth and humour enhanced the lives of countless colleagues and generations of pupils over a long and successful career. In that same year Colin Whitfield died, fondly remembered and greatly missed as a loyal colleague, all-round sportsman and dedicated teacher of Design Technology, until his career was cut short by ill-health.

In 2003, after a protracted illness, borne with characteristic fortitude, the school was again diminished by the death of Alun Hughes, in turn, highly regarded Head of History and Head of Sixth, whose personal and academic standards will long be remembered by pupils and colleagues alike.

Two much loved and respected former members of the Welsh department died, each after a lengthy period of illness, Marilyn Bassett in July 2004 and Freda Watkins in August 2007; two quite different characters, their personalities, diligence and long-term commitment to school and subject will be long remembered.

On 23 January 2012 the death occurred after a too brief retirement of Frank Terrell, former head of English. His flair and dedication were matched only by his thoughtfulness. Frank had time for everyone and was, in the truest sense, a gentleman.

This stained glass window above the Boys' Entrance illustrates the intention that the school should teach practical and technical skills as well as academic subjects.

As indicated elsewhere, Governors have immersed themselves energetically in the life of the school and striven to ensure its continued success. Digby Jones, Mal Hopkins and Sally Winter had strong family links with the school and all brought the benefits of great dedication and a wealth of relevant experience to the position of Governor, Digby as an experienced local politician, Mal as an expert in the field of health and safety and Sally as a practising educational psychologist. Their deaths, in 1995, 2003 and 2008 respectively, were therefore a cause of great personal sadness as well as professional loss to the school.

The Changing Curriculum

Pupils and teachers revisiting the school after twenty years' absence would be astounded by the scope and nature of curriculum change. There are statutory frameworks for Work-Related Education, Careers, Personal and Social Education and Education for Sustainable Development and Global

Citizenship. Accompanying all this has been the extensive development of Personal, Social and Health provision, with the school now offering support facilities for pupils, including a drop-in centre offering confidential counselling from health professionals. Also Key Skills have been introduced, an area where Cyfarthfa has achieved excellent results.

Information Technology, of course, is an example of the new subject choices. In the 1980s, it was studied as a discrete subject by a few pupils, but in the 1990s at Cyfarthfa, as elsewhere, the subject burgeoned. Educators and pupils recognised its tremendous potential with the expansion of the Internet and the development of e-mails. IT became ICT, or Information Communications Technology, and today every subject includes ICT in its schemes of work and every student studies it to at least the age of 16, with many progressing to post-16 study. Pupils learn through VLEs (Virtual Learning Environments) such as Moodle, increasingly used across the school. In 2008, the school became one of the first secondary schools in Wales to achieve the BECTA ICT Mark. Computer suites and interactive white boards proliferate across the school, while teachers in all subjects increasingly use this important resource.

Design and Technology is another example of such change, with traditional workshops giving way to CAD/CAM suites and the ultra-precision of the laser cutter, all enabling a real improvement in the quality of work produced by pupils and in their preparedness for the high-tech world of the 21st Century. Data-logging facilities in Science, Apple Mac design facilities in Art and 'Sibelius' software in Music testify to the powerful impact of ICT across the school.

Enterprise Related Education

The social and economic challenges facing Merthyr Tydfil remain formidable and the current period of government imposed austerity dispels any hopes of an economic quick-fix. All the more relevant then – together with the school's emphasis on providing its pupils with the qualities and skills they require in the modern world – has been the emphasis Cyfarthfa has placed on work and enterprise-related education.

Boys planning group work

The school has been a staunch supporter of the Education Business Partnership (EBP) since its inception in 1989, consistently involved in activities to stimulate the creativity and entrepreneurial talents of its pupils. Project Dynamo, the Sony Business Challenge and Young Enterprise schemes have been enthusiastically embraced. In the South-East Wales Stock-Market Challenge, Cyfarthfa pupils won first prize in 2005 and second in 2009; in 2007, the Regional EBP Young Entrepreneur of the Year Award came to the school; Cyfarthfa's pupils submitted the Best Business Plan in the Sony Small Business Challenge of 2007; and the school's team were area finalists in Young Enterprise 2009.

Since 2008, in emulation of the BBC television programme, the Business Studies department has operated its own *The Apprentice* competition, complete with 'Lord Sugar', in the form of headteacher, Alan Pritchard. This highly popular competition reveals and encourages the amazing confidence, initiative and enterprise to be found in Cyfarthfa's student body. Winners of this demanding competition to date are: Leanne Haines (2008), Tsoane Hill (2010) and Connor Matthews (2011) – the competition was not held in 2009. In 2010, a *Junior Apprentice* competition was initiated, and its winners so far have been Sophie Evans (2010) and Carey Evans (2011).

The EBP Compact Award Scheme encourages all pupils to focus on good attendance, punctuality and team-work. The prizes provided by the school for Compact success, ranging from paint-balling sessions at Pentyrch to ice-skating and ten-pin bowling at Swansea, are greatly appreciated and provide an added incentive; but the real prize is the development of attitudes and habits which will stand pupils in good stead throughout life.

To complete the picture of enterprise and work-related education developed at Cyfarthfa over recent decades, there is the excellent careers guidance provided by Careers Coordinators and a full-time adviser based at the school. The finishing touch is the highly popular and well supported Careers Convention which has been held at the school biennially over the past decade.

The consequence has been a transformation from a broadly academic curriculum to one offering life skills and expanding vocational provision - by 2012 Cyfarthfa was offering 11 BTEC qualifications to its 15 to 16-year-old pupils – with a concerted effort made to achieve parity of esteem between the academic and the vocational.

Expanding Horizons

The distinction between curricular and extra-curricular activities inevitably blurs in a school like Cyfarthfa, with its focus on maximising the holistic development of its pupils. It is a great strength that so many staff and pupils give freely of their time and energy to create an additional dimension of experience and achievement, enriching both school and community.

Music

Cyfarthfa's musical talent has thrilled and delighted audiences at venues ranging from St. David's Hall, Cardiff, to St. David's Church, Merthyr Tydfil, where in an almost unbroken tradition going back to the 1970s, the school annually reaffirms its place in the community of Merthyr Tydfil, in a carol service characterised by exuberance, joy and moments of spell-binding beauty.

Individual Cyfarthfa students under the tutelage of the department have long achieved great success in the wider musical sphere, most recently: Emma Baxter and Dean Godfrey, who were members of the National Youth Choir of Wales in 2000; Nicholas Brill, instrumentalist in the National Youth Brass Band in 2005 and 2006; Rhiannon Jones, chorister in the National Youth Choir in 2005; Rachel Roberts, member of the National Youth Orchestra of Wales in 2009 and 2010; and Luke Hier, National Youth chorister in 2011. Luke's younger brother, Thomas, has maintained the family tradition, including solo performances, with 'Only Boys Aloud' in 2010 and 2011.

Art

An extensive range of extra-curricular courses and activities provided for pupils, include a comic book workshop held in 2006, the collage workshops run by professional artist, Suzanne Carpenter, in 2006 and 2007, the screen-painting workshops held in 2008 and 2009, portraiture and ceramics workshops held between 2006 and 2010, and the Creative Animation project for GCSE pupils, run in conjunction with Glamorgan Gates in 2009. Add numerous visits to galleries and museums in Cardiff, Bristol, London and Amsterdam, plus competition success by such talented artists as Carmen Wong, Callum Thomas and Emily Harris, and you have a picture of the lively and fulfilling diet of artistic activities provided for, and undertaken by, Cyfarthfa pupils in recent years. Talent has been evident in public exhibitions, such as those at Cyfarthfa Museum in 2008 and 2010, the creation of a children's corner in St David's Church in 2006, success in 2008 in a competition to design a mural for a walkway in the town and a series of paintings for Prince Charles Hospital, completed in 2009.

Portrait workshop

English

The nature of English as a subject makes it particularly adept not only at delivering oral and literacy skills and nurturing a critical appreciation of literature and the communications media, but also developing skills and knowledge associated with citizenship and a wide range of extra-curricular topics. In 1999, a highly successful literacy fair was held in Lower school, involving a colourful range of rap artists, writers, poets and story-tellers. In 2000 the department's production of Dylan Thomas's *Under Milk Wood* enthralled audiences on both sides of the Atlantic, achieving great acclaim when performed at Winchester High School's state of the art auditorium in Massachusetts, USA.

'Desert Island Books', a competition for pupils and staff, was held in 2004, the year in which the visiting Black Cat Theatre staged a memorable performance of *Romeo and Juliet* at Upper School. The Literacy Day in

Author Tom Palmer who spoke to boys about the importance of reading.

2008 was a milestone event, linking the English and PE departments and showing through sport – especially, perhaps, to the boys – that literacy can be 'cool' after all. Members of the Cardiff Blues rugby team, Cardiff City Football Club and numerous sports journalists made memorable contributions, and Scott Quinnell presented copies of his recently published book to pupils.

In 2008 the Cinetig Film Project combined cam-corder skills with historical research to produce 'Back to the Future at Rhyd-y-car Cottages', a DVD currently available at St. Fagan's Museum of Welsh Life.

Shot at Dawn

What better way to bring citizenship home to students than by encouraging them to be instrumental in changing a law? The opportunity to do this arose around Armistice Day, 2005, when, in conjunction with a GCSE module on War Poetry, pupils investigated the case of Private Harry Farr, a First World War soldier, shot at dawn for alleged cowardice. They wrote letters arguing either for or against pardons for Private Farr and the 305 other British servicemen who met the same fate. A selection of these letters was posted to the Home Secretary, and in January 2006, the Cabinet Office informed the school that they had been forwarded for the attention of Don Touhig MP, Minister for Veterans. He was so impressed by the quality of the pupils' arguments that he arranged to visit the school to discuss the matter with them.

The pupils then learned another lesson about our democracy, for before the planned visit could take place, Mr. Touhig fell victim to a government re-shuffle, losing his ministerial position. He did, however, visit Cyfarthfa some two weeks after the law pardoning Private Farr and his comrades was passed, and the visit ended with an invitation to tour the Houses of Parliament, an invitation enthusiastically taken up by some 40 Cyfarthfa students.

Mathematics

Typical of its desire to challenge and excite pupils has been the department's involvement in the United Kingdom Mathematics Challenge, established by the UK Mathematics Trust in 1996 with the aim of advancing the mathematical education of young people. The department annually enters approximately 100 candidates for the Junior Challenge, around 40 candidates for the Intermediate Challenge, and again around 40 sixth form mathematicians for the Senior Challenge. Since the mid-90s, Cyfarthfa students have excelled, regularly securing high levels of success at Bronze, Silver and Gold certificate level, and on two occasions achieving the highest accolade, entry into the Maths Olympiad. This was achieved by Adam Ridley in 2001 and again by Jarrod Williams in 2010. Unsurprisingly, Adam went on to secure a First Class

Honours degree in Mathematics at Swansea University in 2009, while Jarrod at the time of writing is a Maths undergraduate at Oxford University.

Design and Technology

Technical flair of a high order has been an essential ingredient in a string of engineering successes registered by the school's technology students, including becoming Post-16 Welsh Regional Winners of the Formula 1 Schools Challenge in 2004 (Nathan Wise, Andrew Kendall, Christopher Richards, Michael Palmer and David Phillips) and team triumph in the Engineering Education Scheme of Wales in 2005 (Jac Evans, Ben Shires and Faisal Dubash). Adam Lloyd's achievement in winning the Student Innovation Wales Award 2004 was outstanding. In 2003 a £4,500 grant was secured from Ford UK toward equipping the Design Technology workshops.

Science

Science at Cyfarthfa has enjoyed excellent links since the 1990s with the Education Business Partnership, involving pupils in real-life challenges with an emphasis on problem solving and team-work, requiring them to put into practice the abstract principles which they have learnt in their science lessons. Lower School pupils have been involved in such tasks as constructing giant tetrahedrons from straws; around 50 pupils participating annually in the GE Engineering Challenge in conjunction with GE Aircraft Engines. Older pupils have been involved in a robotics workshop, building and programming their own robotic vehicles; while others have had to build their own self-propelled buggy, conveying a 500gm bag of sugar, across a bridge – also of their own construction.

Every effort is made to inform pupils of the latest scientific developments and issues, from the new Herschel Telescope, so effectively illustrated and explained at a 'Science Made Simple' event at the school, to the nature of comets and asteroids, including their potentially devastating effect on life on earth, graphically explained in a 2008 lecture by Dr. Paul Roche of

Engineering and Design Challenge pupils

Glamorgan University, a frequent visitor to the school in recent years. In 2009 an Australian forensic scientist visited the school to challenge a large group of Applied Science pupils to solve a murder mystery, using the latest forensic techniques, including finger-print and DNA analysis. The fascination and excitement can be imagined, as over 100 sixteen and seventeen-year-olds were transformed into hands-on 'scene of crime' officers for the day.

The jewel in the crown, however, has been the extremely ambitious and successful trips organised in 2008, 2009 and 2010 to the USA and Latin America. In March of both 2008 and 2010, groups of around 30 visited NASA's Kennedy Space Centre in Florida and the Johnson Space Centre at Houston, Texas. They stood just 200 metres from the space shuttle 'Discovery' as it underwent final preparations for its 2010 launch; they visited the military establishment at Cape Canaveral, where America's first astronaut was blasted into space; they witnessed the array of rocketry, culminating in the enormous Saturn V, which propelled US astronauts

At the NASA Kennedy Space Centre, Florida

ultimately to the Moon; and they experienced for themselves the ATX Astronaut Training Experience, the zero gravity wall, the centrifuge and Multiple Axis Trainer, on which US astronauts routinely prepare for their missions. Perhaps most challengingly, they took part in a Mission control/Shuttle Crew simulation which confronted them with the nerve-jangling realities and split-second decision-making characteristic of human space flight.

A post-script to the 2008 visit came in October of that year, when Mr. George Abbey, former Director of the Johnson Space Centre and the man responsible for selecting all the Apollo astronauts who went to the Moon, visited the school. He was so impressed by the comments received from NASA staff who had dealt with Cyfarthfa pupils on their visit that he wanted to meet them while on a visit to Britain, and thank them personally.

No less exciting was the 2009 visit to Costa Rica. Taking in fantastic volcanic scenery, rain-forest, caves and an amazing array of flora and fauna, the trip delivered to Cyfarthfa pupils a wealth of natural history and local culture that most of us experience only through our television screens. To explore subterranean chasms, zip-wire through the tree-tops of tropical forests, see humming birds and spider monkeys, experience the atmosphere of the Costa Rican rain forest, and actually handle tarantula spiders and rhino beetles the size of your palm – all this stimulated, excited and left an indelible impression.

The Humanities

History, Geography and Religious Education remain extremely popular as subject choices for 15-16-year-olds. All three successfully teach not only their core subject skills and knowledge but also include such important themes as global citizenship, sustainable development and spiritual and moral issues.

As well as supporting large numbers of pupils at AS and A Level, many of whom have gone on to study at such prestigious universities as Oxford, Durham, Warwick and St Andrew's, the History Department has encouraged an appetite for historical research in many of its younger pupils, which has led to notable success, including two first-place awards, in the Welsh Heritage Competition. It has also organised popular and regular visits to such locations as Llancaiach Fawr, Penhow Castle, Westminster, the Imperial War Museum, Berlin and Auschwitz.

Susan Taylor, Head of Geography, has been extremely successful in establishing educational links between Cyfarthfa and schools in Third World locations. First came Port Moresby School in Papua New Guinea, in a link established with the support of the British High Commissioner there, and subsequently recognised by the British Council as 'exemplary practice'. This resulted in exchange visits by staff of the two schools, the development of inter-school pupil links, and high quality educational materials which have been used at Cyfarthfa High and its associate primaries.

Since 2007, links have been developed with Fukuchani High School in Zanzibar in a project monitored by UNESCO. Teachers from both locations, including staff from Cyfarthfa's feeder primaries, have visited each other's schools, funded by grants from the British Council and supported by Sazani Associates. They have developed shared teaching

Geography group in Holland

resources and podcasts of work done by pupils both in Wales and in Zanzibar. The project was used as a flagship study by UNESCO, and Cyfarthfa is one of only three schools in Wales to have been accorded the status of UNESCO Associated School.

Geography pupils have also participated in fieldwork at locations as diverse as the Brecon Beacons, the Netherlands, the Gross Glochner glacier in Austria and Mount Vesuvius.

Moral and Spiritual Issues
The RE department has been similarly active and successful, providing spiritual and moral guidance. It never shies away from complex moral issues of interest and relevance to pupils and has responsibility for

monitoring the delivery of the moral and ethical dimension of education across the entire school. To this end, the head of department, Sian Henderson, carried out an extremely thorough audit in 2007.

The department also provides a rich diet of extra-curricular activities. In recent years, 'Going Public', a Christian theatre company has been brought into the school to highlight issues inherent in sexual relationships among young people, encouraging responsibility, highlighting the dangers of emotional and peer pressure and emphasising the option of saying 'No'. The annual RE Day, focuses on the themes of Racism Awareness and Multi-culturalism, typically exciting and entertaining students with authentic displays of Indian Dancing, Chinese Lion Dancing and African Drumming. A valuable part of its teaching is to make pupils aware of the phenomenon of world religion, so important on a personal and social level in our increasingly multi-cultural world. All Year 11 students enjoy an annual Buddhism Day, including guest speakers, creative art work and participation in Yoga sessions.

Speakers from Christian Aid are brought into the school to illustrate and discuss their vitally important work, and each January, to commemorate Holocaust Day, special assemblies are held with, among the guest speakers, holocaust survivors. In 2009, the department organised a student visit to Auschwitz concentration camp,

where pupils could connect the moving testimony of victims with actual experience of the physical environment in which such atrocities were carried out.

Languages
Both Welsh and French within the school have faced challenging circumstances during the past two decades. French has been transformed from a compulsory subject to one competing for pupils at Key Stage 4 (14-16 year-olds) and beyond. Welsh, to some extent, has moved in the opposite direction, becoming a compulsory subject within Wales for all pupils to the age of 16; but this has proved a difficult challenge.

Both departments have responded positively to their respective challenges and the common task of making additional languages appealing and relevant to students, many of whom ask 'Why bother?' in this age of English language dominance. Both departments have focused on working with children in Cyfarthfa's associate primary schools in order to arouse early enthusiasm; French, in part, through the Welsh Assembly's CILT project, and Welsh through normal school visits and curricular links.

Within Cyfarthfa, extra-curricular activities include: visits to France and e-mail links with French students; European Days, complete with croissants for all at mid-morning break; regular residential trips to the Urdd camps at Llangrannog and Glan Llyn (Bala); visits to the Welsh Assembly and the set of 'Pobl y Cwm'; involvement in school and Urdd eisteddfodau. In addition, there are bi-lingual signs throughout the school buildings and displays of the Welsh 'phrase of the week'.

Drama in Performances

There is a long tradition at Cyfarthfa of drama performance, so valuable in developing the enormous performing talent produced by Merthyr Tydfil but also in the effect it can have on pupils' confidence, self-respect and ability to relate to others. Former pupils such as Alex Wilmott, Kelly Williams, Kyle Jones, Emma Cuesta and others have gone on to study and perform in the field of the dramatic arts, and may well in time achieve fame and fortune in that sphere, but there are countless others whose lives have been immeasurably enriched by these experiences. Parents and pupils talk ten years and more on, of the unforgettable experience of being involved, whether on stage, front of house or behind the scenes.

While Helena Mobley, Gary Brame and Peter McAleer of the English Department, all played a major part in sustaining this tradition of school performances over many years, with memorable productions such as *Witness For The Prosecution*, *A Christmas Carol*, *The Corn is Green* and *Aladdin*, to their respective credit during the 1980s and into the 1990s, two developments in particular stand out for their impact and the place they hold in the collective Cyfarthfa memory.

On with the Show!

First, the phenomenal Lower School musicals produced by the irrepressible Allison Lewis and her redoubtable team, ably assisted by Helen Canney and other enthusiastic staff too numerous to name. Allison achieved the apparently impossible – involving all but a tiny handful of the up to 500 boys and girls, in four nights of sell-out performances.

These productions, including such block-buster musicals as *Oliver, Calamity Jane* and *The Wizard of Oz,* enabled the talented young performers to flourish and shine in the character parts - usually appearing on alternate nights in two parallel casts, to ensure no-one was left out of an unforgettable experience, an experience enthusiastically shared by the hundreds of admiring – and usually copiously perspiring! – parents, grand-parents, uncles, aunts, cousins and next-door neighbours who filled the Castle School Hall - almost perversely, the performances were staged towards the end of the Summer Term, when humidity in the hall could reach tropical proportions!

The curtain finally came down on Allison's epic productions in 2009, with her retirement from teaching, but the baton was taken up by Joanna James and Laura Oliver of the Drama department who, again with the invaluable support of Helen Canney and a host of willing staff, produced *Bugsy Malone* in 2011.

The second striking phase of dramatic performance at the school commenced in 1998, with the appointment of Arlene Jones, under whose talented direction, a series of ambitious productions were undertaken, including such diverse works as the dynamic and gritty teen musical *Grease*, Arthur Miller's dramatically challenging *The Crucible*, the complex and highly cerebral *Our Country's Good* by Timberlake Wertenbaker, Pinter's sinister and unsettling *The Birthday Party* and Godber's hilarious *Bouncers*. Arlene Jones left to become a lecturer at UWIC but the high standards she set have been maintained by Joanne James, who, with the able assistance of her co-producer, fellow drama specialist, Laura Oliver, and the enthusiastic support of innumerable other staff, continues to foster the impressive talent residing in Cyfarthfa's student body. Thus, 2010 witnessed an outstanding performance of *Little Shop of Horrors* at

Upper School, while July 2011 brought the bitter-sweet experience of the final Lower School summer performance, with a no-holds-barred production of *Bugsy Malone*.

Finally, March 2012 saw a production of *The Wedding Singer*, which played to packed houses at Cae Mari Dwn and achieved levels of performance and consistency which must mark a pinnacle even in Cyfarthfa's rich history of theatrical endeavour. The impact of the show was amazing and a fitting tribute to the on-going tradition of drama at the school.

Drama also introduced its own international dimension to pupil experience at Cyfarthfa, with visits undertaken to Winchester High School, near Boston, Massachusetts, in 2000, 2002 and 2005, to perform *Under Milk Wood*, *Our Day Out* and *An Insult to My Brain*, respectively. Indeed, it was from this that the tradition of annual sixth form visits to Boston during the 2000s grew, providing a taste of North America, its colleges, sports and city life, with visits to Harvard and the razzamatazz of American football or ice-hockey games a regular feature.

Sporting Diversity and International Honours

A significant trend during the 90s, accelerating as the new millennium progressed, has been the diversity of sports played by Cyfarthfa's pupils, with extremely impressive levels of performance and success. These include participation in the Duke of Edinburgh Award scheme with an outward-bound trip to Canada in 2007 and regular upper and lower school skiing trips to France and Switzerland.

On an individual level, commencing in 2001, Sarah Taylor achieved distinction in Judo, representing both British Schools and the Welsh Judo Association, while one of the school's most talented athletes, Danielle Bale, represented Wales. 2003 was again a notable year, with Alice Bevan, who in time would become a triple Welsh international in athletics and hockey, gaining her first Welsh colours. Daniel Williams represented Wales in the high-jump and Lee Idzi in soccer. In this year also, Serian Ganesh,

Skiing in France

one of the school's longest serving internationals, represented Wales at hockey, a feat she was to repeat for three further years. Jonathan Bennett also left his mark with impressive track and field performances and still holds three school records in the 100m, 200m and long-jump.

At around this time too, the basket-ball years began, with Cyfarthfa's own Harlem Globe Trotters, Daniel Pullman and Glyn Davies, both capped in 2006 (Daniel went on to captain the Welsh side) and Thomas Ellis capped for Wales in 2010.

In 2007, Jack Bush and Mitchell Allen furthered their already secured Welsh international credentials by going on to represent Great Britain, in golf and judo respectively. 2008 was another prominent year with Josh Flye, Shay Ralph, Rhys Walker and Thomas Farrar-Evans playing rugby league for Wales, Matthew Davies winning Welsh cricketing honours and Christoher Soanes swimming for his country. Other outstanding performers of recent years include Elliot Morgan and Toby Roper, elite hockey players, and Declan John, who has represented Welsh Schools in soccer since 2011, has appeared on numerous occasions on Sky TV in soccer's Victory Shield and subsequently become an assistant professional at Cardiff City FC. Rebecca Hunt and Chloe Lloyd achieved outstanding success at cycling and soccer respectively in 2010, while international honours at rounders were gained in 2011 by Mollie Jones, Hannah Bevan, Chloe Lloyd and Kelly Bourne. Finally, excellence and consistency were shown by Jade Croot, who succeeded in becoming Welsh Junior Karate Champion in 2011 and again in 2012.

Rugby
When Gareth Francis joined the PE staff at the school in the late 1980s, having previously taught at a small Cardiff school without a history of first XV rugby, he was amazed at the intensity of local derbies against such schools as Vaynor and Penderyn, and greatly impressed by the skills and physical strength of such notable team members then as Ian Thomas, Darren Ingrams (also an extremely talented soccer player), Hugh Parry, Neil Morgan, Anthony Hughes and Simon Phillips.

Titanic encounters with all the local schools continued throughout the 90s at 'The Wern', and physical stature was certainly not always on Cyfarthfa's side. One notable team of the period, including Alex Thomas and brothers Christopher and Andrew Bedford, was particularly inspirational in the sheer guts and determination which brought them success against usually far bigger opponents.

Numerically, the largest school rugby squad of the 90s was that which included Mark Cushen, Ian Gilchrist, Richard Lewis, Ian Sweetman, Keri James, Neil Young, Mervyn Matthews, Paul 'Davo' Davies, Gethin Griffiths, Michael Bennett and David Evans. In team spirit and sheer determination to succeed, there was not another team like them, and their commitment to training and pride in representing the school transformed them from a side which hardly won a match at junior level into one which hardly ever lost as seniors.

If earlier teams had sometimes been Davids pitted against Goliaths, the same could certainly not be said of the squad including Ashley Powell and Anthony Mee. They could never use lack of size as an excuse for losing –

Rugby squad in Canada 2012

not that they often had to find such an excuse, as their success rate was phenomenal. Anthony went on to represent the County at under-16 level and only narrowly lost out on international selection. He was renowned (or notorious, depending on your perspective) for his 'dump' tackles, long before they were officially invented, and could also throw the discus a seriously long way.

Another outstanding player of the 90s was Andrew Young, who also played for the County. Andrew an exceptional all-rounder, regularly represented the school at athletics. Another exhibiting this combination of athletic prowess and excellent rugby ability was Gareth Williams, who went on to win a Welsh schoolboy cap and to captain Merthyr RFC. In 2002, one of the school's great characters, Jonathan Watkins, played rugby for Welsh Schools, the beginning, he will tell you, of an illustrious career. How he never had a senior cap for Wales is beyond him! In recent years the team has undertaken overseas tours to Australia in 2006, Canada in 2008, 2010 and 2012, and to the USA in 2012.

Charitable Activities

The school has had links, past and present, with various charities. In the late 1990's, Lower School enjoyed a positive relationship with Lepra - educational and fitness-enhancing for the pupils and financially beneficial to the charity – which saw on one occasion, hundreds of pupils enthusiastically participating in a sponsored aerobics event which raised a staggering £4,000 to assist in the fight against leprosy. In 2003, the first of a sequence of 'Spellathons' was staged at Lower School, since when, the event has raised £10,000 for charity. Cyfarthfa's pupils regularly participate in Comic Relief and Children in Need and in 2012, school events supported the local Mayor's Appeal, while the school also contributes to Marie Curie and Macmillan cancer charities. A typical year sees Cyfarthfa pupils and staff raising in excess of £4,000 for these excellent causes.

A Vibrant Sixth Form

A healthy and dynamic sixth form suggests a thriving school, and throughout the period covered by this chapter, under a succession of dedicated sixth-form heads (Alun Hughes, Elizabeth Phillips, Allison Wallbank), Cyfarthfa's sixth-form flourished, maintaining high levels of academic performance at AS and A Level, and providing relevant education and training for post-16 students - all the more laudable for maintaining a positive budget at the same time!

In a diverse range of school and community-based activities, from Buddy Schemes to the Hype drug mentoring scheme, from Sports Relief to Children in Need, from public speaking to, in the case of many pupils, over 200 hours of Community Action, Cyfarthfa's post-16 pupils have enriched the community and palpably grown as individuals in the process. Meanwhile, an extremely effective pastoral structure has helped individuals navigate the often difficult passage between adolescence and adulthood.

Senior pupils

Estyn inspection reports testify to the value to the school of having such a vibrant sixth form: 'The contribution made by the sixth form to school life is significant and represents a strength of the school' (2003), and 'The sixth form adds to the ethos of the school.' (2009).

Sixth form pupils' confidence, sophistication and, undoubtedly, affluence, across the years is captured well in the transformation of the school-based Sixth Form Christmas Fancy-Dress Party of the 1990's into the style and elegance of the current sixth-form Prom, replete with the latest in fashionable elegance and impeding the flow of traffic on the Cardiff-bound A 470 on certain dark December evenings with fleets of stretch limousines! Since the first was held at the Park Hotel, Cardiff, in 1996 the tradition of the sixth form Prom at Cyfarthfa has gone from strength to strength. In 2005, Jury's Park Inn at Cardiff became its home.

It has become a massive school function, attended by over 200 students and many staff. Crucially, it is organised entirely by the student leadership team themselves, and the previous year's Head Boy and Head Girl are always invited along as a mark of gratitude and respect.

But the wealth of character-forming activities, which contributes so much to individual development and to the well-being of school and community, has not been achieved at the expense of high academic standards. On the contrary, the school banding tables released in 2012 place Cyfarthfa within the top 19 per cent of schools in Wales.

An indicator of the levels of academic success achieved by Cyfarthfa's sixth form comes in the form of the average points score per candidate, with Cyfarthfa students bettering or equalling the Welsh figure in five of the seven years from 2003 to 2009 – in 2009 by a staggering 752 points to 688!

Why Change?

Why then was the decision taken in 2010 to deprive Cyfarthfa of its sixth form in 2014? This decision both angered and dismayed an overwhelming majority of the sixth form student body at the school who, of their own volition, actively campaigned for its retention, believing that there was no easily transferable recipe for the unique experience and levels of success and fulfilment that it provided.

Discussions on the need to reorganise post-16 education in Merthyr began in 2001, when the Welsh Assembly's department for education funded a study that identified a need to improve provision for those aged 16 and over. That the department funded such a study was in line with its vision of post-16 academic and vocational education in Wales being provided, not by sixth forms, but within large post-16 institutions. Various subsequent reports built on this vision and the argument in favour of change was finally set out in a Consultation Document issued by Merthyr Council in February 2010.

The rationale for change was based upon three issues. The proportion of post-16 young people in education, employment or training within the borough was below the all-Wales average; the performance of Merthyr 15-16-year-olds at GCSE was below the all-Wales average; the size of sixth forms in Merthyr schools was predicted to fall from well over 600 to around 550 by 2021. None of these applied to Cyfarthfa. In fact, post-16 numbers at Cyfarthfa had been the highest in the Borough, and were projected to continue to be so, usually exceeding the combined sixth form numbers in two out of the three other high schools.

The proposed solution to the post-16 educational problems said to exist, was a brand new £33 million 'learning facility' to be sited on Merthyr College land, involving demolition of the existing – in fact, recently refurbished – college buildings. The site and new building would be known as the Merthyr Learning Quarter (MLQ) with the cost funded by the Welsh Assembly.

Contrary to the clearly expressed wishes of so many pupils, parents and staff who responded to its consultation process, the local council voted on 28 April 2010 in favour of the MLQ by 20 votes to 8. The reality, therefore, is that to tackle the twin problems of underachievement and falling numbers which beset the Authority as a whole, the proven and cherished standards of Cyfarthfa's sixth form have been sacrificed.

Along the way to that decision two possibilities were dismissed. One was to make Cyfarthfa Castle the centre for sixth form education and training in Merthyr. The other was a compromise solution which would have permitted Cyfarthfa at Cae Mari Dwn to retain responsibility for academic courses at post-16, its proven area of greatest strength, while allowing its pupils to avail themselves of the impressive range of vocational options and cutting edge technology that the Merthyr Learning Quarter would offer. This compromise, known as the 'Hub and Spoke' model, was, however, firmly rejected by the Assembly.

From September 2014 all of Merthyr's secondary schools will only receive pupils aged 11 to 16. With that decision made, it is essential that the new arrangements are successful. Cyfarthfa High School has been engaged for some time in a series of discussions concerning the new curriculum and ways in which pupils can be prepared for the transition to the Learning Quarter. But the task of replicating the successful post-16 formula which Cyfarthfa evolved over many years will be more challenging than many appear to recognise.

Goodbye to the Castle

The departure of 16-plus pupils to the Learning Quarter will enable the remaining pupils in the Castle to move to Cae Mari Dwn. No longer, after July 2014, will there be Cyfarthfa pupils in the Castle: it will be a bitter-sweet moment. It breaks a fond association with a unique setting that extends back to 1913. Successive pupils have enjoyed the idyllic surroundings of Cyfarthfa Park throughout the seasons and the singular atmosphere of William Crawshay II's 1825 mock-gothic construction, with more than a hint of Hogwartian magic.

Unfortunately, however, even Paradise had its serpent, and while most former pupils harbour fond memories of their Castle years, the building itself has had problems of water ingress and structural deterioration over the past twenty years which have imposed major financial burdens on both school and local authority. And in recent years the increased volume of traffic in the Park has resulted in pupils being confined to the school premises, even during lunch-times. Sadly gone are the lingering lunch-time strolls, the lakeside promenades, and the hectic lunch time football games on the Pandy pitch.

It will also end a long era during which the PE department has contended valiantly with the day-to-day problems inherent in sharing space with the general public, not to mention the occasional unexpected arrival of a circus on the Pandy field or a fishing competition around its athletics track – the perimeter of Cyfarthfa Lake! The use of the dedicated outdoor sports facilities at Cae Mari Dwn will be a great contrast and boon.

Cae Mari Dwn

For the first time since the school became comprehensive in 1970, Cyfarthfa will have all its pupils on one site, relieving the pressures on school finances and teaching staff of a split-site existence. Although still frequently referred to as the 'new' school, the Cae Mari Dwn site has been functioning as Cyfarthfa's Upper School since September 1981. Alterations and new buildings now accommodate the greatly increased use of ITC equipment; provide improved facilities for disabled pupils; house new laboratories, classrooms, study areas and common-room facilities; while offices have doubled in area to cope with administrative demands. Not the least factor in all this was the increase in pupil numbers by approximately 50 per cent between 1990 and 2010.

Sporting facilities have also been transformed. September 2003 saw the benefits of school/community cooperation with the opening of the Astro-turf all-weather pitch at Cae Mari Dwn, accessible to the school between 8 am and 5 pm weekdays with community use in the evenings and at weekends. This approach reached its zenith with construction of the impressive sports hall, opened for pupil and community use in 2008, while the adjacent playing fields became available for use in September 2010.

The extension and development of the Cae Mari Dwn building carried out by the Merthyr Authority in recent years in preparation for the school's single-site status have been of a high standard, providing an excellent physical environment for future generations of Cyfarthfa pupils.

The Royal Visit

On 26 April 2012, the school was honoured by a visit from Her Majesty, Queen Elizabeth II and Prince Philip, as part of the Monarch's Silver Jubilee tour of Wales. There was a terrific atmosphere in Cyfarthfa Park, as thousands, including students from the Borough's schools and members of the general public greeted the Queen and the Duke of Edinburgh with tremendous enthusiasm.

The Queen meets former pupils, 26 April 2012

Headteacher, Alan Pritchard and Gareth Morgan, Chair of Governors, escorted Her Majesty and the Duke into the Castle and there they met illustrious former pupils, the Governors and the leadership team of the school, while the school choir sang 'Calon Lan'.

Once in the school library, the Royal Party were nobly entertained by pupils Tom Hier and Sophie Davies, who sang to the assembled group, and gifts were presented by Curtis Evans and Rhiannon Carr, current Head Boy and Head Girl. It was a great day for the school and a significant milestone on the path to its centenary in 2013.

In Conclusion

In the years since 1990, supported by the excellent foundations laid down under the diligent headship of Dennis Bennett, pupil numbers have grown from around 1,000 to a peak of 1,537 in 2010 and, after a period of

Merthyr-wide falling rolls, settling at 1,413 in 2012. There has been continual progress in academic achievement, with 2011, the most recent year for which statistics are available as this chapter goes to press, witnessing the best ever GCSE results, with 69 per cent of pupils achieving the equivalent of five good passes (A-C grade) and 94 per cent achieving 5 passes over all (A-G grade), placing Cyfarthfa in the second-highest achievement band in Wales.

At post-16 too, the period has witnessed consistently high levels of academic achievement, placing Cyfarthfa's sixth form among the most successful in south Wales. Each year around 80 pupils from Cyfarthfa enter a wide range of universities, including Oxbridge and other top UK institutions and Harvard and Princeton in the USA. The drive for the highest standards was illustrated at 'A' Level in 2011 when Daniel Thomas achieved an excellent four As and Hannah Kennedy a truly outstanding 4 A*s and an A (the highest grade possible) in the Welsh Baccalaureate.

Sadly, sixth-form education will leave the school from July 2014. However, any lingering regret over the demise of the sixth form will certainly not affect Cyfarthfa's determination to strive, as ever, for the greatest possible success of all its pupils.

As this story ends another begins. In August 2012 Alan Pritchard retired after 20 years' outstanding service to the school, 16 of them as Headteacher, a period of leadership characterised by the utmost concern for people – both pupils and staff – and a determination to enable them to fulfil their potential.

His departure marks another first for the school as it comes under the leadership of a female Headteacher. Carolyn Meade, honours graduate in History from Leicester University, joined the school as Head of History in 1990, gained promotion to Curriculum Manager in 1997 and became Deputy Headteacher in 2002. Carolyn takes over as Headteacher with the best wishes of all who care about Cyfarthfa's future, in the knowledge that she has the drive and vision to steer the school through the challenges and opportunities that lie ahead.

Carolyn Meade

This chapter opened with a truism concerning change, and ends reflecting upon that old Chinese curse: 'May you live in interesting times.' The 23 years since 1990 have been extremely 'interesting times' for all who have been part of Cyfarthfa High School, though to have shared in the fortunes and experiences of those countless pupils and staff involved could not be further from a curse – indeed, it could even be considered a blessing!

THEY MADE THEIR MARK

JOE ENGLAND

Our deeds determine us, as much as we determine our deeds
(George Eliot)

If you had to pick around 30 former Cyfarthfa pupils who have made a mark in one way or another, who would you choose? It would not be easy; it would certainly be controversial. In Merthyr we all have our heroes and opinions and surely there will be debate over why this chapter contains some names and not others.

A major limitation has been space. Over the 100 years of Cyfarthfa School's existence thousands of girls and boys have passed through, felt its influence and built careers. Many company directors and executives, research scientists, professors, artists and professional people do not appear here. Perhaps they should. To anyone who feels unjustly left out a sincere apology is offered; as one is also offered for any factual errors that may have crept into the accounts given.

Fortunately, a very much fuller list compiled by Mansell Richards, who helped with the research for this chapter, has been deposited in Merthyr Central Library. His remarkable list names over 100 former pupils and should whet the appetite of any future researcher who decides to examine further the lives and achievements of pupils of Cyfarthfa and the other schools in Merthyr Tydfil.

How then were the subjects here chosen? A major consideration has been the contribution made in their professional work, but that has not been the sole factor. In several cases the impact made upon the lives of others has been crucial. Time and opportunity have also influenced selection. It takes time to build a career and for a life to be seen in perspective. That is why so many of our achievers made their mark in the second half of the twentieth century and why so few are drawn from the twenty-first.

Time and opportunity also explain why so few women are included. For most of the twentieth century less was expected of women in career terms. The difference can be seen in the number of academically able girls who went to training college rather university; the number who became secretaries or 'personal assistants' rather than top administrators, although it was often the 'PAs' who made enterprises tick. In addition, the restrictions imposed by motherhood, and the unchallenged assumption that the raising of families was primarily a woman's responsibility, seriously hindered the blossoming of many professional careers. Attitudes are changing, glass ceilings are beginning to be shattered, but progress is slow and the past constrains the present.
A desire to show the range of achievement has also influenced selection. We could easily have found 30 male professors and businessmen but that would have given too narrow a picture. Consequently, we have included sportsmen as well as scientists, musicians as well as millionaires, photographers as well as professors.

Should there be such a chapter? Is it not unnecessarily elitist, emphasising a few at the expense of the many? At a time when it seems to have become almost a ritual for newspapers and television programmes to report, without reflection, the worst aspects of Merthyr society, it is a pleasure to highlight the positive contribution made by Merthyr people to society at large. And these names are just the tip of a very large iceberg.

They appear in alphabetical order and include three knights of the realm, a cabinet minister, an internationally-renowned fashion designer, two opera singers, a famous actor, a theologian, a test pilot, an artist, a Welsh soccer international, a European boxing champion, a photographer and film-maker, senior company executives, musicians, writers and millionaires, historians, leading government advisors on atomic energy, social policy, food safety and computer systems, and some whose efforts have quietly touched many lives. Here they are.

Mansel Aylward

For most of his illustrious career as medical general practitioner, research scientist, university professor and a chief advisor to the UK and Wales governments, Mansel has continued to live in Merthyr. He won a state scholarship from Cyfarthfa in 1961 and graduated from the London Hospital Medical College, returning to Merthyr as a general practitioner. In 1974 he founded Simbec Research Ltd., and from 1974 to 1985 was President of its subsidiary, Simbec Research Inc, New Jersey USA. In 1979 Simbec Research won the BBC Company of the Year award and in 1980 gained the European Small Company Award.

In 1985 he joined the UK Civil Service in Cardiff as the Regional Medical Officer and in 1988 became Senior Medical Officer at the Department of Health and Social Services in London. In 1990 he was appointed Principal Medical Officer. From 1996 to April 2005 he was Chief Medical Adviser, Medical Director and Chief Scientist to the United Kingdom's Department of Social Security and then the Department for Work and Pensions. He was also Chief Medical Adviser and Head of Profession at the Veterans' Agency, Ministry of Defence, playing a key role in developing and evaluating the UK's medical assessment for incapacity (the All Work Test). He led the Corporate Medical Group on the UK Government's Welfare Reform initiatives and made a major contribution in establishing the new postgraduate diploma for doctors in Disability Assessment Medicine. He was closely involved in developing the UK's successful 'Pathways to Work' initiatives and framework for vocational rehabilitation.

Sir Mansel Aylward

With the devolution of health care to Wales he became from 2005–2009 Chair of the Wales Centre for Health. In October 2008, during the 60th year of the NHS, he chaired the Bevan Commission, which brought together international experts to provide advice to the Minister for Health and Social Services. In 2009 he was appointed the first Chairman of Public Health Wales, an NHS Trust responsible for the delivery of public health services at national, local and community level in Wales.

His interests lie in the social issues arising from health inequalities, economic inactivity, rehabilitation, and social exclusion in South Wales. He has published widely in these areas and in 2006 became Patron of The Shaw Trust which provides training and work opportunities for people disadvantaged by disability, ill health, or other social circumstances.
He is Director of the Centre for Psychosocial and Disability Research at Cardiff University and Professor of Public Health Medicine. In 2011 he was appointed Professor at Auckland University and in this role makes frequent visits to New Zealand. He is also visiting Professor at various European and North American universities and has served as a consultant to the United States Social Security Administration.

He was made a Companion of the Order of the Bath (CB) in the Queen's Birthday Honours List 2002 and knighted in the Queen's New Year's Honours 2010 for services to health and healthcare.

Randall Baker

Randall attended Cyfarthfa in the fifties, graduated from Swansea, and then held a Rockefeller Fellowship at the University of East Africa (1965), gaining in 1970 a London Ph.D. in Geography and Economics. He left Africa in 1970 and was at the University of East Anglia for 16 years before leaving for the USA. That was the beginning of a career in academe and consultancy that has taken him all over the world. He has lived in Uganda, the USA, Saudi Arabia, the Fiji Islands, Azerbaijan, and since 2008 has made his home in Sofia, Bulgaria, where he holds a Distinguished Professorship at the New Bulgarian University with which he has been connected since it was no more than an idea in 1991. In September 2012 he retired as Provost of the Diplomatic Academy in Baku, Azerbaijan and returned to his Chair in Sofia.

Throughout his career his focus has been the crossroads where environmental research and public administration meet in a concern for the sustainable management of the planet. From 1975–78 he was Reader and Dean of the School of Development Studies, University of East Anglia, also participating in UNESCO's Man and Biosphere Programme, Paris.

He has lent his expertise and knowledge to policymakers all over the world, serving as consultant to the Asian Development Bank and the cabinet of Fiji; advising the government of Bulgaria on its entry into the European Union; the government of Serbia on higher education; and the government of Azerbaijan on renewable energy sources. In addition, he has helped to establish post-graduate degrees in public administration in Azerbaijan, Bulgaria, Spain, Bolivia, and Lesotho, and environmental studies programmes at Kazakhstan Institute of Management, and at the University of Khartoum, Sudan. He was a two-time Fulbright Senior Scholar in Bulgaria in 1992 and 2002 and Dean and Professor of Academic Affairs, Azerbaijan Diplomatic Academy, 2011.

As professor and director in the School of Public and Environmental Affairs in Indiana University, Bloomington, from 1986 to 2002, he took the lead in internationalizing the curriculum, introducing students to new countries and cultures and expanding their horizons through exchange and overseas study programmes that he developed with universities in the Netherlands, France, Bulgaria, Haiti, and Thailand.

For his impact upon generations of students around the world who now occupy significant positions in business and civil administrations, he has received awards and honorary degrees from Moscow State University, Sofia University, Indiana University, the Bulgarian Academy of Sciences, the National Institute of Development Administration, Thailand, and the Western University, Azerbaijan.

He is the author of a dozen books ranging from academic discussion of environmental management and public administration, to personal memoirs.

Desmond Barry

What is it about Merthyr Tydfil that produces so many writers? Is it the tumultuous history, the extraordinary characters, its community spirit? Whatever it is, poets, novelists, journalists and historians seem to thrive on the Merthyr air. Des Barry, former resident of the Gurnos Estate, is the most recent to make a mark as a novelist. But, unlike most of the others, his writing is neither rooted in Merthyr, nor in Wales. True, the novel he wrote first (although it was the second to be published) was about Merthyr, but the others come from a much wider range of experience. A restless traveller, he has lived in London, Brighton, Rome, Tuscany, Massachusetts, San Francisco, San Diego, New York and Tibet.

He attended Cyfarthfa in the late 1960s, took a degree in history at University College, London, worked at the Fawcett Library, London, and subsequently taught English in Italy. In 1986 he moved to the USA where he did a bewildering array of jobs; but finally in the mid-1990s he enrolled on a creative writing course at Columbia University, New York. His subsequent novel, *The Chivalry of Crime* (2001), set in the American West between 1863 and 1893, and for which he did exhaustive research on Jesse James, was voted Best First Novel of the Year by the Western Writers of America and was shortlisted for the 2002 Wales Book of the Year Award.

His second novel (although largely drafted first), *A Bloody Good Friday* (2002), recounts the events of a violent Good Friday night in Merthyr in the 1970s. Entirely fictional it nonetheless has echoes of 1831 and more recent legendary local characters. His third, *Cressida's Bed* (2004), is set in India and Bhutan during the Indian Independence Movement 1930–31. It is surely not a coincidence that as a history graduate his first and third books were historical novels.

His short stories and non-fiction have appeared in *Granta, The New Yorker,*

The Big Issue and in the anthologies *Wales, Half Welsh* (2004), *London Noir* (2006) and *Sea Stories* (2007). His play *Jetlag* was performed in Cardiff in 2007 part of *3Cities* which included work from theatre groups from Buenos Aires and Melbourne. He collaborated with Uruguayan photographer, Diego Vidart, to produce 'The Falkland Diaries', an exhibition at the Wales Millennium Centre in 2007. His direct dialogue and candid descriptions are not for the staid. For the past ten years he has lived in Cardiff and taught creative writing at the University of Glamorgan. Des coordinates the Far South Project which involves 40 participants from seven different countries: filmmakers, musicians, web designers, photographers, and dancers. Under the name David Enrique Spellman he wrote and drew *Far South*, a multi-platform novel with weblinks. Barring death, he says, he has no intention of letting anything stand in the way of his continuing travels.

David Chappell

In 1954, when David was 12, he found himself with a mouthful of mud on Cyfarthfa Park's Top Field and decided that rugby was not for him. Fortunately, it was at that time that he came under the influence of inspirational orchestral teacher Claudia James and took up the violin. He later said it was much the better experience. By the age of 13 he was a member of the National Youth Orchestra of Wales where he played for six years, eventually becoming leader of the orchestra. He was also a teenage winner at the National Eisteddfod. Building on these achievements he won an Open Scholarship from Cyfarthfa to the Royal Academy of Music. There he took the significant step of abandoning the violin and took up the viola; a real turning point, for the viola 'consumed my life'.

After graduating from the Royal Academy he played in the Royal Opera House Orchestra (with fellow Cyfarthian Harold Nash) and then joined the London Symphony Orchestra, considered the best orchestra in Europe at that time. Over the years with that orchestra he toured 25 different countries playing in all the world famous concert venues.

Then one day the orchestra arrived in Miami. 'I was so intoxicated with this city that I knew it had to be my home'. Within an hour of arriving he had discovered that the position of principal viola player in the Miami Philharmonic Orchestra was vacant. For more than 30 years he was principal viola player for the Miami and State of Florida Philharmonic Orchestras. During that time, in addition to playing the classical repertoire, he played on the soundtrack of Hollywood films and with backing bands and string sections on recordings with Sammy Davis Jnr, Liza Minelli, Count Basie, Tony Bennett and many others.

Gordon Davies

Gordon became a schoolboy soccer international while at Cyfarthfa where he also gained A levels and in 1973 he went to Madeley College of Physical Education to be trained as a teacher. He then returned home to teach in Gwernllwyn junior school, Dowlais. An instinctive player and a natural goal-scorer with the wonderful knack of being in the right place at the right time he played for Merthyr Tydfil FC in the late 1970s and scored 30 goals in his first season with them. His talent was soon spotted and he joined Fulham in 1978, scoring the winning goal in his first game for the club. He spent six years with Fulham and then had a year with Chelsea before going to Manchester City for a transfer fee of £100,000, a large sum in those days.

However, he returned to Fulham in October 1986. This second spell at Fulham lasted five years, at the end of which he had become Fulham's record goal-scorer, with 159 league goals in 394 appearances and, taking into account cup and other games, 178 goals in 450 appearances. At the end of his Fulham career, the club granted him a testimonial which was played against a Wales XI. He then had short spells at Wrexham and Northwich Victoria, and retired from the game in 1993. He still maintains links with the Fulham club and acts as a host for the club on matchdays.

He won 16 full international caps for Wales between 1979 and 1986, making his international debut on 21 November 1979 against Turkey. His

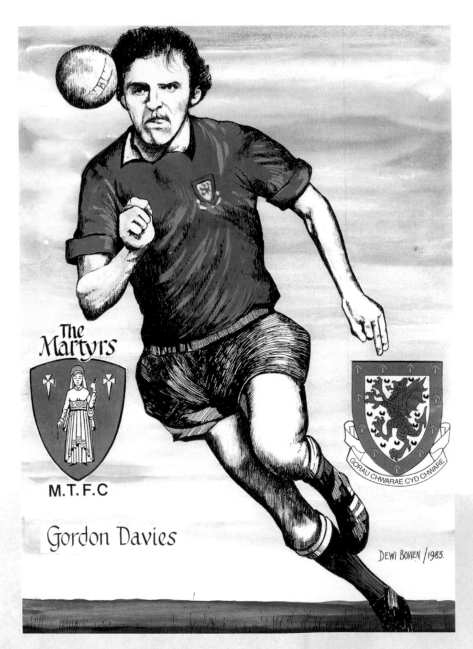

Gordon Davies

final international game was against the Republic of Ireland on 26 March 1986. Gordon stands with a select group of Merthyr-born players who have played professional soccer at the highest level. He is also the only player to score a hat trick both for and against Chelsea in league games.

Howard Denner

Few achieve prominence in two completely separate careers. Howard has done so with startling success. A pupil at Cyfarthfa in the late 50s he graduated from University College, Cardiff, with a degree and then doctorate in biochemistry. After further research at the universities of Miami and Cardiff he joined the Food Science Division of the Ministry of Agriculture in 1972 and remained there until 1996.

During his first ten years with the Ministry he became recognised internationally as an expert on the safety assessment and use of food additives. The UN Food and Agriculture Organization and the World Health Organisation drew on his expertise when drawing up international standards for permitted food additives. Later he headed the Division dealing with food commodity standards, nutrition and the microbiological safety of food. He set up new programmes to detect food adulteration and was the main instigator of the National Diet and Health Survey and also of the establishment of the Committee on the Microbiological Surveillance of Food, which he later chaired. Other significant posts included Chairman of the Codex Committee on Fats and Oils and Assessor on committees that evaluated the safety of novel foods especially food from genetically modified plants and animals. He became Chief Scientist (Food) from 1992–96.

However, throughout his life he had been a keen amateur photographer with a particular interest in candid photographs of people in the street. His photographs were accepted in International Salons of Photography and he was later invited to judge entries for such exhibitions. He was awarded the distinction AFIAP (Artiste de la Fédération Internationale de l'Art Photographique) in 1972. He photographed old Georgetown in

Not a Cyfarthfa schoolgirl. A Howard Denner portrait of Katherine Jenkins

Merthyr before it was redeveloped and had a one-man exhibition of these photographs in a London gallery in 1974 which was favourably reviewed in *The Guardian*.

As he became more and more senior in the Ministry, he was frustrated that he had less and less time for photography. In a somewhat spectacular career change, in 1996 he decided to retire from the Civil Service to follow his passion. With complete disregard for advancing years, he became a freelance, specialising in photographing live music especially rock, blues and jazz concerts. He has photographed many festivals including Glastonbury, New Orleans Jazz Festival, London Jazz Festival, Cheltenham Jazz Festival, Bishopstock Blues Festival and countless individual concerts ranging from Tina Turner, Madonna, Elton John and Tom Jones to B B King, Eric Clapton and Sonny Rollins in venues ranging in size from small jazz clubs to Wembley Stadium.

His photographs have been published extensively in all of the national newspapers, in *Radio Times*, in popular music magazines such as *Mojo* and *Q* and in specialist magazines like *Guitar Techniques*. His photographs have appeared in publications abroad as well as in books and many now illustrate various websites.

Ronald Vivian Ecclestone (1923–1954)

Ronald of Woodlands Place, Twynyrodyn, achieved distinction as a pilot in three distinct spheres, although he is best known in Merthyr for being the first RAF pilot to break the sound barrier. Curiously, the RAF Museum is not able to confirm this officially, for no record seems to have been kept, but his family believe this is so and that it occurred in August 1951. His parents presented to the school a bronze memorial plaque in his memory which records that date.

But before that he had a considerable combat record in World War II. He served as a Royal Air Force pilot with 218 Squadron attached to Bomber Command where he flew heavy bombers, Stirlings and Lancasters. His

IN COMMEMORATION OF THE LIFE AND WORK OF
FLIGHT LIEUTENANT
RONALD VIVIAN ECCLESTONE, D.F.C.,A.F.C.
A FORMER PUPIL OF THIS SCHOOL,
AWARDED THE DISTINGUISHED FLYING CROSS IN WORLD WAR II,
HE RECEIVED THE KINGS COMMENDATION
FOR VALUABLE SERVICES IN THE AIR IN 1949
AND IN AUGUST 1951, BECAME THE FIRST
ROYAL AIR FORCE PILOT TO PIERCE THE SOUND BARRIER
BEING DECORATED WITH THE AIR FORCE CROSS
IN MARCH 1953.
HE WAS KILLED ON 14TH JULY 1954, WHILE TESTING
THE PROTOTYPE HANDLEY PAGE "VICTOR" AIRCRAFT.

The plaque to Flight-Lieutenant Ronald Ecclestone, DFC, AFC

skills as a pilot also enabled him to fly Hurricanes and Spitfires in Bomber Defence. He flew many combat missions and was awarded the Distinguished Flying Cross for bravery in February 1945. Immediately before the German capitulation in May 1945, when the heavy bombers' offensive ceased, his squadron dropped food supplies to the starving Dutch people, and subsequently its aircraft were busily employed ferrying liberated British prisoners of war to England from the Continent. In the 1949 New Year Honours he was awarded the King's Commendation for Valuable Service in the Air and that year he successfully completed the rigorous Empire Test Pilots School course and with this qualification was engaged in development flying for the RAF, successively at Marham, Boscombe Down and Farnborough aerodromes. It is during this period that he is believed to have flown faster than the speed of sound, a feat that was then rare and referred to as 'breaking the sound barrier'. He served for a year in the Directorate of Operational Requirements at the Air Ministry. He held the rank of Flight Lieutenant and in the 1953 New Years Honours was awarded the Air Force Cross.

In April 1954 he joined Handley Page, Ltd. as the company's deputy chief test pilot, and less than three months later, on 14 July 1954 he was killed while testing a prototype Handley Page 'Victor' aircraft at Cranfield. The tailplane failed while the aircraft was making runs over the airfield and the plane broke up. None of the crew of four escaped, although unlike his fellow crew members Ron Ecclestone had an ejector seat and possibly could have chosen to save himself. He was 31 years of age. Sadly, he was not scheduled to fly the Victor on that day but accepted the task so that the senior test pilot could carry out a rescheduled demonstration of another aircraft to a foreign sales delegation.

Andrew Haines

Andrew was a pupil in Cyfarthfa from 1975–1982 and there met his wife Caroline (nee Fletcher). Andrew's year was one of the few that experienced Cyfarthfa on three sites – Georgetown, Castle and Cae Mari Dwn. From Cyfarthfa he went to King's College, London, and graduated in History, subsequently completing a Masters in Business Administration at Kingston University in 1995.

He began full-time employment as an Operations Management Trainee with British Rail following a holiday job as a left luggage clerk. That turned out to be the start of a career that has involved meeting each of the last five prime ministers. After a variety of very different jobs and promotions and following the privatisation of the railways Andrew, aged 36, was appointed in 2000 Managing Director of South West Trains, Britain's biggest train company. The company went on to win Train Operator of Year twice and Andrew was headhunted to join First Group as Managing Director of their Rail Division in 2005.

Andrew Haines

In 2007 he took direct responsibility for First Great Western, commonly known at the time as Worst Great Western due to its poor performance and declining reputation. In 12 months Andrew and a largely new management team transformed the service and laid the foundations for a major programme of infrastructure investment.

In August 2009, for an initial three-year contract, he was appointed the first Chief Executive of the Civil Aviation Authority, a post of international significance. The CAA is responsible for all aspects of aviation safety, the economic regulation of the three biggest London airports and of the National Air Traffic Services, the licensing of airlines and tour operators and the oversight of UK airspace.

During the Spring of 2010 he appeared in almost daily television news bulletins to underline the potential danger of the Icelandic volcano eruption and its associated ash clouds. Thousands of flights were cancelled whilst the UK CAA led the way in identifying a new global approach to manage these risks.

In January 2012 he was reappointed Chief Executive of the CAA for a further five years. Justine Greening, then Minister for Transport, said: 'Since his appointment in 2009, Andrew has helped bring fresh thinking to the CAA while maintaining the UK's excellent record in aviation safety'. The Chair of the CAA, Dame Deirdre Hutton, welcomed Andrew's reappointment: 'Since joining the CAA he has put in place important changes to modernise the organisation and build on its strengths, to ensure an aviation industry that is safe, delivers choice and value for consumers, and takes steps to reduce its environmental impact.'

Robert Haines

When Robert Haines' book of photographs *Once Upon A Time In Wales* was published in 2008 more than one person assumed they were photos from the nineteenth century. In fact they were photographs of Heolgerrig and Merthyr people taken in 1971–72 when, soon after leaving Cyfarthfa

School, he was a student at Westminster University. The photographs had lain for nearly 40 years in a box until, rediscovering them, he realised they were a unique record not just of the people but of a time and place. The book brought him wide recognition, with features in *The Guardian, The Independent* and *The Times* and exhibitions of the photographs were held in at West Midlands galleries, the National Museum of Wales, and in Cyfarthfa Museum.

After gaining a degree in Photographic Arts from the University of Westminster in 1974, where he also received the Margaret Harker Prize in recognition of outstanding photographic practice, he worked as a photographer, journalist, freelance camera operator for the BBC and as a film maker. His photographs and features have been published in *The Sunday Times, The Daily Telegraph* and many magazines and books throughout the world. He has exhibited his work in Arles, Geneva, St Tropez, Paris and China. His film *Tommy Gravedigger* was broadcast on BBC2 and he is the winner of various Arts Council of England bursary awards.

His film *Astronauts, Vikings and Ghosts* looks at how, over a period of 40 years, life has changed for the people of Merthyr Tydfil. It won Best Documentary at Newport International Film Festival 2011. It has been described as 'a remarkable portrait of a community – poetic and elegiac, funny and touching. It shows that, when looked at closely, no life is ordinary ... and how beautiful life is and how much we should cherish every day. The photographs are stunning and this is a truly accomplished and powerful piece of work'. In 2012 it was broadcast in Germany and France and shown at the International Festival of Films on Art in Montreal.

Lesley Hodgson

Brought up in Merthyr's Mardy district (commonly referred to as 'the bottom of town'), Lesley had to leave Cyfarthfa High School in 1974, before sitting her O levels, when her parents moved to Ireland. She returned to Merthyr in 1994, divorced and with four children. Determined to rebuild her life and recognizing the need for qualifications, she attended Merthyr College and gained a BTEC Nursery Nursing qualification and GCE passes in English and Maths. Finding she preferred the 'academic' subjects she went on successfully to complete an Access In Education Course which gained her entry to the University of Glamorgan.

There, she achieved a First Class Honours Degree in Sociology, and then gained a doctorate after writing a thesis on 'Experiencing Civil Society: Civil Society in Post Devolution Wales'. During these years of study, and bringing up children, she worked part-time as a DJ at parties and weddings, and later as a part-time lecturer at the University.

In 2003 at a ceremony in Cardiff she was awarded the title 'Welsh Woman of the Year' in the 'Most Effective Returner to the Workplace' category.

In November 2004 Dr Hodgson moved from her post as a full-time research fellow and lecturer in the Sociology department to the university's Centre for Life-long Learning in order to help set up the 'Glamorgan Gates Project' in Merthyr Tydfil. By this means she sought to give something back to her home community. Until its closure in September 2012 due to lack of funding, GATES provided informal learning using art, culture and media technology to inspire people and encourage them into more formal education, employment volunteering or social engagement and personal development. With over 500 projects and over 14,000 participants throughout the borough GATES also helped to start up new business and social groups – and provided them with ongoing help and support.

Lesley continues to lecture to professional conferences on civil society issues and is collaborating on a research project into the lives of migrant workers in present-day Merthyr. She is vice-chair of the Global Village Festival and in 2012 was appointed a board member of the Arts Council of Wales.

Jason Howard

In the past 20 years Jason Howard of Twynyrodyn (he changed his surname from Jones at the start of his career for professional reasons) has firmly established himself as a leading baritone on the international operatic stage, receiving critical acclaim at Covent Garden, the Paris Opera, Chicago, Seattle, New York, Minnesota, Buenos Aires, Salzburg, Frankfurt, and Welsh National Opera. A boy soprano who loved singing in Baptist High Street concerts, it was only after he had left Cyfarthfa that Jason increasingly felt the need to pursue a singing career, despite being a successful member of the Merthyr Tydfil Fire Service where, incidentally, he was capped on the wing for the Wales Fire Service XV.

Two people in particular were extremely important in his early development as a singer. One was Glynne Jones (see the entry below) who encouraged Jason's ambitions and suggested he join the Dowlais Male Voice Choir where he became a baritone soloist. Glynne also introduced him to Martin Hodson, Director of Music at Cross Keys College. It was Martin who, as an experienced singer and vocal coach, gave him lessons, introduced him to Cross Keys Dramatic Society and in due course suggested he should apply for a scholarship at Trinity College of Music. He won the scholarship, won College prizes and then studied further at the Royal College of Music. In 1992, he was the only UK winner in the Pavarotti Voice Competition in Philadelphia.

He began his professional career at Scottish Opera and has sung with all the major international opera companies and orchestras. He is now recognised as an outstanding performer in the French, Italian and German repertoire, with appearances in *La Traviata, Don Carlos, Rigoletto, Macbeth, Nabucco, Il Trovatore, La Bohème, Le Nozze di Figaro* and many more. One review described his debut in *Die Walküre*, as 'the Wotan of his generation'.

Now a Canadian resident, his rich baritone voice, allied to a strong stage presence, have led to his playing lead roles in popular Broadway musicals. He starred in the sensational 1990 Opera North/Royal Shakespeare Company production of *Show Boat* and has toured the USA and Britain in

Jason Howard

South Pacific. His numerous recordings cover both operatic roles and classic Hollywood musicals. With the double centenary of the births of both Wagner and Verdi in 2013 he is certain to be busy.

Terry Jenkins

Terry, another from the Dowlais assembly line of talent, entered Cyfarthfa Boys' School in 1945 and played both rugby and cricket for the school – he was a fine wicket-keeper batsman. He then went to University College, Cardiff, where he graduated with first class honours in Pure Metallurgy, being top of his year, and played rugby and cricket for the University first teams.

In 1955 he entered the Atomic Weapons Research Establishment at Aldermaston and retired from there in May 2004, establishing during those years an international reputation as a consultant and senior adviser on nuclear safety to the British, American and Jamaican Governments.

In 1970 he went to Jamaica for 30 months to advise the government and industry on nuclear safety and set up a bureau of standards. While there, in his free time, he played rugby for Kingston and Jamaica. In 1975 he was appointed to a senior position as manager of a large facility making radioactive parts for underground tests in Nevada and in July 1979 conducted the Queen on a tour of the facility.

In May 1997 he visited Iraq as part of a United Nations Nuclear Weapons Inspection team in a search for 'weapons of mass destruction'. In 1998 he was 'borrowed' by the USA Department of Energy to advise them on the manufacture of nuclear weapon parts at Los Alamos National Laboratory. Initially for two years, this appointment extended to six years. During this time he made significant improvements to the safety of their operations and advised on the design of a future manufacturing facility. He left the USA in 2004 for a belated retirement.

Phillip Joll

Phillip Joll

Phillip attended Cyfarthfa in the early 1970s where he was part of the Glamorgan Schools Rugby Squad. In the sixth form he studied science subjects with the intention of becoming a doctor but really wanted to be a singer. He was accepted by the Welsh College of Music and Drama but, after hearing him sing, Glynne Jones (see profile below) arranged an audition for him with Frederick Cox at the Royal Northern College of Music, Manchester. He passed the audition and studied there from 1973 to 1977, and then spent another year at the London National Opera Studio. Without Glynne's help I would never have gone to Manchester, he says.

He made his professional début with the English National Opera in 1978 and his powerful dark baritone and imposing physique have made him a natural choice for many leading roles. In 1979 he joined Welsh National Opera, singing several principal roles in the *Ring* cycle 1983–5. He made his Covent Garden début in 1982; and his American debut as Donner in Wagner's *Das Rheingold* at the Metropolitan Opera, New York.

He has a large repertoire in German, Italian, and English operas and has sung at all the major British opera venues and at San Francisco, San Diego, Seattle, Arizona, Rio de Janeiro, Sao Paolo, Opera Bastille Paris, Bordeaux, Dresden, Stuttgart, Cologne, Frankfurt, Munich, Karlsruhe, Dortmund, Brussels, Amsterdam, Turin, Palermo, Bologna, Barcelona and in Korea and Bangkok. He has also appeared with leading orchestras throughout the world in a repertoire including Verdi's *Requiem*, Beethoven's *Choral Symphony*, Mahler's Symphony No. 8 and the Vaughan Williams *Sea Symphony*, and has broadcast frequently on radio and television. On disc he has sung in the complete recordings of *Tristan Und Isolde, Parsifal, The Greek Passion* and *Cavalleria Rusticana*.

In recent years he has returned to live in Merthyr whilst continuing professional engagements around the world.

John Ithel Jones (1911–1980)

When immigrants flooded into Merthyr Tydfil from the countryside in the early nineteenth century they literally had to build a new town. A priority was to build their own Nonconformist chapels and from those chapels Merthyr, for over a hundred years, has sent preachers into the wider world. John Ithel Jones, brought up in Dowlais during the inter-war depression, was one of the most prominent communicators of the gospel in both English and Welsh.

After attending Cyfarthfa he graduated in both Welsh and philosophy in Cardiff before becoming a Bachelor of Divinity. Later he gained an MA with a theological dissertation. After completing his studies at the South Wales Baptist College he was ordained minister of Gilgal, Porthcawl, in 1936, moving to Horfield, Bristol, in 1940 and Haven Green, Ealing, in 1950. In January 1958 he was appointed Principal of the South Wales Baptist College and lecturer in Christian Doctrine and the Philosophy of Religion at the University College, Cardiff, later becoming Dean of the Faculty of Theology. He also served as Moderator of the Free Church Federal Council of England and Wales and as President of the Baptist Union of Great Britain (1967–68).

As a lecturer and preacher he received many invitations from Europe and North America and was guest-speaker at Cyfarthfa's Fiftieth Anniversary Service at Zoar Chapel on 16 May 1963. In 1965 he was invited to preach in the meetings of the Baptist World Alliance in Miami Beach, Florida, and subsequently lectured at various centres in the USA, receiving honorary degrees from the Eastern Seminary, Philadelphia, and the Baylor University, Texas. In 1968 he was invited to preach in the 125th Anniversary of Collins Street Baptist Church in Melbourne, Australia. As a result of this visit he was inducted as minister of Collins Street in September 1970 where he remained until his death in December 1980. Shortly before his death he had accepted an invitation to be appointed Principal Emeritus of the Baptist College in Cardiff.

John Ithel Jones

His publications included *Temple and Town and Other Sermons* (1961); *Ein Capel Ni* (1966); *The Holy Spirit and Preaching* (1967); and *Facing the New World and other Sermons* (1968).

Llinos Jonathan

A pupil of the 1970s, Llinos Jonathan left Cyfarthfa Grammar to read French and English at Royal Holloway College, London University. Graduating during the rise of consumerism within Thatcherite Britain, Llinos began her career with the country's largest retailer, J Sainsbury. There she was at the vanguard of sourcing and creating 'Own Label' product lines, now a core offering with every retailer across the world. Her prize-winning marketing ideas were soon being used by Heinz while she became a major influence behind the re-invigoration of the Crosse and Blackwell brand.

Building on her success she joined Nestle, the world's largest food manufacturer, where her marketing skills were honed at their international training centre in Switzerland. Whilst with Nestlé she gained international advertising awards for her work and pioneered developments in healthier convenience food for adults (less sugar and salt), and fun style food for children (she created the first spaghetti shapes in tins). Her increased interest in developing products for children led her to accept the position of UK Marketing Manager for Fisher Price Toys in the late 1980s, where she continued winning creative and media awards for her work with advertising and promotions.

The 1990s saw her change direction and move into the newly emerging Business to Business marketing arena, with the Post Office seeking new revenue opportunities through the fast evolving world of telecoms. During this period she became an early exponent of the potential for the newly emerging world of mobile telephones, and was approached by BTCellnet to join them. It was here that Llinos developed her enthusiasm for identifying the benefits of technology for business. Headhunted by Motorola, the network and mobile giant, she led a European team that moved essential operations, such as police and emergency services, from old fashioned analogue systems into the new digital arena.

In 2002, she moved to technology giant Invensys, a company specialising in business systems and climate control research. Initially with a European role, in 2010 she was appointed Director of this global company, with a brief to take high tech business solutions into the rapidly emerging markets of China, Brazil, India and Russia. Although a frequent global traveller, her links and enthusiasm for her local town and happy memories of the school that started it all remain strong.

Aubrey Jones (1911–2003)

Aubrey Jones from Penydarren was one of the most able pupils who passed through Cyfarthfa in the 1920s. The son of a miner and a teacher, he won a scholarship to the London School of Economics, where he achieved a first in economics and won the 1933 Gladstone Memorial Prize and the Gerstenberg postgraduate award. He did not, however, pursue an academic career.

After a brief time with the International Labour Organisation (an arm of the League of Nations) in Geneva, he joined *The Times* as a sub-editor on the foreign desk (one of his colleagues was Kim Philby), served at the Paris and Berlin offices and left Germany in 1939 three days before war was declared. He spent the war in military intelligence in North Africa and Sicily, attaining the rank of captain. His meditations on politics during this period resulted in a book *The Pendulum of Politics* (1946) in which he declared his conversion to Christianity and Conservatism. After two failed attempts to enter the Commons, he was elected the Conservative member for Hall Green, Birmingham, in 1950.

In 1949 he joined the British Iron and Steel Federation as assistant to the Director, and became its Director in 1955. But later that year Anthony Eden made him Minister of Fuel and Power, where he was a strong advocate of nuclear power. In 1957 Harold Macmillan made him Minister of Supply. His proposal that his department should be transformed into a Ministry of Technology was shelved, only to be implemented later by Harold Wilson. After the 1959 election Macmillan abolished the Ministry of Supply and, although Aubrey was offered another post, his frustration caused him to choose the back benches. He accepted a number of company directorships and never held Cabinet office again.

In truth, his Toryism was not in tune with the increasing emphasis on free competition in industry and commerce favoured by his party. He believed in government holding the balance between competing economic forces and enlisting their aid in planning the economy. It was entirely consistent therefore that he accepted an invitation from Labour Prime Minister, Harold Wilson, in 1965 to become chairman of the newly formed Board for Prices and Incomes. Its task was to review pay settlements and price rises. Its carefully argued reports contributed greatly to understanding the processes of collective bargaining and the weaknesses of British industry.

After Labour lost the 1970 election, he returned to the world of business, chairing Laporte Industries and Cornhill Insurance and holding many directorships. He remained an advocate of incomes policy and his book *The New Inflation: the politics of prices and incomes* (1973) summarised lessons learned from experience. At odds with the free market policies of Margaret Thatcher ('I could not be a member of that government') he joined the Liberal Alliance party in 1981. In 1981 he published *Oil: The Missed Opportunity* and in 1985 *Britain's Economy*.

He possessed vision – understanding that technology would transform our thinking, industry and society – but was a loner, out of tune with modern Conservatism. As he once observed: 'My Welsh heritage has given me an independence of spirit – unlike most of my old Etonian cabinet colleagues, I had my own ideas.'

Glyn Jones

Glyn Jones (1905–1995)

Born at 16 Clare Street, Glyn Jones was one of Wales' foremost writers in prose and poetry in the twentieth century. He wrote numerous short stories, three novels and four volumes of poetry. His best novel *Island of Apples* obliquely comments upon his school days at Cyfarthfa and in *The Dragon Has Two Tongues*, a fascinating study of Anglo-Welsh authors, he reveals that it was at Cyfarthfa 'that I awoke to the marvel of English romantic poetry'. His Christian belief and his love of Merthyr and of Wales are evident in all his work.

A pupil of Cyfarthfa Boys' School from 1916 to 1923, he entered St Paul's College, Cheltenham, to train as a teacher. His earliest poetry was published in 1933, and in 1935, on the suggestion of his friend Dylan Thomas, he wrote a collection of short stories, entitled *The Blue Bed*. One of the stories, 'I was Born in the Ystrad Valley', reflected his experience of teaching in the slums of Cardiff.

A collection of his poems appeared in 1939, with another in 1944, *The Dream of Jake Hopkins* and in that same year came a second book of short stories *The Water Music and other stories*. In the 1950s and 1960s came his three novels, *The Valley, The City, The Village* (1956), *The Learning Lark* (1960) and *The Island of Apples* (1965). In 1968 he published *The Dragon has Two Tongues*, an autobiographical and critical work examining the effect of education, religion and politics on Welsh writers between the two World Wars. This was followed by his *Selected Poems* in 1975, and two collections of stories, *Selected Short Stories* (1971) and *Welsh Heirs* (1977).

His life spanned most of the twentieth century and his commitment to writing in English whilst, at the same time, respecting the Welsh language made him an important figure in Welsh literary circles. He always encouraged young Welsh language writers in their work, stressing that there was only one dragon, though she spoke with two tongues. His writings, however, never strayed outside Wales and its people.

He was elected President of the Welsh Academy and was awarded an honorary Doctorate by the University of Wales in 1974. He was also an

Honorary Fellow of Trinity College, Carmarthen and in 1988 he was made an honorary member of the Gorsedd of Bards. The Glyn Jones Centre, opened in 2005 in Cardiff, exists as a base for writers and a space for visitors to gain information on the practice, publication and promotion of writing.

Glynne Jones (1927–2000)

Glynne from Dowlais, a Cyfarthfa pupil in the 1940s, went on to become one of Wales' foremost choral conductors and an accomplished broadcaster. An exuberant and flamboyant personality, his first job after studying music at University College, Cardiff, was as music teacher at Merthyr County Grammar School. His annual school concerts in the 50s, especially his initial *Messiah* in Zoar Chapel, will never be forgotten by choir members and those fortunate to be in the audience. At the same time, from 1955 to 1965 he conducted the Merthyr Philharmonic Choir and Rhymney's Silurian Singers who, under his baton, won the prize for choral singing at the National Eisteddfod in three consecutive years, a record.

In 1965 he became music advisor to the County of Monmouthshire where he promoted the County Youth Orchestra and initiated the Gwent Musical Trust, but in 1962 he undertook a task that lasted almost 40 years – conducting the Pendyrus Male Voice Choir. From the beginning he aimed high, bringing new works into the traditional Welsh choral repertoire, and always seeking new audiences. I remember going to Cardiff gaol with him and Peter Hill to arrange a concert for the prisoners.

He made significant contributions to the future careers of Jason Howard and Phillip Joll. His first concert with the Pendyrus in 1962 was at the Queen Elizabeth Hall. The choir achieved international fame, becoming in 1979 the first choir from Western Europe to tour the Soviet Union. In 1994 he was made a Fellow of the Welsh College of Music and Drama for services to choral music. In 1996 he was appointed MBE. A street in Dowlais is named in his honour.

Glynne Jones

Julien Macdonald

Julien attended Cyfarthfa High School in the 1980s where, quiet and polite, he early displayed an individual sense of style, the wide orange stripe in his hair whilst in Lower School (the Castle) earning him the nickname 'Duracell'. In Upper School he frequently wore a long black coat draped around his shoulders and black nail varnish. These flashes of individuality did not prevent him from being well liked by the staff and his flair for design and art was supported by his Art teacher, Lorraine Buck. Initially Julien dreamed of being a painter after seeing Monet's water lilies in a Paris gallery whilst on a school trip.

From Cyfarthfa he went to Brighton Art College where he studied Fashion Knitwear and then went on to the Royal College of Art, where he gained a Master's Degree. Julien's early interest in textiles and design (apparently he was taught knitting by his mother) blossomed into a triumphant career. Soon after the success of his RCA graduation show in 1996 the international designer Karl Lagerfeld recruited him as Head Designer of Knitwear for Chanel and Karl Lagerfeld.

In 2000, aged 29, he was appointed successor to Alexander McQueen as Creative Director at the Paris Haute Couture house of Givenchy, and in 2001, he was named British Fashion Designer of the Year. In 2004 he returned to London to concentrate on his own label. His creations have been worn by stars such as Gweneth Paltrow, Anjelica Houston, Madonna, Dame Shirley Bassey, Katherine Jenkins, and Naomi Campbell. He also redesigned the uniforms worn by all sales and operations staff at British Airways. In recent years he has appeared as a judge on the popular television programme 'Britain's Next Top Model'.

He frequently returns to Merthyr and when, in 2006, Julien was awarded an OBE for services to the fashion industry, he said 'I'm very proud of where I come from. I went to a great Welsh school and I thank them for my education and training which brought me to where I am today'.

Julien Macdonald

Philip Madoc (1934–2012)

When, in December 1951, Cyfarthfa put on a production of *Macbeth*, Twynyrodyn's Philip Jones possessed a self-assurance and feel for language that made him the obvious choice for the starring role. He carried it off splendidly. It was some years, however, before he took up the acting career that many of us who saw that production forecast for him. With A levels in Latin, German and French he graduated from University College, Cardiff, with a degree in classics and modern languages. He then went to the University of Vienna, where he became the first foreigner to win the Diploma of the Interpreters Institute. A natural linguist, he spoke at least seven languages, including Swedish, Russian and Albanian. Initially he worked as an interpreter at international conferences but finding the work boring, successfully applied for a scholarship at the Royal Academy of Dramatic Art. He was then 24.

From there he began an acting career under the name Philip Madoc that lasted for over 50 years and made him one of Cyfarthfa's most recognized former pupils. He made his television debut in the 1961 BBC Sunday Night play *Cross of Iron* – as a German officer, a role he played more than once with great effect. As the SS officer in *Manhunt* (1969) the World War II series he showed he was ready for major roles. And as the captured German U-boat captain in a 1973 episode of *Dad's Army*, in peaked cap and white polo-necked sweater, he played a scene remembered by everyone as a comedy classic.

In a variety of television roles he worked with the best of British actors – Pamela Brown, Diane Cilento, Judi Dench, Brewster Mason, Kenneth Branagh and Emma Thompson. The first of his four different roles in *Doctor Who* began in 1969, but it was as the vicious Huron warrior Magua in the 1971 BBC series *The Last of the Mohicans* that he made his name. That was enhanced when he played with great authority the title role in Elaine Morgan's *The Life and Times of Lloyd George* (1981). There was rarely a British television series that did not feature him in one or more episodes: among them *The Avengers; The Sweeney; The Goodies; Brother Cadfael; Porridge*; and *Midsomer Murders*. Between 1994 and 2002 he played DCI Noel Bain in the television series *A Mind to Kill* that was broadcast on S4C as *Noson yr Heliwr*. He also appeared in a number of films.

Philip Madoc with Arthur Lowe in Dad's Army

His stage career began straight after RADA when he joined the Royal Shakespeare Company. He returned to that Company in 1991 to play Professor Raat in *The Blue Angel* and the Duke in *Measure for Measure*, productions that opened the new Other Place theatre in Stratford-upon-Avon. Over his long career he played many leading parts including Iago in *Othello*; Anthony in *Anthony and Cleopatra*; Macbeth; Shylock; Dr. Faustus; and Falstaff in *The Merry Wives of Windsor*.

His distinctively rich sonorous voice was heard on many audiobooks including *The Canterbury Tales*, the works of Dylan Thomas, and Buddhist writings. For BBC radio he played King Lear, Prospero in *The Tempest* and, in 2011, Stalin in *Life and Fate*. In 1994 he was made a Fellow of the Royal Welsh College of Music and Drama and in 2001 received an honorary degree from the University of Glamorgan.

Ursula Masson (O'Connor) (1945–2008)

Ursula was born in Penydarren into a Catholic family, entered Cyfarthfa in 1956, and subsequently gained a degree in English and Philosophy at Cardiff University. She spent three years in Australia as a journalist on the *Sydney Morning Herald* where she gained a reputation for writing with fairness and insight on religious affairs.

Upon returning to Britain she married Rob Masson and enrolled at the University of Keele for an MA in Victorian Studies, which she gained in 1975 for her thesis, *The Development of the Irish and Roman Catholic Communities of Merthyr Tydfil and Dowlais in the Nineteenth Century*.

After her divorce from Rob, she worked as a civil servant, cleaner and sauna attendant before, in the 1980s, she taught adult and community groups in Swansea. There she became involved in film-making with the Swansea Women's History Group and in the mid-1990s was appointed to teach British and Welsh political history at the University of Glamorgan. She enthusiastically researched women's role in party politics in the late nineteenth and early twentieth centuries and wrote a thesis for which she received a doctorate from the University of the West of England.

Ursula was one of a small band of historians who began to uncover the lives and significance of the ignored half of the population of Wales – the women. She was one of the founders of the Women's Archive of Wales and from the Heritage Lottery Fund obtained resources which enabled road shows to travel throughout Wales publicising women's history. In 2006 she was named a national 'Woman of Achievement'. Less than a year before she died the Centre for the Study of Gender in Wales was launched at Glamorgan University, another of her initiatives.

In 2003 she became joint-editor of *Llafur*, the journal of the Society for the Study of Welsh People's History. As vice-chair of the Society I often spoke to her about Cyfarthfa and Merthyr, as well as wider topics, but it was some time before I learned that she was battling with breast cancer. She determinedly carried on her work, which included editing the minutes of the Aberdare Women's Liberal Association and revising her thesis for publication. The first of these appeared in 2005 as *'Women's Rights and Women's Duties': The Aberdare Women's Liberal Association, 1891–1910*. Her revised thesis was published by the University of Wales posthumously and is a valuable contribution to the history of Wales – *For Women, For Wales and For Liberalism: Women in Liberal Politics in Wales, 1880–1914* (2010). The annual Ursula Masson Memorial Lecture is held by the University of Glamorgan.

John Percival Morgan (1916–?)

Among the large number of former Cyfarthfa boys and girls who served honourably during World War II, the memory of one is revered in a corner of Italy to this day. On 18 June 1944, two German soldiers were killed and a third wounded by Italian resistance partisans in the Tuscan 'city' of Civitella in Val di Chiana. Many inhabitants, fearing a German reprisal, fled to the countryside; but when the Germans discovered this, punitive action was postponed. After three days most villagers returned in the belief that their innocence was understood.

On 29 June, more than a week later, when the local inhabitants were feeling secure, SS units of the Goering division entered the town at dawn and moving from house to house shot the men, many still in bed. At the church, where people were gathered for early mass, they lined up the men, including the priest, and five by five machine-gunned them to death. Within one hour 161 innocent men and boys were executed. The SS then looted, mined and burned the houses. Altogether during that day 212 men, women and children in the immediate district were killed. Some of the dead women were found completely naked. The ages of the dead ranged from one year to 84 years. Approximately 100 houses were destroyed by fire; some of the victims being burned alive in their homes.

A week later, on arriving with advancing British forces, Captain John Morgan, from Pant, organised army lorries to bring food and blankets to the desperate women and children, without electricity, food or shelter. After the war, John Morgan returned to his job at Lloyd's Bank in Merthyr and later in the Channel Isles. But in 2001, 58 years later, his widow Barbara and son Keith were invited to a moving ceremony in Civitella, where John was posthumously honoured by the townspeople for his humanitarian act. A street was named in his memory – Costa Cap John Perceval Morgan – and a plaque in Italian and English erected. The plaque reads:

> In memory of John Percival Morgan,
> Father O'Shea and their friends
> of the 8th British Army, who gave
> Precious aid to the survivors of
> 29th June 1944 massacre
> Civitella 6 May 2001

Harold Nash

I still remember the trombone performance Harold Nash gave at the school eisteddfod in 1947 when winning the instrumental solo: beautiful tone, complete control, and an impish choice of music. He was a natural, instinctive player from a Salvation Army background and a member of the local band, as well as the famous Parc and Dare Band. That September, at the age of 15, he entered the Royal Academy of Music having won an entry scholarship. By his third year at the Academy he was often playing with the Royal Philharmonic Orchestra. When the time came to sit his final exams he went to the Principal to request that he could sit one of the written papers on another day as there was an important rehearsal at Glyndebourne. 'Certainly not, you should make a decision which one you want to choose.' He left the Academy and joined the RPO; he was nineteen.

In 1953 he joined Sadlers Wells Opera on first trombone and in 1956 he was invited by Raphael Kubelik to join the Royal Opera House orchestra, where he stayed for 41 years. In an interview with Warwick Music in 1995, he was asked why he had stayed so long with the same orchestra. He replied, 'I've thought about this a lot. It's lack of ambition on the instrument partly. I don't really want to be the best trombone player in the world. What I enjoy is taking part in the opera. You're part of a tremendous show. It's real life drama going on up there, with wonderful singers, scenery, costumes. At the end of *Othello*, for instance, when all sorts of mayhem has happened on stage, there's this deafening silence and the trombones enter playing those growling chords. That's not a musical thing to me, it's an emotional experience. You live for the operas, the good singers, and the good conductors.'

He has composed, taught (which he enjoyed enormously), been a recording artist, and played with some of the greatest instrumentalists and conductors of our time. He does not have a high opinion of conductors but picks out Beecham and Carlos Kleiber as among the finest. Of Kleiber he said, 'He has the emotional range, he takes tremendous chances, the intellect is marvelous, the shows are just a joy to play in.' He provides his own summary of his career: 'I have been very fortunate to have worked in so many different and interesting areas of the profession, while the Royal Opera House has paid the mortgage and provided me with a first class interactive free seat for thrilling performances listening to the world's most wonderful singers; and even joining in with them at times'.

Leslie Norris (1921–2006)

Born in Cyfarthfa Row, Georgetown, and brought up in the inter-war Depression, Leslie left school at 17 and found work as a clerk in the Town Hall. At 19 he joined the Royal Air Force and trained as a pilot, but was injured when he collided with another plane on the ground while practising landings. He contracted blood poisoning and was invalided out.

Leslie Norris

He returned to Merthyr, and in 1948 enrolled in the teacher training college at Coventry and subsequently at the University of Southampton. Later he gained the research degree of MPhil. He became a teacher, a headmaster, and then a lecturer at Bognor Regis College of Education.

He had begun writing poetry as a Cyfarthfa schoolboy, and published some in 1947 but it was 20 years later that his first substantial collection *Finding Gold* was published. After that his reputation as a poet and short story writer steadily grew. Several of his poems refer to Merthyr. 'An evening by the Lake' recalls his schooldays 'in a comic gothic castle, built for a fat ironmaster' and 'Elegy for David Beynon' remembers his school friend who died protecting schoolchildren in the school at Aberfan.

In 1973 he accepted an invitation to be Visiting Professor at the University of Washington in Seattle and the following year he resigned his post at Bognor Regis to become a full-time writer. He continued to visit the USA, published his first collection of short stories *Sliding* in 1978 and in 1983 was invited to teach for six months at Brigham Young University in Utah. It was there that he settled until his death. He was appointed official Poet-in-Residence at the university and later Professor of Creative Writing.

Altogether he wrote a dozen volumes of poetry, numerous short stories and essays and also two books for children. His *Collected Poems* and *Collected Stories* were both published in 1996. His poetry is deceptively simple, carrying considerable emotional power. His reputation in the USA and Britain grew steadily and before his death he had been recognised as an important Anglo-Welsh writer. He was also a perceptive critic, commenting on the work of fellow poets Edward Thomas and Vernon Watkins, and publishing an affectionate study of *Glyn Jones* (1973). A plaque to his memory is in Merthyr Central Library.

Geoffrey Olsen (1943–2007)

Geoffrey, also from Georgetown, attended Cyfarthfa in the late 1950s where his art teacher was Dewi Bowen. Afterwards he studied fine art at Newport College of Art, Cardiff College of Art, and later as a scholarship student at the Academy of Fine Art, Munich. The poet and critic Tony Curtis has described him as 'one of the most original painters to come from the Welsh valleys'.

He used energetic, bold, free-flowing oil paint in layers reminiscent of the impact of humans upon the landscape. The result is that his works are complex, highly personal and not easily categorized: neither literal nor abstract they draw the viewer into contemplation of the scene and its history, whether the brutal scars of industrialisation, as in Merthyr; the impact of quarrying and Roman settlements in Gloucestershire; or the very different light and landscape of Miami. In its layering his work captures the relationship between landscape, memory and human intervention upon nature. These techniques emerged after years of childhood play on the Georgetown Tips; a landscape where man's impositions upon the landscape were only too evident.

During the 1980s he made an important series of works in response to the Cotswold landscape and its very specific archaeology and topography. In 1992 he was a visiting lecturer at the Studio Art Centers International in Florence, and this influenced his painting to include references to Renaissance fresco painting. In 1999 he was awarded an Abbey Award In Painting at the British School at Rome to continue and develop these interests. In 2000 he was artist in residence at Cheltenham Art Gallery and Museum. His commitment to teaching and the communication of his ideas informed a whole generation of students in the UK and abroad. From 1978–2001 he lectured and taught at Oxford Brookes University and in 2001 he was appointed Associate Professor of Painting and Director of the MFA Visual Arts program at Florida International University, Miami. Many of these students are now practising artists as a direct result of his teaching. In works such as 'The Place of Burial Series', first shown at the Newlyn Art Gallery in 1990, and 'The Extramural Series', shown at the

Museum of Modern Art, Machynlleth in 2000, he achieved dream-like, unsettling images.

He exhibited widely from the 1970s, including the Ikon Gallery, Birmingham, Camden Art Centre, London, the Corcoran Museum of Art in Washington DC, the Cheltenham Museum and Gallery, the National Library of Wales, the National Museum of Wales and the Glynn Vivian Gallery, Swansea.

Johnny Owen (1956–1980)

John Richard Owens, a quiet, generous and shy boy from Gellideg, entered Cyfarthfa from Georgetown Secondary Modern School in 1970, Cyfarthfa's first year as a comprehensive school. His appearance and character were in total contrast to what happened when he stepped inside a boxing ring. Then he became an opponent with determination and strength that seemed impossible to summon from such a frail looking body.

He began boxing at the age of eight and steadily made a name for himself in Welsh amateur boxing circles. (He dropped the 's' after Owens because there was already a boxer named Johnny Owens.) He represented Wales on 17 occasions, winning 15 of the contests and in a distinguished amateur career he won 106 fights out of 124.

His style was one of perpetual motion coupled with skill and knowledge. Unlike his hero, Jimmy Wilde, he was not a big puncher but would wear opponents down, smothering their best work while raining in his own shots from the first bell to the last. His thin, wiry, almost skeletal frame led to him being called 'The Matchstick Man'. He was also referred to as 'The Bionic Bantam' due to his dedication to training and his relentless pursuit of opponents and astonishing stamina.

After only six professional contests he won, on 30 September 1976, the Welsh Bantamweight Title. In his tenth fight, and with a reputation as a dedicated, tenacious boxer of unparalleled stamina, he won the British Bantamweight Title.

In November 1978 against world rated Australian, Paul Ferreri he won the Commonwealth Bantamweight championship. Just four months later, he went to Almeria, Spain to challenge Spaniard Juan Francisco Rodriguez for the latter's European Bantamweight title. In his first fight on foreign soil he out boxed the title holder for 15 rounds but was declared the loser! It was a scandalous hometown decision.

Johnny came through the episode with his resilience and self-belief intact. After winning a further seven fights, his European title dream returned when Rodriguez was brought over to Ebbw Vale in 1979 to defend his title. Yet again Rodriguez was out-boxed and Johnny Owen was rightfully proclaimed Bantamweight Champion of Europe.

In September 1980 he travelled to Los Angeles to fight for the World Bantamweight Championship against the Mexican holder, Lupe Pintor. He had secured a Lonsdale Belt outright and was the holder of the Welsh, British, Commonwealth and European titles with a record of 24 wins, one defeat (avenged) and one draw in 26 professional fights. But Los Angeles was a fight too far. On 19 September in the 12th round he was knocked unconscious and never recovered. He fell into a coma and was pronounced dead on 4 November, 1980, aged 24.

At his funeral, on the afternoon of 11 November 1980, Cyfarthfa School was closed and thousands of people lined the streets from High Street Baptist Chapel (where he had been a member) to Pant Cemetery where an estimated crowd of 4,000 stood silent in the rain. An Appeal Fund, initially set up to help his family visit his bedside, reached £75,000 and, with the agreement of his parents, was spent on a variety of local causes, including a permanent unit at Prince Charles Hospital. Twenty years later, a memorial to Johnny Owen was unveiled in Merthyr's shopping centre. At the request of Johnny's father, the unveiling was performed by Lupe Pintor.

Helen Phillips

Helen entered Cyfarthfa in 1984. Eleven members of her family, including her nieces and nephews, have passed through the school. Her family members were all sport fanatics so it was no surprise that she enjoyed PE at school, joined the local St Tydfil's Gymnastics Club where her mother was a coach, and also the squash club at Rhydycar. She played squash for Wales while still in school, as did other Cyfarthfa pupils, and coached the junior section at the squash club, developing more Cyfarthfa pupils into international players and national champions. Helen later qualified as one of the world's leading gymnastics judges for the Commonwealth and Olympic Games discipline, Women's Artistic.

But she has also had a successful career as a business woman. In 1992 she graduated from University of Wales, College, Newport, with a degree in business and subsequently worked in many Blue Chip organizations and award-winning companies. As a company director and investor in a variety of successful businesses predominantly in the building services industry, Helen says her success is down to the inspiring people she has worked for and alongside.

With this valuable advantage of being competent in business yet also understanding sport she has brought her expertise in identifying aims, structure and strategy, to sporting bodies within Wales. Since 2001 she has chaired the board of directors of Welsh Gymnastics Ltd, where she has built up a professionally-driven limited company. She is also vice-chair of the Commonwealth Games Council for Wales, and a director of British Gymnastics. Helen also chairs mentoring forums for Women in Leadership through Sport in partnership with Sport Wales and was a Welsh Assembly World-skills Champion in 2011. Her sporting and business activities have enabled her to travel world-wide and her trump card has always been to tell people that she went to school in a castle!

Bill Roberts (1918–1992)

'The Daleks' first appeared on British television screens on 28 December 1963 in an episode of *Dr. Who*. They instantly became a world-wide phenomenon that continues to arouse cultural debate and interest, appearing on British postage stamps and with various web-sites devoted to them. The man who built them was Bill Roberts from Gwladys Street, Penydarren, a former Cyfarthfa School pupil. By so doing he certainly made his mark. Bill was neither the originator of the idea of the Daleks nor the initial designer. Terry Nation, born in Llandaff, Cardiff, was the script writer who came up with the idea of these machine-like creatures and Robert Cusick, a BBC staff designer, developed the idea before engaging Bill Roberts to build them. But Bill put his considerable experience, skill and ingenuity into the task, including using a camera's diaphragm shutter to act as an eye.

He had entered Cyfarthfa Boys' School in 1929 and then in 1936, like thousands of others during the Great Depression, he left Merthyr to find work in the London area. He gravitated to Berkshire, was taken on by cabinet makers where he displayed a natural flair for innovative design and during World War II worked for Miles Aircraft.

In 1947 with two partners he set up Shawcraft Models, which specialised in making moulds and large-scale models for the aircraft, car and film industries. An early film assignment was to build models of the ship Lydia used in the 1951 film *Captain Horatio Hornblower*. In 1956 he bought out his partners and became sole managing director. The firm grew to employ almost 40 staff in Uxbridge and in 1958 produced a 40-foot model of the Titanic for the film *A Night To Remember*.

It was natural, therefore, that Cusick would contact Bill Roberts and ask him to build the original Dalek to a 'pepper-pot' design. It became instantly recognisable as the gliding manifestation of a dark evil force uttering 'Exterminate!' and despite various design modifications the basic original shape remains. Bill retired and sold his companies in 1987 and died in 1992.

A Dalek: feared throughout the Universe

John Spackman

Born in Merthyr, John attended Cyfarthfa Boys' School from 1943–1948 and went on to have a distinguished career in the Army, in telecommunications and in business. He entered the Army when called to do National Service in 1950, took a regular commission in 1952 and continued to serve until 1982 when he took early retirement with the rank of brigadier.

Whilst in the Army he studied at the Royal Military College of Science where he gained a first class honours degree as an external student of London University and went on to take a PhD in Physics. He then served in various regimental and technical staff appointments in Japan, Egypt, Belgium and Germany and in Britain. These appointments included senior military officer at the Chemical and Microbiological Defence Establishment at Porton Down; branch chief in charge of software development for Supreme Headquarters Allied Powers in Europe, and as Director of logistics computer systems, an appointment he held during the Falklands war.

Upon retirement he was appointed an Under Secretary at the Department of Health and Social Security, responsible for the modernisation of all social security systems – pensions, supplementary benefit, unemployment benefit, child benefit, etc, in then the world's largest programme of government computer-based modernisation. After three years he was offered the post of Director of Information Systems for British Telecom. He left BT in 1988 to act as a consultant in telecommunications and computing and was the founding Director of the European Telecommunications Information Services and served as director and chairman of several companies.

In 1994 he was selected for a three-year appointment as the Director of the Management Services Unit for the Government of Malta, responsible for the modernisation of its administrative systems. He is a Freeman of the City of London and a member of the Institute of Directors.

Stanley Thomas and sons

Stanley Thomas (always known as Stan), was born on 4 July1917 and, in the second half of the twentieth century, began a remarkable business career in his home town. He early showed sporting prowess while attending Cyfarthfa Boys' School for in 1933 he became senior schoolboy boxing champion of Wales. From Cyfarthfa he went to the English College of Physical Education, Denmark, where he qualified as a physical education instructor and, on the outbreak of war in 1939, he volunteered to serve in the Royal Navy and emerged after six years' service as a physical training officer with the rank of Lieutenant. Along the way he was one of the first naval officers to qualify as a parachute jumping instructor.

Back in Merthyr, in 1946 he bought a bakery and in 1954, taking advantage of the end of meat rationing, launched his pie-making business – Thomas' Pies. In 1956 he was joined by his son Stanley from Cyfarthfa School. The business then grew rapidly from having two distribution vans in 1956 to having 14 by the end of 1963. In 1964 Stan's other son, Peter, who also went to Cyfarthfa, joined the business and on 1 January 1965 Thomas' Pies and Stan Thomas Ltd were sold to the Avana Group for £175,000. Stan and his sons were engaged on five-year contracts with the group.

In 1968 Peter left to work in Majorca and in 1970 Stan junior founded Peter's Savoury Products and brought his father, brother and sister into the enterprise with Stan senior as chairman. Together they built a company that employed 1,300 people at Bedwas near Caerphilly and which they sold in 1988 for more than £75m.

After the sale of Peter's Savouries the two sons built new business careers. Peter created Atlantic Property Development and Stan junior invested in a Cardiff-based property company that eventually, as TBI, became listed in the top 250 FTSE companies. By then it had diversified into airports, acquiring first Cardiff and then Belfast International and eventually buying an airport group from George Soros that owned and managed 66 airports on four continents. The brothers and their sister Mary were all shareholders in TBI when it was sold to the Spanish company Ibertis in 2004 for £550m. Both brothers continue to be involved in land and property companies. Peter is chairman of Atlantic Property Developments plc which has capital value today in excess of £100m. It was this company, in association with Merthyr Tydfil County Borough Council, that built the multi-million pound Rhydycar Leisure complex which opened in 2007.

Father and sons are substantial donors to charity. In 1984 in recognition of his commercial achievements and charitable work Stan senior was appointed an MBE and in 1992 made a Freeman of Merthyr Tydfil. Peter is chief shareholder and chairman of the Cardiff Blues rugby club and a benefactor of Welsh National Opera. In the New Year Honours list 2011 he received the CBE for services to entrepreneurship and charity in Wales. Stanley junior is chairman of NSPCC (Wales) and was the chairman and leading force behind the development of the first children's hospital in Wales (the Noah's Ark Appeal). In 1994 he was awarded an OBE and in 2000 he joined his father as a Freeman of the County Borough of Merthyr Tydfil. In the 2006 Queen's Birthday Honours he was knighted for services to business and charity in Wales.

Rhodri Walters

Behind the public face of the Houses of Parliament – the Lords and the Commons – a formidable administrative machine ensures that everything runs smoothly. At the centre of that machine in the Lords is Rhodri Walters who since 2007 has held the ancient title of Reading Clerk. In this role he is Head of Corporate Services and one of the principal procedural advisers to the House. But he also takes part in certain House ceremonies where he reads out Royal Commissions from The Queen, introduces new Members to the Chamber, and administers the oath of allegiance.

From Cyfarthfa in 1968 Rhodri won a Meyricke Exhibition to Jesus College, Oxford, and was also a Kitchener Scholar. He went on to earn a

Rhodri Walters introduces Lord Grade (Michael Grade the former TV executive) to the House of Lords in November 2010

highly praised doctorate for a thesis that was published in 1977 as *The Economic and Business History of the South Wales Steam Coal Industry*.

He entered parliamentary service in 1975 when he was appointed a House of Lords Clerk. Clerks are the procedural advisers in the Houses of Commons and Lords. They service Committees, draft their reports, administer the legislative process and occupy some of the key administrative positions. Between 1986 and 1989, Rhodri was seconded to the Cabinet Office to be Private Secretary to the Leader of the House (then Lord Whitelaw, Deputy Prime Minister) and the Government Chief Whip. In that capacity he advised the Government on matters relating to the House and planned and managed the Government's legislative business. In 1989–90 he was a Nuffield and Leverhulme travelling fellow, attached to the US Congress. From 1990 to 1993 he was clerk to the House of Lords Select Committee on Science and Technology, and subsequently

Establishment Officer 1993–2000, Clerk of Public Bills 2000-02, and Clerk of Committees 2002-07. He is a joint author of *How Parliament Works* (6th edn 2006), and contributed the chapter on 'The House of Lords' in *The British Constitution in the Twentieth Century* (2003).

Glanmor Williams (1920–2005)

From 1931 to 1938 Cyfarthfa was graced by a tiny, ebullient and popular Dowlais boy of exceptional ability who blossomed into a scholar of international reputation. The son and grandson of a collier, Glan – as we naturally referred to him – won a state scholarship and read Welsh and History at University College, Aberystwyth, where he graduated with first-class honours. Unfit for military service, he taught at Merthyr's County School from 1942–44 ('among the happiest years of my life') until he was appointed a temporary history assistant lecturer in at University College, Swansea. He rose to be Professor of History in 1957 and there remained until his retirement in 1982.

Under his leadership the department became a power-house of research and publication that established Welsh history as a substantial discipline and a crucial element in Britain's story. His own output was prodigious, continuing long after his early retirement in 1982. His path-breaking book *The Welsh Church from Conquest to Reformation* (1962) was followed by *Welsh Reformation Essays* (1967); *Religion, Language and Nationality in Wales* (1979); *Recovery, Reorientation and Reformation* (1987); *Owain Glyndwr* (1993); and *Wales and the Reformation* (1997). These were accompanied by a flood of scholarly articles, chapters and reviews in Welsh and English that appeared each year.

In 1957 he founded and edited *Morgannwg*, the journal of the Glamorgan History Society. In 1960 he was founder editor of *The Welsh History Review* and in that same year became general editor of the massive *Glamorgan County History*, an enterprise in six volumes that stretched over 30 years.

Sir Glanmor Williams

Although a specialist in the Reformation, his upbringing in Dowlais during the interwar Depression meant that he was fully conscious of the importance of the industrial revolution in shaping Wales. In 1966 he edited a volume of essays, *Merthyr Politics: The Making of a Working Class Tradition* that was seminal in the study of Welsh labour history and in the 1970s he sponsored a project based at Swansea to work on the labour and social history of the South Wales coalfield. A major outcome was the Miners' Library at the University.

He generously gave time to public service. Amongst other posts he was chairman of the Broadcasting Council for Wales (1965–71), a national governor of the BBC, and chairman of the Royal Commission on Ancient and Historical Monuments in Wales (1983–95). He was elected a Fellow of the British Academy in 1986. Publications and honours apart, those who knew him will always remember his geniality, infectious enthusiasm, and his encouragement of young historians. His autobiography *Glanmor Williams: a Life* (2002) fully displays these qualities. He retained his Baptist faith throughout his life and in 1975 served as president of the Baptist Union of Wales. In 1981 he was appointed CBE, and in 1995 he was knighted 'for services to the history, culture and heritage of Wales'. In 2002 he was made a Freeman of the County Borough of Merthyr Tydfil. In 2010, a housing development in Dowlais was named 'Glanmor Gardens', in his memory.

Gwyn Alfred Williams (1925–1995)

They say that lightning never strikes the same place twice, yet close behind Glanmor entering Cyfarthfa came another small Dowlais boy who also developed into a brilliant historian. But 'Gwyn Alf', as he became universally known, (a designation he did not like but could not escape) was also a left-wing activist – the Communist Party, the Labour Party, Plaid Cymru – and blessed with the gift of eloquent oratory which, in later life enabled him to forge a whole new career as a charismatic television presenter.

He won a scholarship to Aberystwyth but went straight into the army in 1943. The comical fragments of autobiography posthumously published in

Fishers of Men (1996) tell how he took part in the Normandy landings, entered Paris, saw the ruins of Frankfurt and Berlin and emerged as a 'bolshy' sergeant.

Finally entering Aberystwyth in 1947 he gained an exceptional First; followed it with a Master's; and then wrote a brilliant thesis for his doctorate at London. The thesis eventually emerged as a book, *Medieval London: From Commune to Capital* (1963), probably his finest work of scholarship. In 1954 he returned to Aberystwyth as an assistant lecturer in Welsh History and quickly gained a reputation as a passionate inspirational speaker. In 1963 he was appointed Senior Lecturer in History at York and two years later Professor. In 1974 he returned to Wales as Professor at Cardiff.

Throughout these years he wrote and lectured prolifically, becoming one of the best-known left-wing historians in the land. His books included *Artisans and Sans-Culottes* (1968), *Proletarian Order* (1975), *Goya and the Impossible Revolution* (1976), *The Merthyr Rising* (1978), *Madoc and the Making of a Myth* (1979), *The Search for Beulah Land* (1980), *The Welsh in their History* (1982), and *When Was Wales?* (1985).

Also in 1985 came the celebrated television series *The Dragon has two Tongues* in which Gwyn the Marxist and the famous broadcaster Wynford Vaughan Thomas debated opposing views of Welsh history. By then he had taken early retirement from his post in Cardiff and launched into writing and presenting films, with the Taliesyn company – some 30 in all were shown on BBC2 and Channel 4.

He carried his audiences along on a torrent of vivid insights, witticisms, and passionate concern for the plight of 'ordinary' people, occasionally interrupted by a stammer that only added to the drama of his presentations. The breadth of his sympathies can be seen from some of the subjects of his broadcasts: Mary Shelley, Sylvia Pankhurst, Pushkin, Iolo Morgannwg, John Hughes (the founder of Hughesovka, later Donetsk), South African apartheid, and the lives of Soviet coalminers. Yet, never losing sight of his roots, he did more than anyone in the academic world to bring before the people of Merthyr and of Wales the significance of their history.

REMINISCENCES

'Education is what survives when what has been learned

has been forgotten'.

(B.F. Skinner)

What memories of your schooldays? Former Cyfarthfa pupils and teachers reveal here what they recall and who they remember. The reminiscences range across most of the 100 years since Cyfarthfa School opened its doors, recalling aspects of the past that may stimulate quiet reflection on years gone by. In some cases they reveal what happened to pupils after they left school. Many more contributions were received than we could use, and most of those that have been used had to be severely cut for reasons of space. Nonetheless a sincere thank you to all who sent in their memories. Reminiscences by Rosentyl Griffiths, Bryneilon Griffiths, Glyn Jones, Beynon John, Gareth Griffiths, and Jill Kemp are taken from the Fiftieth Anniversary booklet published by the School in 1963.

That First Day

In September 1933 I presented myself at the first floor entrance to Cyfarthfa Castle. In that year of grace the upper floor was, of course, a female citadel. As we lined up nervously in the hall where we were sorted into forms, disaster soon overtook me; by the simple expedient of selecting alternate girls for the two forms, I was promptly deprived of both my boon companions. It was a very sober small girl who arrived home that afternoon, much deflated by the triple humiliation of being bereft of her friends and being officially designated the shortest and youngest-but-one girl in the class.

Nan Davies

Those 1950s memories are never forgotten. The boys in black blazers or sports jackets, white or grey shirt, blue and yellow striped school tie, and black shoes; the first year boys with caps bearing the borough's coat-of-arms etched in yellow or gold, in short grey trousers and long socks of the same colour. The girls, always immaculately turned out, in white blouses, dark blue cardigans and skirts, white ankle socks and black shoes and sporting the obligatory school tie.

All of us nervously treading the same paths as boys and girls of earlier (and later) decades, through the lovely, early autumn-hued Park, to the impressive ivy-covered, pseudo-medieval Castle. The glorious flower-beds were soon hidden from the girls as they left the main path to enter the doors of the former girls' school at the rear of the building. The boys meanwhile, traversed the broad front terrace, to enter the main school gates at the far end, (sixth-formers had privileged access via the central arched gateway). Apart from a gleaming, new brown, leather satchel, containing note book, 12-inch ruler, geometry set and pencil case, younger pupils carried an extra canvas bag which accommodated a pair of smooth, flat-heeled gym shoes. These, by a compulsory all-pupil school regulation, were to protect the highly polished upstairs hall floor.

The comfortable environment of the junior school seemed a million miles away, especially during that first mid-morning break when rather innocent initiation ceremonies were carried out. One consisted of groups of new boys being imprisoned by older boys, inside a ruined castle tower, for what must have been about five minutes, but which seemed to many of us an eternity, while a few less fortunate newcomers received an involuntary introduction to the Park's prickly holly bushes!

Mansell Richards

I started in Cyfarthfa Castle Grammar School on 8 September 1952. It was raining heavily and I waited nervously for two older boys, Howard Brougham and John Pritchard, to take me to the school bus which went from Dowlais to the top gates of Cyfarthfa Park. The long walk down to the school was enough to soak us to the skin.

I was led through the quadrangle and was met by an unsmiling J. R. Williams – the Boss. 'In the Hall,' he said, and I was deposited there, amongst other soaking new boys, to start what was, in retrospect, five years of a priceless education.

Fast forward 50 years to 9 September 2002. My grand-daughter, Gabrielle Grant, started in Cyfarthfa High School. It was raining heavily. She was obviously very nervous and I had the great pleasure of driving her up to the same quadrangle. We were met by two senior pupils who directed her into the Hall. I told her, 'Don't look back,' as she might cry. She didn't look back and she didn't cry – but I did all the way back to the car.

Mervyn Saunders

The red double-decker bus meandered down Twyn Hill, up the High Street to Pontmorlais, then turned left at Merthyr General Hospital to finally reach its destination at the Gwaelodygarth top gates of the Park. A mass of buses disgorged hundreds of boys and girls, 120 of whom were about to begin the first day of a new adventure.

The prefects looked like giants to a very small 11-year-old boy in 1957. They dished out lines for the slightest perceived misdemeanours, saying '100 lines by tomorrow, boy' and then rattled off at breakneck speed, 'Deep harm to disobey seeing as obedience is a bond of rule'.

The journey home on the bus was light-hearted although the prefects remained in control. The new boy alighted at Penuel Chapel on Twyn Hill with his school satchel seeming to 'weigh a ton'; but as each year passed it lost its shine and became 'as light as a feather'.

Brian Jones

A classroom in the Castle 1914

It was September 1985 and I remember being absolutely terrified, especially when the bus (number 2 from Twynyrodyn) was running late. We sprinted up the drive and arrived to a deserted and silent school – everyone was in the main hall in Lower School for a welcome assembly. We trooped down the corridor by the Art room, chattering nervously, to be met by Allison Lewis wearing a cross look and shushing us loudly. That was bad enough; but as soon as we arrived in the hall, all eyes were upon us and we got a severe dressing down from Mr Gethin – a totally unforgettable start!

Helen Saunders

The First Girls to become Medical Doctors

I was at the Girls' School in the days of Miss Newton and Miss Davenport, both dignified and dedicated, and both strict disciplinarians. One felt shy donning for the first time the Girls' school uniform, blouse and blue gymslip, black shoes and long stockings and a straw-boater (called a 'straw-bengie') with a hatband of blue and gold with a shield depicting St Tydfil and the letters MSS – Merthyr Secondary School. A dark hat was worn in winter. Outdoor shoes were changed for black gym-shoes so that the beautifully polished floors would not be scratched.

The barrier between the boys' and girls' schools was attacked when my sister Rosentyl was permitted to attend classes downstairs that were not available in the Girls' School. We were the first girls to qualify as doctors from the school.

Bryneilon Griffiths

I have very warm feelings for the Girls' School, and the Boys' School, for I commenced in the former, and ended in the latter!

In the Girls' School only two courses were open to the pupils – either to take up commercial work, or to go to a Teachers' Training College – the majority taking the latter course. I had always thought of medicine as a career and, having passed the Senior Oxford examination with Matriculation exemption, found myself ill-equipped to start a medical career, as I had no training in physics and pure chemistry, the essential basic subjects for the first year Medical Course. These were considered boys' subjects and were not taught in the Girls' School.

The one route open to me was to enter the Boys' School, and this was made possible by the efforts of Miss Davenport, the headmistress, and the kindly co-operation of Mr Fleming, the headmaster. I had to learn chemistry and physics from the very beginning and therefore had to be a member of all the classes from the first form up to the sixth, and also had to work in the laboratory, independently, under the instruction of Mr Evan Lewis Davies in Physics, and 'Sarnicol' in Chemistry.

Chemistry laboratory 1914

I was given a small room, situated between the chemistry and physics laboratories. Here I was able to experiment to my heart's delight. The oxidation experiment such as mixing red lead and magnesium powder, producing a small incendiary bomb, particularly fascinated me. On one occasion, the caretaker, whose house overlooked my little room, came scurrying over to see what happened. He had seen the flames fly up and his daughter had taken shelter under their kitchen table. My room was often filled with smoke fumes. Sarnicol's remark rings in my ears, 'I'll be scraping you from the ceiling one day'.

In my little private room (as I called it), I was provided with a personal drawer, and this, when I returned from lunch, I very often found full of oranges and chocolate bars supplied by the boys. Today, girls and boys are taught together, and I am glad I made the start successfully!

Rosentyl Griffiths

Between The Wars

Cyfarthfa Castle Grammar School set in Cyfarthfa Park was something – a target for boys and girls after passing the 'Scholarship'. I was so proud when I was told that I was top of the Borough of Merthyr Tydfil, which was shared with Lona Davies, who was the daughter of Mr Davies the Head Master of Cyfarthfa Boys School. This was the start of my secondary education in 1925.

The teachers were all unmarried, as in those days married women were not employed as teachers. When I was in the third form we were told that we could study commercial subjects, bookkeeping, shorthand (Pitman) and typing so I was pleased to learn these new subjects as they helped me when I left school to take an office job doing invoice typing. Later in life this enabled me to become secretary to the managing director of a firm in London.

Lunches were provided for the pupils at school for half a crown per week (12.5p). Transport to the school was by 'shanks pony'- no buses or cars then to convey us to and from school.

My last day at school when I was seventeen ended with my friend Ailsa Hawkins and myself going down to the lake and throwing in our school hats and report books to the waters below. My father never forgave me for this daring action.

A few years after leaving school I met my future husband, Brynmor Jones, who had also been a pupil at Cyfarthfa at the same time I was there. We had so many memories to share of our antics at school. It is great to know that my daughter Marilyn, grandson Andrew and grand-daughter Adele all attended Cyfarthfa Castle Grammar school and have all done well in their respective careers.

Elsie Jones

Merthyr was a grim place in the 20s. The queue of men at Pontmorlais going to the Labour Exchange and the numbers standing about in the

High Street, were a depressing sight even for school children, but the Castle and the Park were a joy, and to me, uplifting. I shall always remember the spring show of flowers in the gardens on the south-east side of the castle and the bank of rhododendrons in bloom.

Margaret Williams

I passed the scholarship examination from Abermorlais Junior and entered in September 1932. I walked to the School each day from where I lived in Tudor Terrace through the Quar entrance with my friends: Marion John, who lived next door to me and Kathleen Fry from Cromwell Street. We walked home for lunch each day.

Miss Davenport, the Headmistress, taught us to walk properly, to speak properly, clearly and grammatically; the best pupils in this training were awarded yellow girdles to wear as part of their uniform. She produced a Shakespearean play each year and it was always excellent. All the costumes were made in the School's sewing classes. A Christmas Party was always a highlight of the year; they were wonderful and all the food was made in the School's cookery classes. There was never much to be had in the way of fine food at home in the 1930s so jellies and blancmanges and cakes of all sorts were doubly tasteful.

I sat the Central Welsh Board (CWB) examinations in my Fifth Form and gained distinctions in Latin and Greek. I entered the sixth form but left for a part-time telephonist job in the local Post Office. Then I went full-time as a telephonist at the Merthyr Tydfil Exchange.

My husband-to-be went to Cyfarthfa in the 1930s, my older sister Winnie also, and my two eldest sons attended in the 1960s.

Jean Williams, née Morris

I became a pupil in 1937. It was like a parachute jump into another world of spacious class rooms with high ceilings, polished floors and surrounded by picturesque gardens. In one of the towers was a well-equipped library which was always referred to as 'the round room'. Many of the Art lessons

Girls were taught ballet and gave an annual concert

were taught in the Museum. My favourite subjects were Latin, for which I won a 'Dictionary' prize, and Mathematics.

I can recall the distress I felt when I had to leave at the age of fourteen. I had progressed very well but the cost of education beyond school leaving age was high. My father was an unskilled council worker and poorly paid. Times were hard and I was one of four children so I, very reluctantly, had to leave school where I was happy.

I eventually started work in a grocery shop. The job description was 'Accounts Clerk'. However, it included keeping counters and floors clean. My hours of work were 8.30am to 6.00pm but we were lucky to finish on time. At Christmas time we finished late, sometimes 10pm. No overtime was paid. I finished at 2pm on Thursdays and had one week's holiday per year. Wages were six shillings (30p) per week which helped support the family income. This gave me much pleasure.

I always regretted not being able to realise my potential. In later life, through evening classes, I gained six O levels (now called GCSEs), a BTEC in Pharmaceutical Sciences, and A levels in Law and Psychology.

Winifred May Arthur, née Holland

Wartime Evacuees

I wonder if it is appreciated just how much work went into arranging the evacuation. It was a major operation to arrange a special train from Folkestone to Merthyr, but at the same time the evacuation of Dunkirk was still taking place – for this the Southern Railway alone put on 586 extra trains. At the same time a small group of people in Merthyr had to plan for the schooling and housing of about 2000 children. And all this had to be done in a matter of a few days. There was the Dunkirk spirit, in East Kent people were prepared to fight on the beaches and in Merthyr other people were doing their bit by offering homes to a large number of children, essentially refugees. I don't know if anyone in Merthyr was honoured or received an award for this work, they certainly deserved it.

Leonard W. Bean, evacuee

Soon after ten o'clock that summer evening, we had all been placed in billets. We woke the following morning to look upon a town of distressing streets, but lying in a broad valley banked by high rolling mountains, bright in the morning sun, and filled with people we came to know as friends with an understanding sympathy as native to them as their hills and their singing. When we remember that Merthyr was one of the most depressed areas during the last 15 years and that to be workless for years has been a common experience of many of the men, we salute these people for their courage and their faith.

A. P. evacuee

When the initial reticent politeness had worn off, there was a resentment against the whole affair; against the town being so industrial, against the slag-heaped countryside for being so different from our Kentish greenery, against our being so far from our families and the danger they were in, against the strangeness of the accent; in short, the futile resentment that Merthyr was not Folkestone. This hostility soon evaporated. Who on earth can be proof against warm, voluble friendliness?

The grandeur of the scenery taught me that my beautiful, fertile Kent could be considered cluttered and sickly-green. Quite early on the slag-heaps had a beauty for me, as did the morning wetness gleaming on identical rows of slate roofs, showing one behind the other in shades of grey, lightening in intensity towards the horizon.

The years between 14 and 18 are very impressionable, and the impression is one of generous, open-hearted people. There were some of us, who, after settling down, sprinkled their speech with 'there's lovely' and used 'see' after every phrase. There were others who so adopted the country that they married local people. I did neither, but I shall always be grateful that my years of evacuation were spent among people who taught me so much and took us so completely to their hearts.

Jill Kemp, evacuee

Many who were in Cyfarthfa School between 1941 and 1945 will remember Manfred Linder because he stood out as the cleverest boy in the school. Manfred was born at Chemnitz near the Czech-German border, the son of well-off parents who were able to pay the German government to allow him and his sister Bella to leave the country in 1939, just months before the start of the war.

The British government would not allow such children into the country unless British Jews took responsibility for them. Adverts were put in the Jewish press asking for sponsors and as a result the two children arrived in Merthyr in April 1939, Manfred to live with the Moscovitchs and Bella with the Bernsteins. Manfred's mother and father also managed to escape and found sanctuary in Santiago in Chile.

Manfred spoke no English when he arrived. Yet he attended Abermorlais school and passed 'the scholarship' with flying colours. It was therefore no surprise to anyone when in 1945 he gained the Central Welsh Board Certificate with eight distinctions and a credit. It was the second best result in the whole of Wales.

After the war Manfred and Bella sailed to Chile and he entered the University of Santiago despite knowing no Spanish! He became Manager of Electrical Operations for the whole of Chile and later worked for the World Bank.

Alan N. Owen

In the summer of 1944, John Davies, a young London evacuee and first-year pupil at Cyfarthfa Boys' School, lost his life while playing with friends on the high moorland above Pant. He unknowingly picked up a live bomb. After throwing it against a stone, a large blast left him with serious head and leg injuries from which he died the following day. The community of Pant was distraught that a young boy sent to the relative safety of the valleys, had nonetheless been killed by a German bomb. In the year 2000 a headstone-memorial was placed on his grave in Pant Cemetery.

Mansell Richards

From the 40s into the 50s

What I remember most about my years at the Castle School is the music. The choir led by Lewi Geoger became the joy of my life. As soon as I joined she had me singing duets with Eirfron Morgan in school concerts. We used to practice on Saturday mornings and I would meet Eirfron at the Quar gate to the Park and we would sing at the top of our voices all the way to school.

The orchestra, conducted by Claudia James, was incredible. Looking back at the range of pieces they played I am amazed. My love of classical music was nurtured at Cyfarthfa and has never dimmed. When my husband Brian and I emigrated to Canada I joined a professional opera company and sang in the chorus. Happy days!

Dorothy O'Halloran, née Small

Keir Hardie Shield Winners 1948-49. Back row (l-r): Gilbert Crook, Billy Ansel, Bernard Jones, Eddie Connors, John Felton, Robert Parry, Leslie Treen. Middle row: Jackie Cowhig. Seated: Roy Richards, Elwyn Davies, J.R. Williams (Head), Mansil Morgan (Capt.), Dan Jones, Peter Ward, John Aris.

Through the archways scurrying, memories crowding fast,
Back the years are scattering, borrowing the past.
Children's laughter echoes through hollow, empty halls.
Children's secrets burrow in thickly-fashioned walls.
Voices in the Library, voices on the stairs,
Voices moved in single file, or whispering in pairs.
Walking endless corridors, pictures on the walls
Painted by Old Masters, but newer masters call.
Scenes of Christmas Parties; classes in the park;
Museum for the art class. Park gates closed after dark,
Prefects with their coloured shields displayed upon their chests.
Mistresses determined to make us do our best.
Junior Druids posing in mini-bardic robes;
Urdd Eisteddfod looming: 'A oes heddwch?' called.
Girdles for deportment; gym shoes when indoors
Not to leave a single mark on brightly polished floors.
Crisp, white blouses for the girls, gymslips neat and flared,
Blazers with the Martyr's badge tenderly conferred.
Ginghams, for the girls again, for summers in the sun,
Panamas, with navy bands, the Martyr on each one.
Prayers began the day for all, rousing hymns were sung,
In Welsh on Wednesday mornings; taste of native tongue.
Order marks for small misdeeds, conduct marks for graver.
 Always there are eyes alert for infantile behaviour!
Hockey sticks are brandished, with gusto and with glee,
Rugby boots are meeting some unsuspecting knee.
Tennis courts in summer. Cricket for the boys
In gentlemanly flannels – none of rugby's noise.
Swimming, double period, on Friday afternoon.
French exam tomorrow – oral first of June.
Offerings in Cookery, burnt beyond recall,
Explosions in the Chem Lab, eurythmics in the Hall.
Dogfish for dissection, frogs to probe with flair,
Formalin, not perfume, floating on the air.
Pythagorean triangles, equations algebraic,
Verbs declined in various tongues, suitably exotic.

Stitching seams in Needlework, for garments still unworn,
Learning facts and reading maps, stifling a yawn.
Kings and Queens and Wars galore, dates to memorise.
Heat and light and magnetism. Milton to revise.
Shakespeare's plays to learn and watch; Stratford trips as treats.
Virgil, Wordsworth, Cicero, Dickens, Swift and Keats.
Satchels crammed with books to read, homework to prepare,
Tests for Latin, French and Greek must be done with care.
Choir practice after school, or in the luncheon break,
Orchestra for others – lovely noise they make!
Rushing, late as usual, through rhododendron lanes,
To Top Field or Pandy, for long-forgotten games.
Past the 'vanished' summer house, nestled in the wood,
Countless scores of children, trying to be good.
Pupils sent from Dowlais, Pant or Penywern,
Merthyr, Penydarren, hoping they would learn.
Trusting in their teachers, to show them all they knew,
Hoping they would grasp enough to simply see them through.
Green hills call across the lake, swans glide slowly past.
Ducklings on the top ponds, haunt of nature class.
Sitting on the terrace, on summer afternoons,
Fountain softly playing its simple, peaceful tunes.
By Museum archway, cannons on each side
Made in Crawshay's foundry stiffly stand, with pride.
Through Museum's entrance, Merthyr's past is laid:
Out of bounds antiquities, carefully displayed.
See the small Welsh kitchen: nature under glass;
Strange Egyptian relics; anything which lasts.
Watched by Crawshay's family; ghosts within its walls,
Tenants of a later age permeate its halls.
Madrigals and music class, horse-play in the gym,
Wallbars and the ropes to climb, stiff in every limb.
School plays in the hall: Madoc's first *Macbeth*.
Scenes of first romances, faithful 'unto death'.
Hearts engraved on benches, initials carved in time,
Memories of yesterday, recorded line by line.

Proud hearts beating strongly, in navy, piped with gold,
Where history was written, while history was told.
Nurtured by the motto: 'Rhinwedd o flaen clod' –
(Virtue Before Fame) was the youthful code.
The world of books lay open, learning shaped the key.
The effort called for – costly; the knowledge given – free.
Shades of Castle Grammar, scurrying along,
Pass before my eyes again and, swiftly, they are gone.
Studious and mischievous, faces from the past;
Faces that will linger, as long as memory lasts.
Cyfarthfa holds their secrets; their lives enshrined in stone.
Shapes belonging to the past, whispering alone.

Mary Atkins

Cast of The Tempest 1952: Michael Allen (centre) as Prospero

I proudly entered Cyfarthfa in 1953 having run only in the Pontsticill village sports day and swum very badly in Pant baths. The PE teacher in Cyfarthfa at the time was the glamorous Sylvia Robson. When she left to get married in 1955 she was succeeded by Clare Crowley.

Clare Crowley had lunchtime hockey practices and I progressed to the first team quite quickly. We played our home matches on the 'top pitch' which was full of potholes and narrowed towards the top pond end. The side line was also the try line for the boys' rugby pitch which never seemed to bother us. Visiting schools were not impressed but we loved the field and were very successful.

The boys usually had a rugby match against the same school in what we called a 'double fixture' and, since we were still segregated from the opposite sex in all but lessons, it gave us an extra interest on Saturday mornings. Away matches were great as we all went on a Morlais Services bus, usually to the Rhondda. We flirted with the boys and sang the popular songs of the day all the way there and back. We were dropped off in town and went to the Central Cafe proudly carrying our hockey sticks with our boots tied on the end – we hadn't heard of hockey bags!

In the summer we enjoyed athletics and, although we had no facilities, managed to do well. The girls at that time were not outstanding but we always qualified for the Glamorgan County finals at Maindy Stadium in Cardiff. The boys' team was excellent. The outstanding memory for me is of Elliot Fine, a superb sprinter, who went to Cardiff on the Friday to stay with family because he could not travel on a Saturday, the Jewish Sabbath. He walked to Maindy to take part.

Jane Type, née Wilding

In the 1960s

Form 4A of Dowlais Junior School, in 1962 passed the 11+ examination and proceeded, as we were destined to Cyfarthfa Castle Grammar School. My mum and dad went there, separately but within a year or two of each other, in the 1930s. A class of my contemporaries at Dowlais, whom I had befriended through eight years of infant and junior schools, failed the 11+ and progressed to the local secondary modern school at Gellifaelog. I barely saw any of them ever again! Within a decade we Dowlais boys would not have qualified to attend the Castle, living as we were outside what became the Cyfarthfa School catchment area.

We, the A class at Dowlais, had been groomed the entire final year with homework to pass the 11+. One of the twins in the class was somehow allocated a place at the 'County'; her mum intervened as soon as the results were declared and the twin was transferred to join her sister going to Castle. What struck me the most in those first unsettling weeks at Castle was seeing someone write left-handed. I had never seen that before.

There were four forms in the first year, A to D, bizarrely numbered from the outset as Form 2; there was no Form 1. Gerald Protheroe, my lifelong friend, and I were enrolled into Form 2D and immediately informed by various teachers that we were an elite stream, to be fast-tracked towards O levels in four years instead of the regulatory five, thus allowing the luxury of three years in the sixth form to attend to university entrance.

I reckon I saw the very best of years in my youth – the 1960s – and some of the best years of Cyfarthfa Castle. The teaching staff was caring, dedicated, professional and decent. Latin was dutifully followed to O level as part of that streaming and I have always felt fortunate to have been in receipt of the academic grounding and discipline of that subject. It was always a pity, on reflection, that Welsh was not part of the syllabus beyond year two, where a choice had to be made between French and Welsh in preparation for O level. Maybe the frantic years of D streaming were worthwhile, but I still query their necessity and ultimate ends. A broader syllabus of arts and sciences would have been preferable in my opinion.

Huw Williams

The girls' choir that sang in 'Night of the Stars' at the Theatre Royal, 22 May 1960

In some ways the Castle wasn't an ideal school for me. I had not one, but TWO sisters-in-law teaching there; I couldn't put a foot wrong without it getting back to Mam, the supreme ruler! I remember my music lessons in particular, in the magical round library, firstly with Gwylim Jones and later Derry Prothero. I also remember very fondly my rather posh English teacher Vince Lee who expertly encouraged my love of words.

I'll never forget the school trip with him to *Macbeth* at the RSC in Stratford, (of course, never dreaming that I would one day perform there myself). Apart from the gorgeous Helen Mirren as Lady M I remember vividly that Nicol Williamson (as Macbeth) kicked over a stool in Act I and there was an inappropriate titter from the audience (of mostly school kids). Well, he stopped the play, came out of character and gave us all a row! Happy days indeed.

Jason Howard

Cyfarthfa chess team 1966-67 with Ian Hopkins and Vince Lee

In the 70s

As one of the first cohort of pupils to go to the new Cyfarthfa Comprehensive School in September 1970, I remember the trepidation with which I walked into the old Secondary Modern School at Georgetown. A vivid memory is of the art classes where a new student teacher, dressed flamboyantly in the style of the day (purple tank top and flares), had our class listen to a new album – Simon and Garfunkel – and then draw one of the songs we heard. These included 'Homeward Bound', 'Sounds of Silence' and 'Somewhere They Can't Find Me'. I still recall the visual interpretation of that music by some of my 11-year-old classmates.

As Third Formers, we transferred up to the 'Big' School. The Castle! We were of course banned from entering the wonderful woods that surrounded the Castle at breaks and lunch time. But, what 13-year-old boys could resist? The huge conker trees, shedding their shiny fruit in autumn, proved a particular attraction.

Memorable teachers include Miss May Treharne (Latin) who also taught my father! I can still chant the Latin grammar which she instilled in to us all those years ago. Mr Gethin (Welsh), who was also Deputy Head, Mr Wiley (Languages), whose voice seemed to carry throughout the castle when he shouted. Mr Lee (English), and Miss Jane Owen (Maths) who also taught my father, epitomised teachers who were part of the fabric of the old Grammar School.

The final lasting memory, apart from playing cards in the Sixth Form Common Room, is of dancing down the long drive of the school, at the front of the Castle, with classmates, the day on which our O levels finished. The sight very nearly caused Miss Owen to drive her elderly car into the deep ditch alongside the drive!

I would never have guessed at that time that I would end up being responsible, amongst many other things, for 140 schools and the education of nearly 30,000 children. I only hope that I can influence their experience and that they too will have fond memories of their time at school.

Mark James
[In 2012 Mark, Chief Executive of Carmarthenshire County Council,
was awarded the CBE for services to local government.]

I entered Georgetown, the lower school, in September 1970. I was put in 2A2, a class of real characters. Also in 2A2 was Ann Foster, who I was later to marry in 1983. She didn't like me much then. Old Georgetown was a great part of Merthyr. My father worked in the bus station and I would pop over there to see him at dinnertime. Georgetown had a chip shop, two or three sweet shops, the RAFA club and what seemed like loads of pubs. There was also no rule stopping you from going into town at dinnertime so we were all introduced to the delights of the cafes – the Model, the Queen's and upstairs in Liptons. The school was a real landmark in the area and it was a very good way to ease the transition from small Caedraw to the much larger Castle school.

I enjoyed every minute of my time in the Castle School. This is not down to anything in particular, more that its setting, its atmosphere, its teachers, its pupils all collectively served to make a lasting impression on me and one for which I will always be grateful. I don't think we realised how great the surroundings were in Cyfarthfa: the lake, the woods, the park. The best was the pitch and putt golf course. How many schools had a pitch and putt on their doorstep? Many a free lesson in the sixth form was spent chipping around the course. I got a ball stuck in a tree once and threw up my club to knock it down. Of course, the club got stuck as well. I lost my deposit.

One of the more negative things about Cyfarthfa, and probably of most schools in the 1970s, was a lack of any careers guidance. I was quite clever, so was my girlfriend Ann, and it was assumed that pupils like us would just go to university. While I never regretted my choice to go to Swansea to study history, a bit more discussion would have been welcomed. Anyway, Swansea it was, and I achieved a first class degree in my chosen subject.

Phil Star

The thing about 2B3 was that it was made up of kids from Swansea Road or other council house children, and to say that we were boisterous was an understatement. We were type cast as troublesome children, and tended to live up to that image. There were a lot of well-off children in the school who were always going on skiing trips and the like, and the teachers seemed to be a lot nicer and more tolerant to those than to us. (This could be because they were a lot better behaved than us!) This caused an even bigger gap between us and them.

It was about this time that there was a lot of bitter rivalry between Pen-y-dre, Afon Taf and Cyfarthfa. Our school was in a poor state of repair; windows were broken and ceilings collapsing. The strange thing was that we all felt great pride in the school. I always remember a gang from Pen-y-dre going on about their new swimming pool and I can't remember who, but it was someone from Swansea Road, who piped up: 'Yeah, you've got a pool, but we've got a lake, four ponds, a park, and we go to school in a castle. So get lost'. The Pen-y-dre kids could not answer this and strode off. This was from a boy who, if asked, would have said that he hated school. But it was our school, and even though you would have had to beat it out of him, he was proud of it.

Colin Rees

Netball team 1970-71. Back row (l-r): Lynne Davies, Angela Hudson, Janice Flye, Yvonne Williamson, Christine Morgan, Vivienne Head. Seated: Lyn Williams, jane Type, Susan Hamer, Elaine Mahoney.

My two and a half years in Cyfarthfa High School (September 1970–
December 1972) coincided with the introduction of the comprehensive
system in Merthyr and with the building of Pen-y-dre High School, so I
was part of two sets of sixth-formers moved over from Merthyr County
Grammar School while the move was effected from the County
Grammar School to the new site of Pen-y-dre. During those two years,
the sixth form in Cyfarthfa was double the normal size.

The larger sixth form had many benefits. Under Brian Evans, head of
music, the mixed choir won the National Urdd Eisteddfod School Choir
competition in successive years. One of the singers in that group, Philip
Joll, my cousin, went on to become an international opera star and sang
with Pavarotti in the open air in Cardiff Castle, with peacocks shrieking
in the background!

Opportunities to take leadership responsibilities as Head Boy, captain
of a sports team and leader of the Christian Union also provided
formative leadership experience. I have no doubts that I would not
have studied history in university, or even applied to do so in Oxford,
had it not been for Mansell Richards.-His infectious enthusiasm,
interest in those he taught, and constant encouragement left a lasting
impression. He is, without doubt, the best teacher I have ever had,
including all those who taught me in Oxford! For many years I have
been the international director of The International Fellowship of
Evangelical Students (IFES) which brings together 450,000 evangelical
students in 152 countries around the world.

Lindsay Brown

I was at Cyfarthfa from 1975–1982 so spanning the three school sites –
Georgetown, Cyfarthfa Castle and Cae Mari Dwn. At the Upper School
site we were fortunate to have an excellent history teacher in Philip

Atkinson and another with the name of Elizabeth Tudor (we always felt she was destined to be a history teacher with a name like that). I can still quote my most memorable mention in a school report. It was from Ian Hopkins our long-suffering Maths teacher. 'Andrew's O level result was undoubtedly the zenith of his mathematical career'. In many ways Ian was right, though I do now have under my control a team of around 30 economists and statisticians.

Other teachers who stand out include our A level English teachers Trevor Jones (who drove to school in a van with blacked out windows) and Miss Aldred who made up for her diminutive stature with a fiery temper and zeal for the subject and it was a sadness to many of us that she retired early due to illness.

The school gave me and others like me from very ordinary working class backgrounds a grounding, a work ethic and a determination that has allowed us to succeed in our chosen paths. By the time I was in the Lower Sixth the roof above our English classroom often leaked and I used to engineer it so that the desk of the girl in front of me was always in the firing line for the drips. It took her a while to catch on. In some ways she's not changed a bit. There aren't that many happily married people who can say that they sat next to their wife at school. So if I had to point to the one thing about the school that has had the greatest impact on my life it would probably have to be that leaky roof.

Andrew Haines

I started at Cyfarthfa in 1975 with the first two years at Georgetown and the remainder in the Castle. I recall thinking that Georgetown school was very big with three buildings making up three sides of the playground. The fourth side was a high brick wall topped with barbed wire, beyond which, and at a lower level again, was a factory bottling carbonated drinks. Immediately beyond the school boundary towered a coal tip which had been reduced to half its original size sometime after the Aberfan tip disaster.

Three under-15 soccer Internationals, 1979: Kevin Rogers, Tony Rees, and Jonathan Jones

After Georgetown, I moved to the imposing 'Castle'. Behind the Castle a series of portacabins housing woodwork and metalwork climbed the hillside. I can recall standing in the rain waiting for the rooms to be opened.

I haven't touched on being the Headmaster's son. This was a difficult experience in the early years with the majority of the boys suspicious that I was always going to 'grass them up' and the teachers nervous in case their lessons were criticized. As I progressed through the school my contemporaries accepted me more, and being appointed Deputy Head Boy by a combination of my peers and teachers reflected this. So I am grateful to record that my education at Cyfarthfa High School was intellectually and socially stimulating, preparing me for university life and the workplace beyond.

I applied to Gonville and Caius College, Cambridge, to study medicine but was told that I failed to get a place 'by a whisker' in a year when fewer candidates were accepted than usual. I regret not trying again when my A level results showed that I had gained three A grades and distinctions in both the Special Papers I had taken. Instead, I accepted an offer from King's College, London, where I obtained a first class honours degree in Physiology, and my medical degree, before becoming a Fellow of the Royal College of Surgeons and an Upper Gastro-intestinal Consultant at the Royal Bournemouth Hospital.

David Bennett

In the 80s

Whilst at Cae Mari Dwn, I'd walk to school up the hill, sometimes meeting up with friends on the way and hoping to catch a glimpse of Julien MacDonald as he left his house to see what he was wearing that day! Life changed when I passed my driving test and I got a little red mini which I'd drive to school and park around the side near the kitchens. I remember leaving school one day and not being able to find my car – some of the sixth form boys had hidden it from me by lifting up the back end and wheeling it around the corner like a wheelbarrow!

Helen Saunders

I joined Cyfarthfa High School in 1988 from Heolgerrig Primary School, following in the footsteps of my two older brothers. For the first two years I was based at Cyfarthfa Castle, at the time this didn't seem unusual. Later in life, when I showed people photos, they thought I must have been very privileged to go to a school in a castle.

The school gave me the opportunity to complete work experience at the Simbec research company in Merthyr, something that inspired my interest in the sciences. In my latter years at Cyfarthfa I attended a week long Human Rights course in Harlech, and also a Youth Leadership course based in Cardiff, where Nigel Walker the ex-Wales sprinter and rugby player spoke on leadership, a fascinating insight into some of the skills that would be expected of me in my working life.

I went on to obtain nine A grades at GCSE and chose to study A levels in Biology, Chemistry and Mathematics. I was taught Chemistry by a truly inspirational teacher. Mrs Manning had studied at St Hilda's College, Oxford, and took a small group of us to the college for an open day. Her enthusiasm was infectious and so I rather nervously agreed to apply to Oxford and to take the entrance exam. Mrs Manning helped me with application forms and also coached me in her lunchtimes. I was offered a place at Hertford College reading Biochemistry and to this day I know none of that would have been possible without Mrs Manning's support.

I am married to a man I met in London but whose family are from Merthyr and whose dad and grandmother both went to Cyfarthfa School. We have even brought a piece of Merthyr to Twickenham – as we have named our house Cyfarthfa House to carry on the great memories the place holds!

Joanna Adlam

My family came to Britain with nothing when we escaped from the communist oppression in Vietnam in 1980. After a short stay at a refugee camp in Hampshire, we were housed in Merthyr on a housing association estate. I started my schooling at Cyfarthfa a few days before my 12th birthday. I had only been in the UK for ten months. I could not speak English when I arrived, but I had picked up enough English during the ten months such that I could understand what people were saying and make myself understood.

However, my written English was very basic so it was a very daunting experience for me when I first attended Cyfarthfa. I did not always understand what the teachers were saying or what I was meant to do when I was given homework. The first year at Cyfarthfa was very stressful because of the language barrier. However, by the end of the first year, my English had improved enough to enable me to take in what I was being taught and things just progressed very well from there.

I made some very good friends at school which made school enjoyable. However, I was not at school for enjoyment. I wanted my family to have a better life than living on benefits on a council estate. It was not nice that we did not have much money. Every week when my mother did the weekly shopping, she would worry about the embarrassment of not having enough money to pay when she got to the till and would have to put some food back. We could not afford to buy clothes but had to wear second hand clothes that other people were kind enough to give to us. I hated queuing up for my dinner ticket every morning at school, which was only given out to children of poor families. It made me feel very self-conscious.

For five years at Cyfarthfa, I worked very hard and passed ten O levels, nine 'of which were grade A, including a grade A in English language, which, to me, was the most challenging as English was my second language at the time. After Cyfarthfa, my family moved to London, so I studied for my A levels in London. I then went on to university and got a First Class Honours Maths degree. My qualifications enabled me to get a very good job in Actuarial Consultancy.

I remember Cyfarthfa warmly as it made the most impression on me as a child newly-arrived from a foreign land. It provided me with the opportunity to learn and be successful with my exams. It was my first exposure to British culture where I could mingle with other children, learn about how they live, think and behave. This helped me to socially integrate, without which I would not have grown to feel this to be my country and my home.

Tien Dodd Du

That Special Building

Whenever I go up the A470 towards Brecon and I have a friend in the car I point to the castle in the park as we go past and say, 'That's where I went to school.' A school in a castle, with a quadrangle, a round library; a museum full of mummies, and assegais and opium pipes; teachers who wore gowns; and a lot of kids who like me grew up on housing estates. The environment in which students learn is crucially important to developing insight and imagination: It was a cauldron for the imagination with its spiral staircases, its glass panelled reference library, the dusty anarchy of the round library attic, the woods surrounding the school, the museum full of ancient artefacts connecting everyone in the school with the roots of nature and lost civilizations – Egypt, Greece, Rome – whether they were aware of it or not.

Desmond Barry

Half my school life passed away in talk and argument, Religion, Politics, Welsh Rugby, Welsh Nationalism – subject flowed into subject; learning flowed in through talk; wit grew unobserved. Beyond the lake and the river, the crumbling red brick and stained iron of the old works wove its own stark pattern into the carpet of the mind ... Cyfarthfa was a school for the real and the imaginary, for quickening and sobering ... Academic success was only a part of its gift to pupils.

Gareth Griffiths

School tower by Dewi Bowen

I went to a school in an environment that members of the rich upper middle classes eagerly pay out thousands of pounds a year to gain for their children. The school was a mock Gothic castle set in many acres of its own woodlands and had beautifully laid out lawns and flower beds. A huge lawn in front of the castle swept down to a boating lake.

But Cyfarthfa School reflected the town it served. It was a melting pot of people from different races and different economic backgrounds. I mixed with boys and girls from Chinese, Spanish, Italian and Irish backgrounds as well as the more mundane English and Welsh. We mixed easily with those from comfortable affluent family backgrounds and those whose parents were unemployed and who found it a struggle to buy even the basics of the school uniform.

Mario Basini

The mystical school Hogwarts of course doesn't really exist ... does it? Who on earth ever went to a school in such a grand setting as Hogwarts? Well actually I did, along with many others who were fortunate enough to attend Cyfarthfa High School. Rather disappointingly, none of our teachers wore pointed magician's hats or carried a magic wand, unless you count a cane which was largely frowned upon by the time I graced the doors of this spectacular school.

Kevin Davies

Fellow pupils

No doubt there were many decent, steady, undistinguished pupils in Cyfarthfa then, boys like myself lacking the staunchless energy, the cunning, the intellectual toughness, to become dedicated enemies of learning and steady flouters of its rules and conventions. I can only say that I remember very little about them. Most of the boys for whom I felt anything like warm friendship seem to have chosen to spend their school days in a state of merry desperation, as resourceful dodgers of homework, liars of transcendent genius, tormentors of the less ruthless masters ... what has happened to them, all those generous, friendly, idiotic and fearless creatures?

Glyn Jones

My ignorance of science I blame upon a lively character I shall call 'Jack'. 'Jack', later to be decorated for bravery as a flier in World War II, was one of my form mates in the Physics class (1937–38). I might have learned something of the mysteries of what we laughingly described as 'the foundations of science' if 'Jack' had not been around. But what chance had Ohm, the inclined plane, the pulley, or the angle of the refraction of light, when that comedian was performing. He moved restlessly round the lab like some hungry beast of prey; he surreptitiously fiddled with the apparatus so that we were denied the results so confidently predicted; he tried to apply pads soaked in ether to our noses as we stood in the dark room, allegedly watching some experiment. He convulsed us with laughter as he stood like a robot in front of the class, obligingly offering his large tough hands for further punishment after he had already taken the prescribed dose.

Beynon John

It was during the 1939–45 war and Rees was his surname. I do not recall, or maybe never knew, his Christian name. He was a Prefect, a demi-god. I was insignificant, a second former. He was always 'Rees' to me. He was slight, dark haired with an easy manner and ready smile and at lunch in the Dining Hall he sat at the head of our Form Table. His duties included dishing out the puddings. When it was rice, once a week, it was delivered in a huge enamel tureen, and I prayed for 'skin', but with so many hungry competing mouths I rarely got any.

Until one day, as he was stirring the newly arrived tureen, I began bouncing up and down like a yoyo on the hard wooden bench and blurted out: 'Please Rees, please can I have some skin.' The effect was magical. 'Skin!', said he, and burst out laughing and when my turn came with a swirl of the ladle he deposited the finest piece of skin imaginable on to my plate, chuckling the while and murmuring, 'Skin!'.

That ritual was repeated for the rest of the school year. He would always catch my eye, whisper 'skin', grin and give me a big bit. When the year ended he left and I next saw him smiling and chatting near the Staff Room in his RAF pilot's uniform, with wings. He was killed six months later when his Blenheim was lost over Brest. I will not forget him.

J. C. Price

The Teachers

My father insisted that a good time to practise was first thing in the morning before school. Unfortunately the school was over two miles away, which resulted in me constantly being in trouble for being late. On one occasion, just as the headmaster, J. R. Williams, was about to cane me, he said, 'So why are you always late for school, Nash?' I explained about the trombone and my early morning regime, to which he declared, 'Well, do you think you'll make a living doing that?' Anyway, one thing he did was to write to the Royal Academy of Music applying for a scholarship, which I gained. I was fifteen at the time.

Harold Nash

Mr Havard Walters who taught Welsh had been at the school since the 30s and one of his tasks was to teach us the Welsh National Anthem and also the school song, the first two lines of which were:

Ienctyd y Castell, Caer I Ddysg a Hedd
Gloewn Ein Harfau I'r Gad Ddi-gledd

Many a time he would despair at the 'Wenglish' of most of us, moaning that we were 'a lot of Dowlais Cockneys'.

Brian Jones

Miss Treharne, known secretly as 'May Fag' due to the continual cough she had, was our form mistress in 1957. She taught Latin and the answers to the day's lesson would be on the blackboard, as she often forgot to clean them off after the last lesson of the previous day. We would hurriedly write down the answers. She cottoned on to that after a while, much to our dismay.

I vividly remember my first Latin text book, the inside cover of which had been scribbled on by previous pupils. I did, however, manage to salvage a little verse from it. It went: 'Latin is a subject dead as dead can be; once it killed the Romans, now it's killing me'. The class laughed at that. There is probably someone out there who can take credit for writing it.

During my time we were well aware of the discipline. If the boys had detention on three occasions it would lead to the cane. I well remember one master coming into our class, cane in hand, and calling out the offending boys. He then added, 'Come with me, you've qualified'.

Dawn Davies

I particularly remember Dan Jones, the sports master, with whom I got on well. My time at Cyfarthfa was thoroughly enjoyable. I swam and played rugby for the school and in 1956 I became the flyweight schoolboy boxing champion of Wales, following in the footsteps of my father 23 years earlier. But I also enjoyed Music and Maths and when I left school to join my father's business, Maths was particularly useful and without question helped me to become a successful businessman. My thanks go to all those teachers who encouraged me.

Stan Thomas

I entered the castle in 1960. My first form master, Vincent Lee, must undoubtedly take pride of place. He taught English and History and the first topic he taught me: '*What History owes to the Jews*', made a deep impression on me. Mr Lee had that rare talent of being able to make history stimulating, and the interest that he fostered has remained. By contrast, my attempts to learn Latin were not a great success. Miss May Treharne laboured mightily to make Latin grammar interesting, an uphill task, and tried to ease the way by teaching our class to sing 'London's Burning' and 'Ba Ba Black Sheep' in Latin.

Were teachers aware of the nicknames we applied to them? Most were innocuous enough, affectionate even, like 'Willie Welsh' or 'Tommie Art', but there were also 'Nero', 'Fizz' and 'Twiddles'. The headmaster was known simply as 'The Boss' and we were in awe of him. When he walked into a classroom, we jumped to attention, as soldiers in an army. One of his first decrees was that we learn the school song, *Ienctyd y Castell*, and although I wasn't Welsh-speaking, I did learn it. I also learned the first few lines of the 'alternative' version – '*Boys of Cyfarthfa, Smoking in the bogs, Going down to Parkers, Betting on the dogs ...*' How did it continue, I wonder?

As one of the few Jewish kids, I didn't attend the morning assembly, but never really understood why. I could clearly hear the hymns floating out of the hall, and can still tolerably sing *Calon Lan* and *Cwm Rhondda* in Welsh.

Family rumour had it that my great-grandfather had been a pharmacist and these genes asserted themselves in Mr Fisher's chemistry laboratory. Just hearing the hiss of a Bunsen burner transports me back still to that magical place, with its mysterious Kipp's apparatus, Erlenmeyer flasks and the peculiar Woulff Bottle. Not to mention the 'vigorous chemical reaction' that reared its head a little too often when over-enthusiastically adding hydrochloric acid to metal filings. But I wanted nothing more than to work in a laboratory, and did later become a chemist with the National Coal Board. Thank you Mr Fisher!

Robert Fraser

Derry Prothero: a really good teacher who encouraged us all to do well. There was only a Music class of seven, one of whom was Jason Jones, now transformed into Jason Howard, the opera singer. Derry would let us go up into the tower room above the Round Library on wet dinner times. It was worth taking music for that really. History with Cliff O'Shea – another entertaining and comfortable teacher; Geography with Ron Roberts – he was completely mad (or so it seemed), but also a very good teacher. Scripture Knowledge (not RE) with Steve Barnes: probably my favourite teacher in the school; a real gentleman.

When I started teaching myself I like to think that I modelled my style on Messrs O'Shea, Roberts and Barnes. They were all laid-back, humorous and calm. I was probably none of these, but they were really influential.

Phil Star

Mansell Richards was an enthusiastic, newly-appointed History master with a love and concern for that subject. The Tudors and Stuarts, the European Renaissance and Reformation movements seemed matters of utmost concern to my class of over twenty bright, intelligent students.

Economics A level was in the hands of David Mills, an adult graduate from Cambridge University who had a worldly, informed view of current affairs, constitutional matters, of economics and of politics. Geography, offered in parallel with Geology, attracted a group under the benign control of John Alfred Evans who went on to become head teacher of Pen-y-dre Comprehensive School, the successor to the County Grammar. Field trips around South Wales informed us of the earliest making and shaping of the Rhondda Valleys and of river capture in Breconshire.

The other popular subject at A level was English. I often regretted not choosing English for I regard Vince Lee one of the finest of English masters. He brought poetry to life as part of the O level syllabus covering Keats, Tennyson and Browning. Shakespeare took on new and fuller meanings. His interpretation and masterful critique of *Henry V* I have never seen bettered or equalled anywhere, on stage or in print. Here was, I am convinced, a truly exceptional teacher who died tragically young within a few years of my leaving Cyfarthfa in 1969.

Huw Williams

My first ever exam was supervised by a teacher called Jones. I'd finished the exam quickly and turned around to see if my best mate had finished too. My mate smiled and lifted up a cartoon he'd drawn of a character based on our teachers in a Goon Show world. Jones called us out to the front. 'You were talking during exams,' he said. 'What happened?' He asked me first. I was terribly confused and afraid. How could I tell him the story of the Telly Goons, the cartoons we were making, the funny stories?

'I turned round and he called me, Sir,' I said. It wasn't true. All my friend had done was to show me a picture. I was mortified at my betrayal. Jones slapped both of us hard across the face with the flat of his hand and told us we'd get zero for the exam. My left ear rang for days. Later our real Maths teacher, the wonderfully good-natured Ian Hopkins, asked us what had happened. We told him and he reinstated our marks.

I remember a school cruise to Gibraltar, Alicante and Lisbon on the SS Devonia. I read Moby Dick, saw people and places that were fascinating because their languages and cultures were so different to mine. I became conscious that there was a huge world to explore, full of colour and sound and image. I also fell in love with my first girlfriend and we kissed on the foredeck among all the other first time lovers away from their parents for two weeks. Ian Hopkins was the great facilitator of that trip, even if he had a rough time as the Devonia rolled and dipped through the Bay of Biscay, Ian's face so wan and green.

It was Trevor Jones who was responsible for seeding my love of great writing. Trevor was a short man, with dark curly hair and always wore a gown. His enthusiasm for Shakespeare guided us through *Macbeth* and *The Merchant of Venice*, in our first and second years. What amazing stories.

Particularly when Trevor Jones, in his understated way, having us act out the plays in class, with a knack for casting that made us aware of all the tensions and prejudices exposed in the writing. He also introduced us to great poetry: especially Blake, Yeats and Auden. Poetry was cool for a small group of us: French poetry by Baudelaire, Verlaine, Mallarmé, and Rimbaud. I studied these with a Mrs McPhail, who was young, good-looking, with long dark hair but who always seemed a little depressed. I hope she wasn't.

Desmond Barry

Dewi Bowen would always emphasise that we should walk tall, head up, shoulders back, not slouch, and hands out of our pockets. Our art classes were always very good.

Now we come to Mr Gethin or called, but only in whispers by us boys: 'Gethin'. I was never taught by Mr Gethin, but he was a legend in Cyfarthfa. The corridors were an ideal place to lark about and try to impress girls. Mr Gethin would stride out of his room into the corridor and bellow *dawel* just once and the corridor would be completely silent and we would shuffle past trying to look innocent. Nobody ever answered him back or gave him any lip. He would stand like a grey-haired sergeant major in the middle of the corridor with his cane up the sleeve of his tweed coat with elbow patches. He could have been on a parade ground in Aldershot.

Mr Bennett was truly the academic headmaster – walking the corridors in his black gown. He was the only teacher to do that, in our minds he was on a par with a professor. Mr Bennett took no prisoners, but you would always get a fair crack of the whip and a second chance with him. You never heard him raise his voice or lose his temper, a thing unknown to us, but he commanded your respect. Because of this image of a very learned man who knew things we from Gellideg Estate could never know or be able to understand, it was a powerful image and one you could not forget.

Colin Rees

After being browbeaten by my parents, I reluctantly signed up to do Latin: it was one of the better decisions I was to make during my school days. I loved it. There were just a handful of students and our classroom was sited at the back of the main school building in a sort of Portacabin. It felt cosy and comfortable. There were books and maps and statues in the room and Mr Wiley was an inspirational teacher. We worked our way through Virgil, Catullus and Plato. He told us about Masada and allowed me to borrow a book about it. I felt very privileged to be allowed to take this beautiful book home. I was good at it because it made sense and I liked the logic and beauty of the stories Mr Wiley told us.

I studied geography for both O Level and A Level. The O Level teaching by Mr Bennett was rigorous, interactive and challenging. We went on field trips which involved me getting soaking wet in a river in Ystradfellte. I was the tallest in the group, so when it came to nominating a pupil to enter the water in order to measure depth, width etc. I was an obvious choice. The trip fell on the day of the Cup Final and was not popular with the boys in the group.

We learned some things by rote: 'an arête is a knife edged ridge ...a cirque, cwm or corrie is an armchair-shaped hollow formed where more snow falls in winter than melts in summer', but we all did well in the exam. I can remember the boys in the group being told to stand in front of a row of desks and then move forward: the middle boy was stopped by the desk whilst the others walked into the other desks from each side. It illustrated how waves move forward and erode each side of a headland: this, at a time when teaching was rarely innovative. The usual teaching method in most subjects was copying from the board or death by worksheet. But geography, at least at O level, was different and very memorable. Pupils who were part of that class still share memories of it.

Deborah Prosser

Cyfarthfa was the school I wanted to go to. Although my father taught there (and before her marriage, my mother too), I had never been inside. The school had seen some recent investment, with a new assembly hall/performance area/gym erected in the area formerly occupied by the Castle's stables. So Cyfarthfa in the 1960s was quite a grand place to an 11-year-old!

In those days we all began in form 2, moving through forms 3, lower 4, upper 4, to form 5 where O levels were taken. I never came across any other school which followed this numerical system. (Doubtless at some point it had been logical to someone. I wonder why?) Early on we were told that 2D would miss the lower fourth and if all went well would take O Levels in four rather than the usual five years. The idea was to spend a third year in the sixth form and so be better prepared for university applications. So we were pushed, most of us survived pretty well.

Some of the older staff had been at the school since well before World War II and were a pretty awesome lot, and as they retired, there were few duds amongst those who came to replace them. I chose History, English, Economics and Welsh for A Level. The third year sixth was very useful to those of us who wished to sit the entrance exams for Oxford and Cambridge – which I did, to read History – and to those who needed to take the odd re-sit.

Soon after I had left school I remember being asked by May Treharne for my honest assessment of how I thought my education at Cyfarthfa compared with that received by my contemporaries at Oxford. I had no hesitation in saying that Cyfarthfa compared very well. The quality of teaching both to O and to A level had been high and extra support had been offered in languages for those of us who needed it for college entrance exams. I think we benefitted from being in a co-educational environment (well almost co-ed, some segregation survived) and in a school which was pretty well grounded in society – socially we were a well-mixed lot. And of course, exotically set in a 'Gothick' castle and acres of parkland, the school exuded a strong ethos; it aimed high and we were proud of it.

Rhodri Walters

As a young violinist at the school, I remember playing the Preludium and Allegro by Fritz Kreisler in the gym at the lower school in Georgetown. An ambitious choice as it was one of my first public concerts anywhere. I was lucky enough to have met Terry Strachan during my earlier school years, who, although not my main teacher, taught me for a while at both lower and upper schools and with whom I was, a few years later, to join in a performance of the Bach double violin concerto in a concert in the upper hall in Cyfarthfa School. Terry was a lovely man, valuable inspiration and, with students' interests at heart. I remember him with fondness.

Derry Prothero was another who provided valuable support. A very good pianist, Derry was also a gifted choir trainer. In *his* round library, my musical appreciation was honed, often accompanied by fellow students, the pianists Ceri and Delyth Williams. I was the third pupil in the school's history to become the leader of the National Youth Orchestra of Wales, following in the footsteps of Anne Hooley and David Chappell.

Pat Hill stands out as an inspirational teacher. Strangely, some of the subjects that made the least impression on me during my school days have been the most useful and absorbing. Technical drawing, coupled with wood and metal work provided me with some background to design and manufacture an adjustable chinrest for violinists. My A level tutor in economics., David Painter, would probably like to know that I managed to sell some of these creations to my colleagues at a sizeable profit perhaps rounding off the use to which my time at Cyfarthfa was put.

Alun R Thomas

I had little natural aptitude in Maths. Mr Rogers was amazingly patient. He would explain something to the class and then ask if everyone understood. I would almost inevitably say that I didn't. He never grew impatient – or, if he did, he never showed it – and would take as long as it needed to sort me out. Thanks only to his teaching, I am living proof that it possible to get a good O Level in Maths without being able to count!

Mr Bowen also had a huge impact. When I was in the sixth form, I used some of my free lessons to take up pottery which I adored. I still only have to smell damp clay and I am mentally transported into that pottery studio next to the downstairs art room. Some smells there were not so pleasantly evocative – I don't think I'll ever be able to forget the stench that there used to be when he was boiling up horrible ingredients to make glue.

My A Level teachers were all outstanding. Miss Aldred had taught me since I was in Form 2. She was a tiny woman with an enormous personality. I don't think any of my other teachers ever frightened me as much as she could when she was annoyed about something. She was also totally inspiring. It was she who really triggered the love of medieval literature that played a big part in my choice of degree.

Mr Barnes was almost universally loved. We were a large and sometimes unorthodox A' Level class but everyone responded to him. He was the sort of person in whom we could confide, knowing he would always give us good advice. He was also never shocked – or perhaps he was just good at hiding it – by any outlandish views that we happened to express. Mr Lee hadn't been one of my teachers before Form Six but I was fortunate to have two such very different and yet very good teachers for English. As part of his work with us, he had the unenviable task of making *King Lear* accessible to 16-year-olds.

Mr Richards encouraged my passion for history. He never minded what historical theories I put forward as long as I could back them up by research and he allowed me to argue with him about interpretations. I ended up, at one time, as Head of History in a comprehensive school – I could have had no better role model.

When I received my A Level results, I was stunned. It has become relatively commonplace in recent years for pupils to leave school with a clutch of A grades but when I got three As, I was the first person to achieve that anywhere in the Borough for, I think, 11 years. When the Head told me the results I actually asked him if he was joking – he told me that he didn't joke about things like that!

Val Williams

Many years later, I set up a life skills centre in the heart of socially deprived parts of the borough. As well as being challenging, it is very rewarding, especially seeing people, many of them teenagers, fresh from failing at school, move into employment and realising that they really can achieve so much if they have support and the motivation to go with it. It always amazes me to think that when I was largely under-achieving in school, I was in fact being prepared for a career, many years ahead in my life, where I would understand many of the issues our trainees are trying to come to terms with.

So if you need to ask just how beneficial school was for me, I would respond in this way. It taught me many things and the lessons learnt were not just simply English, science and history. It taught me that just like the cross-country runners who cheated by taking short cuts through the woods to catch up those of us near the front, life isn't always fair. And when I was gifted with the chance of tapping the football into an open net to win the game, only to see my shot stick in the biggest puddle on the pitch, it has taught me to expect the unexpected. And when I was punished for something I didn't do, it was my best friends I could depend upon to believe me. Finally, as my woodwork teacher taught me, if you keep sanding a piece of wood in the right place it will gradually take the shape you want it to be. My thanks go to the teachers who helped me to 'sand' my life into the shape it is now. Thank you very much.

Kevin Davies

Three Headmasters

I began my teaching career at Cyfarthfa Castle Grammar School on 3 September 1966 and ended it at Cyfarthfa High School on 21 July 2002. I taught Physics with some Chemistry and General Science. The head I knew least well was Mr Lloyd Williams who passed away in 1967. At his funeral service in Brynhyfryd Chapel, Treharris, a speaker referred to him as *brenin urddasol yn ei gastell* (a dignified king in his castle) and this phrase has stayed in my mind ever since.

Gwyn Rees

My first Headmaster was Mr Lloyd Williams. He was very keen to foster an academic atmosphere within the school, particularly at sixth form level. I was impressed that the school library, used for private study by the sixth form, compared very well with the library at university in its silence and seriousness of application of the students.

Mr Williams died in 1967. He was succeeded – after a well-run interregnum, during which Senior Master Mr Havard Walters became Acting Head – by Mr John Davies, who was to lead us through the trauma that was the introduction of comprehensive education. He succeeded to a great extent in transforming the appearance of the student body. The girls had always been smart but now the boys, resplendent in blazers, blue shirts and ties rivalled them.

The boys were not angels. I well remember how the tiny Fiat belonging to a lady who had refused permission for members of the senior rugby team to leave early found her car carefully parked in the lower corridor. The culprits were never found; I suspect that Mr Davies (a one–time hooker for Treorchy rugby team) did not pursue the investigation with his usual thoroughness. He departed to become head of Treorchy Comprehensive School.

He was succeeded by Mr Bennett, a native of Senghenydd, who had been a Deputy Headmaster in the West Midlands. A quieter man than Mr

Davies, Mr Bennett noticed things. He set about quietly improving the state of repair and of the decoration of the school, insisted on the immediate removal of any graffiti, and generally oversaw improvement in the physical state of the school.

He caused consternation by insisting on the amalgamation of the two staffrooms in the Castle; for a short time there was almost as much angst over this as there was over comprehensive education! Mr Bennett felt that a mixed school should have a mixed staffroom. The logic of this was irrefutable and the ladies` staffroom and the classroom next door were knocked into one. A certain amount of sexual apartheid persisted with the men occupying the former classroom while the ladies retained their sanctum sanctorum. Full integration took some years to achieve!

Mr Bennett's approach to discipline was quite different from that of his predecessor. Teachers had to be responsible for their own discipline and should not be able merely to send pupils into the corridor to await punishment by a senior member of staff. This approach, received with a distinct lack of enthusiasm by some, eventually bore fruit, and the school became a quieter and calmer place. Cyfarthfa High School seemed to be in the van of educational and social development while retaining what was best in customs and traditions inherited from its contributory Secondary Modern and Grammar Schools.

Ian Hopkins

Success at the Urdd

I began teaching in Cyfarthfa in 1972. It was the start of an episode in which the *Urdd* Eisteddfods were to play a part for many years. My guitar playing was very basic, but I could put together enough chords to allow me to invent tunes. There was no short supply of pop-singers and guitarists. Later, we even had one or two drummers. Early efforts met with moderate success but determination brought rewards. I can think of at least one year in which we won the *Urdd* National Eisteddfod Pop Group Competition. The names of three contributing pupils come to mind — Nina Cockery, Jayne Edwards and Caroline Owen.

I was the proud owner of a stereo, twin-track tape recorder. Jane Type got to hear of this and asked if I was interested in putting together a ten-minute track for use with the *Urdd* Creative Dance Team. I agreed and signed up for a very creative period in my life.

I learned very quickly through watching our team and others what movements went together with what music and, more importantly, what constituted creative dance. We got on famously and between us all we put together a creative dance presentation to be proud of. Success came early and it was not long before we were Welsh National Champions. We managed to produce a high standard of performance for many years. I will always be grateful for the contributions made by Meryl Star, Andrea Samuel, Zoe Treharne and many other pupils.

Huw Morris

When I think of the *Urdd* at Cyfarthfa two things immediately spring to mind: Eisteddfodau and Llangrannog. We began practising for the annual competitions in recitation, music and dance soon after Christmas. The excitement and tension would reach frenzy level by March, when the local secondary schools would compete against each other to represent the county at the eisteddfod, usually held in Pontypridd. I'm sure parents remember spending hours waiting for their children to perform and not being able to understand much of what was taking place! The standard was extremely high and the rivalry between the different schools even higher.

At county level, when the Merthyr schools competed against the other schools, rivalry changed to support, and whenever a Merthyr school was on stage there would be cheering from all the other Merthyr schools. Only the competitors placed in first place would represent the county in the National *Urdd* Eisteddfod held alternately in North and South Wales.

When in North or West Wales we had the excitement of travelling by coach and minibus. I'm sure that hundreds of former Cyfarthfa pupils

Allison Lewis in charge.

have fond memories of 'stuffing' themselves with pop, crisps and sandwiches while singing heartily for most of the way. One memorable trip was when Cathy Druce, a pupil from year 8, who had very recently come out of hospital, together with her mother, travelled all the way to North Wales and won first prize in the recitation for learners under 15!

At our destination we were farmed out to kind families that would host us and friendships were started in this way. This was reciprocated when the National *Urdd* Eisteddfod was held in Merthyr in 1987 and many families opened their homes to competitors from all over Wales. That was the way of a bygone age as the abuse of children in our society means the implementing of child protection laws which forbid such hosting now.

The possibility of appearing in the big pavilion (and on television!) was exhilarating, if not totally draining emotionally. Sometimes we succeeded and sometimes we did not. I was unable to go to one Eisteddfod in North Wales as I was in hospital. I had been teaching duetists from year 8, Faith Nicholas and Laura H, and they were singing in the big pavilion. I was wheeled from my cubicle to the ward where I saw them not only sing but win first prize! Wonderful!

People who made these experiences possible were Ian Hopkins in Upper School and Gwilym Jones in Lower School whose dedication to teaching the choirs was invaluable; Pam Davies, a parent, who accompanied duetists and choirs in the practices; Huw Morris who trained dance groups over many years, Allison Lewis and Jane Type.who trained the gymnasts. Sadly three people.who were also involved are no longer with us: Frieda Watkins, Marilyn Bassett and dear Ray Gethin, Deputy Head -- our 'father'in all *Urdd* activities .

For three weekends in the year we went to the *Urdd* camp at Llangrannog where pupils would have the opportunity to practise Welsh, enjoy the Welsh discos and the folk dancing, They would hear Welsh being spoken naturally as they took part in the activities – quads, mountain biking, skiing, horse riding and skating to name a few. They would see that Welsh was a living language not just a subject on the curriculum.

It is heartening to see former pupils working in Welsh medium schools or as translators or Welsh tutors while others work through the medium of Welsh in the field of nursing. It is a wonderful experience to meet former pupils and speak Welsh naturally to them as they have become fluent Welsh speakers. Their children are also Welsh speakers! That's the fulfilment of any Welsh teacher's dream. *Diolch Cyfarthfa*.

Bethan Jenkins

CHS Dramatic Society 1976–1984

I had been at Cyfarthfa for two years when Mr Raymond Gethin, 'persuaded' me to put on a play. He assured me that several members of the sixth form were keen to take part. During our early rehearsals I discovered that they, too, had undergone that certain brand of Welsh persuasion!

They say ignorance is bliss and I can confirm that, despite three years studying Drama, I was ill-prepared for the demands of a full-scale production. I went blithely to rehearsals, just assuming that everything would fall into place. Fortunately, with the unstinting efforts of pupils and staff, that is exactly what happened. Our first effort on 7 May 1976 was *The Corn is Green* by Emlyn Williams. All the cast were so enthusiastic that they ensured a polished performance. I remember it with great fondness and pride.

The next production in 1977 was *Witness for the Prosecution* by Agatha Christie; a court-room drama which had been a very successful film starring Charles Laughton and Marlene Dietrich. I remember it best for Delyth Jones''s portrayal of Romaine – she just loved hugging that fur coat in her *femme-fatale* way à la Dietrich! The judge was played by Paul Owen then Head Boy, now my GP!

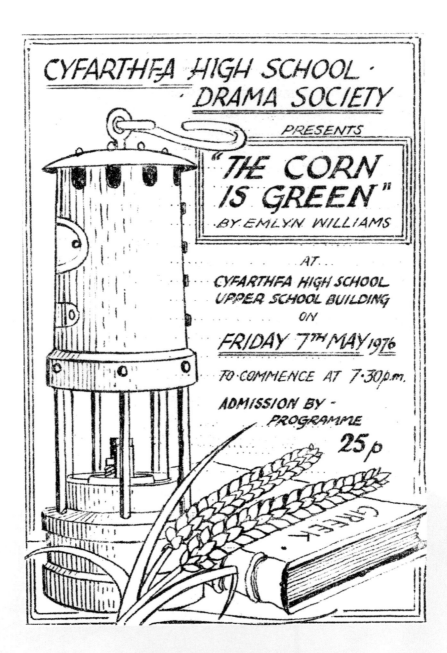

Programme cover: The Corn is Green

By 1978, despite my insistence that I would only do serious drama, Mr Gethin had once again worked his magic and I found myself producing our first musical *The King and I* by Rodgers and Hammerstein. Never mind that it involved several sets – a port in Burma; a royal palace; a royal garden; a horde of young Princes and Princesses and a cast of thousands! If I'd really thought about it we'd never have started. But we did and we did it!

Derry Prothero, Head of Music, had also fallen under Mr Gethin's spell and took charge of all the musical aspects of production. His musical expertise and ability drew technically outstanding performances from our casts. Where music was concerned he was second to none. A young sixth former by the name of Sian Lloyd Davies played Anna. She was so good it's hard to believe she was just 16!

In our first play there were 20 people involved; in this there were 120! (small fry I know in comparison to Mrs Lewis's mammoth events in Lower School). Out of a staff of over 60 at least 20 were involved – a testimony to the dedication of Cyfarthfa staff. After that it seemed natural to go on in 1980 to present *South Pacific*. I'd seen the film, knew the story and songs so why not do it? We only needed a couple of South Pacific islands, some natives and the American World War II fleet! The late Mrs Margaret Jones of the Art Department not only designed the programme but also and more importantly made the shrunken head which Sandra Jones sold on stage every night as Bloody Mary! Our two Deputy Heads were also involved: Ray Gethin, general organizer and David Young on ice-creams and lollies!

An elderly member of the audience was overheard saying how good the make-up was on the young native girl Liat played by Dhilak Dharmasiri. Mr Atkinson as Capt. George Brackett insisted that he couldn't find a native to '... pick a cow or milk a coconut'. Well it almost makes sense!

It was two years before the next production, the seasonal *A Christmas Carol* leading up to Christmas 1982. This was the first production in Cae

Cyfarthfa High School
Dramatic Society

presents

A Christmas Carol

Adapted by Shaun Sutton

from the novel

by

Charles Dickens

Programme 10p.

Programme cover: A Christmas Carol

Mari Dwn. Each production saw new faces appearing, taking the place of those who had left for university or a job. In this play, Robert Purdy took the lead as Scrooge, Robert Evans was Bob Cratchit and a very young looking Arfon Rees was Tiny Tim. Mr Huw Morris, reliable as ever, took the part of Marley.

In 1984 came my last major production, *The Drunkard*. I'd always wanted to do a Victorian melodrama complete with moustachioed villain, fragile heroine and handsome hero. We had sermonizing songs: 'Down With Demon Drink'; a plaintive plea for help in 'Pity a Girl up in London'; AND a chase of the villain around the hall pursued by the kind-hearted yokel George Downton (played by Ian Hughes) and angry villagers; complete with gunfire! This production saw the arrival of two casts with the leads being shared over four nights.

And that was the last. Looking back I wish I hadn't stopped because I had the privilege of working with some remarkable young people whose talent exceeded their years, and with colleagues who gave over and above what was required of them in order that those youngsters could perform. One last recollection: I remember the late Mrs Margot Treharne telling me how worried she was when her son Michael went home after the dress rehearsal for *South Pacific* and when asked what I'd said about it, replied: 'She said it was alright.' Well, they were more than alright; over the years they were all brilliant.

Helen Mobley, née Rees

Special Needs

Not long after the school became comprehensive, a pastoral care system was introduced and I became Fifth Year Tutor. Among the pupils was a group deemed to have 'Special Needs'. These pupils suffered health or social problems of one kind or another and had a very short attention span which made double science lessons challenging, to say the least. However, my memory is how reasonable most of them were on a one-to-one basis, despite their problems, and particularly in the light of some pretty awful home backgrounds. Speaking across the table to one lad, it was obvious that his voice output was not far short of 100 decibels. I said, 'Don't shout at me, I can hear you perfectly well'. He replied 'Oh, Sir, if you don't shout in our house, nobody takes any notice of you'.

One year, with a Special Needs class of 18 boys and at my wit's end as to how to occupy them for a double period each week, I decided to teach them to drive. (Readers will doubt my sanity at this point!). I bought an old Austin A35 car, so decrepit it could barely move, and once a week, at the back of the Castle, attempted to teach these lads starting, changing gear, emergency stops, three-point turns and reversing. The arrangements were – one pupil in the back, one behind the wheel and me in the front passenger seat. Fortunately their attendance was nowhere near 100 per cent but it always amazed me that these lads would wait patiently for their turn in the car, albeit with plenty of comment and banter about their mates' efforts. I like to think that I made a small contribution to road safety (!) but I often wonder what 'Health and Safety' would say about such a thing these days.

Gwyn Rees

Staffroom Memories

Two decades is a fair time to spend at a school, even one as special as CHS: but I could claim three schools for the price of one: Georgetown, the Castle, and then Cae Mari Dwn. My dad Islwyn had taught Welsh and RE at the then Georgetown Secondary School in the early 60s under John Lewis as Head and alongside Owen Caudle, Meriel Thomas, Sandra Jones, Gwladys Owen and Islwyn Rees; characters all.

As a student at Jesus College Oxford I had met Rhodri Walters, son of ex-Deputy Head Havard, Gerry Protheroe, Soccer Blue (well, bench ... !) and Robert Campbell, all CHS Old Boys, and I opted for the school for my teaching practice. 'Gunner' Rees, by then in charge of Lower School, was the first person I met when I arrived in January 1973.

Smiling, confident Cyfarthfa girls

School those days nearly 40 years back was smaller, cosier and perhaps more flexible than today, (the 'long play' bell in Georgetown could be wonderfully elastic!), especially with lower school being the smaller of the sites, but there were genuine challenges for a brand new student teacher. One young lady of Gellideg with white plastic boots and a scarlet asbestos tongue, name well-remembered but omitted here, would be a stark reminder to any who think behaviour is worse now! Bus duty with her and her cronies was a tester, never mind getting her to do some work.

The ladies of my Dad's era, plus Betty Roberts, Allison Lewis and Co were the doyennes of the ladies' staffroom. The male staffroom, far from politically-correct in any sense whatever, was perched alone and un-fire-exited at the top of a narrow, winding, wooden staircase. It was a brave and fearful pupil who climbed to receive punishment at the door of that room, still (just) in the era of the cane and the 'dap'.

Mansell Richards, my mentor when I joined the staff full time from January 1974, and one of my Deputies when I became Head of Afon Taf 20 years later, was an inspiring classroom practitioner, rugby enthusiast and a whizz at the fondly-recalled and dangerously-intoxicatingly-fumed Banda copying machine. He even had multi-coloured copies!

 Staff and pupils adapted well to the inadequate Castle facilities, especially for PE, Drama and so on, while the plumbing and toilet locations were 'different', too! What was achieved in sport and plays and musical productions, alongside academic success, was all the more praiseworthy. 'Up' to the Park's top pitch, 'across' to the Pandy's sometimes stony dust-bowl or boggy mud-patch or 'down' to Rhydycar Sports centre when that opened, PE was a moveable feast for Bernard Evans, Jane Type, Roger, Allison, Bob Coombes and their successors.

However, the likes of Steven Meek, Welsh Soccer Cap Tony Rees, Merthyr AFC's Atlanta hero Kevin Rogers, all-rounder Simon Davies, and Welsh Athletics twins Venissa and Vivienne Head still emerged to their own and the school's great credit, while terrific drama performances graced the cavernous Lower Hall. There was regularly a great noisy atmosphere, too, for Eisteddfodau, with vociferous house backing. The late, truly lamented Cymro Ray Gethin, brother of WRU President Dennis, would call on 'CyfarthFA' for silence or support before orchestrating the Chairing Ceremony. *A Oes Heddwch? Oes, am Ray, rwy'n gobeithio.*

Dewi Bowen (whom God preserve) bossed the Art Department in his own talented, idiosyncratic and inimitable style while the 'Woodwork and Metalwork' Departments under the late Glan Jones and Vic Davies, Owen Caudle and Roger Burgum were nearby. Robert Butcher, friend from our days at Lewis School, Pengam, just preceded me to a full-time CHS post, while the marvellously-humorous Ron Roberts became Head of Geography and brought much mirth to many.

Other arrivals included Rod Walker (Maths) and in English Peter Edwards, son of actor Meredith Edwards. He memorably introduced a pupil-written magazine 'Snobs and Bolts' during a sadly-short stay, before rising to be head of Drama at HTV and the creator of the Merthyr-based TV series *Nuts and Bolts*.

Yet another was Oxford Classicist Len Deas, last Latin master at the school, who once memorably turned up in school wearing the jacket that I had taken to the Oxfam shop the previous week! He became the Reverend Canon LS Deas, Master of the Charterhouse at Hull.

When I started, there was still strict division of staffrooms in the Castle. May Treharne, formidable (on the outside) as Senior Mistress, cigarette in hand, was an imposing presence alongside the coal fire or temperamental geyser in the ladies' quarters upstairs, where the Bettys, Jane Owen and Babs Bowen liked to be nearest the warmth.

Amongst the denizens of the male staffroom alongside the Museum downstairs were Cliff O'Shea, John Hubert Davies of limerick fame, Li Fisher, Tony Whiley (whose sister Pat also taught languages at CHS), the tragically-taken Vince Lee, all-rounder Ian Hopkins, Ray Iverson who would marry the magnificent Meriel, Gwyn Rees, dry and devastating one-liner Mike Wood, smiling Steve Barnes, 'draughtsman' Ron Davies, 'new boys' Gary Brame and Mike Jenkins and meticulous Maths man Dave Young.

Dave was on his way to becoming Monmouthshire Director of Education, but he finished the timetable first! No computers then, just paper, pencil, panic, worry about the wind blowing bits away and remember that you couldn't expect staff to teach one lesson in Castle and the next in Cae Mari Dwn (unless you met the kids at Pontmorlais!). I followed him as timetabling Deputy, and once took it (not quite finished) on summer holiday with me to Bournemouth. Didn't look at it there, mind! The late Trevor Church, who followed DHCB as Head, never quite came to terms with my timetabling timekeeping.

The office staff is of course a vital cog in the school machine. Glynis Williams, Norma Sharp, the unforgettable Eira Smith, Sheila Coombs (Williams) and their colleagues worked wonders (and sorted you out if you needed it!) in the days before computers, and saw the arrivals of another generation of staff in the 80s and 90s.

On the female side of the new unisex staffroom in the Castle (there were still effectively sides to the room, joint or not), the formidable Anne Aldred (whom the kids DID NOT all dread when they really got to know her), Liz

Leese, Margarets Jones and Davies, Helena Mobley, Desna Pearce, Alison Power, Mary Owen, Liz Ikin, Susan Lewis (Hughes), Bethan Jenkins, Anne Jones, Carolyn (Coakley) Meade, Bev Davies, Diane Evans, Helen, to-be wife of David Powell, new Deputy Head Janice Williams and many others joined the ever-present marvellous musketeers, Allison, Meriel, Sandra and Merryl Jones.

When Dewi Bowen 'retired' Lorraine Buck took over in Art and became mentor to a Twyn lad whose fame was to flourish worldwide: Julien MacDonald unfailingly credits her as a major influence on his road to international fashion stardom.

John Battenbo of Aberdare also came to teach Maths and be the smiling butt of several long running jokes. He could never remember that when we were doing the crossword and pretended that the clue was 'overloaded postman', he shouldn't ask 'How many letters?' because the answer was always 'Bloody thousands!'

The 'Staff Cricket Tour', ran for some 15 years and only once involved an actual game. ('It spoilt it', was the verdict). It was originally genuinely intended to centre on a cricket match, whether in Bournemouth, the Wirral, Chester, Manchester, Liverpool or wherever, but that fell through on the first few and after a while we even stopped taking our kit.

The sporting theme was maintained, though, in that an hotelier in Wexford (we liked Ireland) still thinks we were the Staff Golf Society (what time for tee, sir?!), and it was also while playing soccer on a beach near there that we saw *Saving Private Ryan* being filmed, though they wouldn't let us be extras.

There was rarely peace and quiet at the sixth form and staff parties and discos. Sport, drama, school trips and marvellous music under Derry Prothero and Gwilym Jones helped cement the generally fine staff-pupil relationships.

Memorable staff functions and PTA occasions float back to mind, with one of the former, at a Blackwood nightspot on the scorching night of an epic Borg-McEnroe clash perhaps the classic. The Governing Body were often involved at closer than arm's length on the social side, with Gareth Daniel, for one, an irrepressible force. Ray Iverson and his mates began an enjoyable series of PTA Car Treasure Hunts, which I must confess were made rather trickier over the years by Rob Butcher and myself!

The new buildings at Thomastown were certainly an impressive contrast to the Castle in some ways, though there were regrets amongst staff who saw less of the old building. Playing fields, though still hardly alongside, were a big improvement for the Upper School, highlighting the Lower School's deficiencies, but Gareth Francis, Adam Rosser, Sue Overbury and the rest were still up to the challenge.

What other images appear in memory's eye? Snow falling outside the Castle windows; the high ceilings and long chains of the Castle toilets; the prolonged search for a dead and far-from-fragrant rat under the upstairs floorboards in the Castle; the crowded Parents' Evenings in the Hall-cum-Gym at the Castle; Dewi Bowen's drawings and huge murals (black line round everything, please!); Cliff O'Shea's laugh; the smell of the black toner of the Gestetner machine in Ann and Tricia's room; Alan Pritchard arriving for interview as Deputy; Huw Morris and myself taking a group of disaffected pupils on 'Outdoor Pursuits': we'd walk them through the Aberdare tunnel or, through mist and fog, to the summit of Pen-y-Fan. Would we be allowed today? I doubt it!

Enough, I left in 1993. By the time this history of the school emerges the pupils who were 11 then will be about 30 – frightening, isn't it? But I hope they, the terrific people who taught them, and all those pupils of Cyfarthfa before and since, enjoyed the experience and look back on their years at CHS with as much fondness as I do. It is, after all, the people of any institution who make it, and keep it, special. Long may it be so!

Phil Atkinson

THE PARENT-TEACHER ASSOCIATION

Dennis Bennett

The Cyfarthfa PTA was formed in autumn 1973 and its contribution cannot be over-emphasised. Without the PTA, Cyfarthfa would have been immeasurably poorer.

The Executive Committee of volunteer enthusiasts encouraged the School's many activities, advertised its qualities, engaged in many hours of 'hard labour' and provided financial backing when, increasingly, economic constraints plagued the educational scene. Initially, Mansell Richards (Head of History), as Assistant Secretary, drove the Association forward before full parental participation became a practical possibility.

In the very early days of the Executive meetings, Gareth Daniel, as Chairman, with astuteness and warmth, clarified the relationship between teachers and parents, making the important distinction between the professional responsibilities of staff and the responsibilities of the parent members of the PTA. Newsletters were enthusiastically edited and published each term by Bob Thomas (Chemistry Master) throughout the 1970s and 1980s.

The first year programme set the broad and balanced pattern of monthly events, with little modification to the end of the 1980s. Popular events such as dances, car rallies, jumble sales and fayres, were largely permanent fixtures. Interspersed were concerts, talks, demonstrations and, sporadically, more prestigious and grand occasions. The Merthyr Express reported a coffee evening attended by nearly 300 parents in November 1973 as being highlighted by a first class gymnastics display . . . and culminated

Autumn Fayre poster

with the senior girls' choral group singing Bach's 'Cariad Crist' which had gained the Cyfarthfa girls first place at the 1973 Urdd National Eisteddfod.

A Primary/Lower School Cyfarthfa concert on 11 July 1974 was a sell-out, with over 400 people present. It gave immense enjoyment to the packed audience, at the same time providing youngsters from the contributory primary schools a taste of the big comprehensive school in advance of attending it.

Dances and Raffles

At least two dances were held annually, with the Christmas dances the most popular. 'Castle' nostalgia drew back many former pupils who felt privileged to have received their education in such unique surroundings. Tickets cost £1.50 in 1973, rising in later years to £2.50, and raffles brought in more income than ticket sales.

Concerts

School-based concerts and functions were supplemented by PTA musical evenings. Concerts given by the splendid Dowlais Male Voice Choir at Soar Chapel in 1975, and the internationally renowned Polyphonic Choir in 1976 were outstanding. The latter Choir returned again in 1979 to share the stage with the School's Girls Choir which was not overshadowed by its illustrious partner, and was earning a justifiable reputation in its own right! Entrance costs were not raised to match inflation, being 50p for adults and 25p for children!

 In contrast, a block booking for 400 people was made to see The Three Degrees at the Theatre Diamond Club, Caerphilly, on 2 December 1980. It provoked great excitement and pleasure for those whose musical sensibilities were tickled by such well-known and popular entertainers of the time.

Talks

Ossie Bevan reminded a large audience of the historical significance of Merthyr Tydfil. The headmaster toured with the nomadic tribes of British Somaliland, Clive Roberts invited parents to experience Dolygaer Outdoor Pursuits Centre, John Edwards lightened proceedings with his Wenglish research, and Gareth Daniel offered an exhilarating and revelatory dissection of the Probation Service.

Special occasions involved well-known personalities such as David Parry Jones who reflected on his varied professional life as a journalist and BBC commentator, and Alun Williams, the well-known Radio and T.V. personality whose address was a skilful blend of humour and serious comment. Meetings were admirably chaired by Gareth Daniel, a raconteur of considerable experience and success in his own right. On Friday 1 December 1978, the PTA entertained the long running BBC live programme Any Questions, chaired by David Jacobs at the Technical College, no suitable accommodation being available in the School. Because of the speed and intensity of Government educational reform, in 1988 the PTA rapidly arranged a series of lectures given by Peter Davies, of the Welsh Joint Education Committee, and by the Headmaster, to explain the new GCSE examinations, and the new education acts. The Head, in early 1989, spoke on 'Education on the Move'. Teachers, let alone parents, floundered under the sheer weight and flurry of government dictats!

Additional imaginative programming involved Cheese and Wine evenings, floral arranging, wine making and tasting, pottery demonstrating, fashion displays, and rugby film and guest evenings. 'Question and Answer' Forums tackled topics of special interest in the 1970s and 1980s such as the aims of the comprehensive school, raising of the school leaving age, leisure opportunities, corporal punishment, vandalism, truancy, drugs and social deprivation. Plastic duck races on the River Taff, and car treasure hunts following fiendishly devised clues along unfamiliar country lanes to unknown destinations, were very popular!

Fund Raising

Fund raising was an absolute must from the founding of the PTA in 1973. To sustain the momentum of extra-curricular and sporting activities it was paramount to have the finance to support them. Each year functions were pencilled in with the prime purpose of bringing in capital. One of the first uses for monies raised by the PTA was to extend the stage in the Castle Lower Hall cum gymnasium, and provide lighting and electrical equipment for multifarious purposes including theatrical and musical productions. £1,000 was required, and the LEA matched the £500 raised by the PTA so that the work could be completed.

As further evidence of the value of financial support to the School from the PTA in the early days of its existence, a 16mm sound/film projector was purchased for the Lower School, and £800 given towards a new fully furnished Sixth Form Common Room. A new minibus at a cost of around £7,000 became School property on Saturday 31 January 1981. Eight years later, on 19 April 1989 on the terrace in front of the school, the PTA handed over a spanking new 17-seat diesel crew bus for the School's use. At the same time, sums of money, amounting to £1,164 were given to the School for general purposes.

Raffles regularly raised over £500; sponsored fun and seasonal fayres would often top £1,000. The Fun run on Saturday 23 September 1988 raised £1,300; and the Spring Fayre 1988, £1,000. A 200 Club formed in 1980 regularly raised over £1,000 a year.

Government directives propelled parents into power on governing bodies and thus gave them control of the voting. From 1973 onwards PTA nominations were frequently elected on to the Cyfarthfa governing body - Gareth Daniel, Reg. Criddle, Warwick Rowlands - all fulfilled this role and Ray Baker, as a local education officer, serviced the governing body.

My last PTA Annual General Meeting was on Thursday 18 October 1990. Mrs Margaret Williams was re-elected chairperson, Mrs Barrell re-elected Secretary, and Mrs M. Adlam, Treasurer. The PTA was in good and experienced hands. The presidency was handed over to the worthy acting headteacher, Mrs J. Williams.

FRIENDS OF CYFARTHFA HIGH SCHOOL

Diane Roberts and Sue Mulcahy

The flourishing Parent Teacher Association at Cyfarthfa High School, renamed in recent years as the Friends of Cyfarthfa High School, continues to support the aspirations of the school with financial help and community involvement. The Friends also provide a social link between parents, staff and supporters of the school. These social events have included very successful dances at Christmas, New Year and various other times, when the school rocks to the sound of dancing feet and bands such as the Beatles Tribute Band.

Other social events include beauty demonstrations from the Body Shop where ladies have been pampered and polished or had their taste buds tempted by the 'Chocoholics' sales. Auctions have also been extremely successful, whilst the heart-rate has also been raised on the race nights.
Over the years, the Friends have used a variety of methods to raise funds for the school. Bargain hunters amongst pupils and parents have been well catered for by the regular school fetes, held in the lower school. Many a wet sponge has been thrown and many a burger burnt, but fun has always prevailed.
The funds have been used in a variety of ways. There have been donations to departments, who have often used them to enhance their extra-curricular provision. School trips have been high on the agenda, with visits to Granada Television Studios, a Geography field trip to Austria and a Drama trip to Boston amongst them. Kit has been purchased for the school's Rugby/Football teams and also to support the Duke of Edinburgh Award Scheme on their outdoor adventures. Staging for the Drama Department has enabled them to produce the excellent school productions we have

become accustomed to enjoying. Dictionaries have been purchased for lower school as well as a wide range of reading books to support literacy. A recent donation was for benches so that students can relax in their free time in the excellent new facilities at the upper school and the Friends have most recently helped with the printing costs of this Centenary history.

The Friends of Cyfarthfa always welcome new members and anyone interested should contact the school for further information.

Acknowledgements

This book, part of Cyfarthfa School's Centenary celebrations, would not have been possible without the help of a small group of former pupils and teachers at Cyfarthfa School, some of whom, Sandra Jones, Allison Lewis and Mansell Richards, knew the school in both capacities. The other members of that group were Dennis Bennett, Dewi Bowen, Noel Davies, Joe England, Trevor Jones, Alan Pritchard, Alan Rees and Ceinwen Statter.

Dennis Bennett as the architect of Cyfarthfa's transformation into a successful comprehensive school brought intimate knowledge to the group, as did Alan Pritchard who, until July 2012 was the current headteacher. Alan not only provided hospitality for the group's meetings at the school but helped in a variety of practical ways. Carolyn Meade, his successor, was equally supportive. Sandra Jones, Allison Lewis and Alan Rees with their practical common sense and long understanding of the school's development helped to shape the final outcome, while the irrepressible Dewi Bowen enlivened meetings and contributed his unique illustrations to the book.

Ceinwen, a one-time pupil of Merthyr County Grammar School, brought a more objective eye and her experience as a former academic editor and proof-reader with Reading University. With Joe England, who acted as Editor, she saw the book into production.

The four historical chapters were written in sequence by Joe England, Mansell Richards, Dennis Bennett, and Trevor Jones. Dennis also wrote the account of the Parent Teacher Association and tenaciously sought reminiscences from a wide range of former pupils and teachers who are thanked for their responses. Mansell contributed research to the chapter *They Made Their Mark*.

Among those who also helped in various ways were: Margaret Evans, Ian Hopkins, Cynthia Jenkins, David Lewis-Jones, Colin Mulcahy, David

Owen, John Cynog Price, Clive Pugh, Shirley Rees, Granville Thomas, Jane Type, Rhodri Walters, Gilbert Williams, and Huw Williams.

Substantial help with photographs came from David Hines, Dean Cummings, Claire Fry, Lindsay Griffiths, Carolyn Jacob, Howard Denner, Jenny Phillips and Adam Rosser. Alan George's *Old Merthyr* web-site was an invaluable resource for photographs and Alan went far more than an extra mile to ensure their successful inclusion. Warwick Music gave permission for quotations from the interview with Harold Nash. Apologies to those whose copyright we have been unable to trace.

A special thank-you to the Governors, and to the Friends of Cyfarthfa High School for making it possible for the current pupils at the school to receive a copy of this record of their inheritance.

Finally, this account of the first hundred years of Cyfarthfa School would not have been written without Noel Davies conceiving of the idea, and enthusiastically persuading all within earshot that it should be done.

Contributors and Sources

The **Introduction, Chapter One**, and **They Made Their Mark** written by Joe England who was educated at Cyfarthfa Grammar School and Nottingham University. A former senior lecturer at the University of Hong Kong, a Research Fellow in Industrial Relations at Warwick University, and Chief Executive of Coleg Harlech, he is the author of *Industrial Relations and Law in Hong Kong, The Wales TUC: Devolution and Industrial Politics,* and the editor of *Changing Lives: Workers' Education in Wales 1907-2007.*

The sources for Chapter One were *Minutes* of Merthyr Tydfil Education Committee, A.W. Howells *The Development of Secondary Education in Merthyr Tydfil from 1881 to 1970* (M.Ed dissertation, Cardiff 1970); The Cyfarthfa Boys' School *Pupil Register 1913;* The Fiftieth Anniversary Booklet, *Cyfarthfa Castle Grammar School 1913-1963;* the *Merthyr Express*.

Chapter Two

Written by Mansell Richards who was educated at Cyfarthfa Grammar School and Swansea University. He later gained a Cardiff University M.Ed. He began teaching at Stoneham School, Reading before becoming Head of History and subsequently Head of MiddleSchool, Cyfarthfa, later being appointed Deputy Headteacher at Afon Taf High School. In those schools he led projects that won Prince of Wales Committee Heritage Awards - the Joseph Parry Birthplace restoration and the Gateway to Merthyr Tydfil plaques. He contributed chapters on the late Fifteenth to Eighteenth Centuries to *Merthyr Tydfil - A Valley Community (1981).*

The sources for the chapter were *Minutes* of Merthyr Education Committee; A.W. Howells *The Development of Secondary Education in Merthyr Tydfil from 1881 to 1970* (M.Ed dissertation, Cardiff 1970); The Cyfarthfa *Staff Register 1913- 66;* The Fiftieth Anniversary Booklet *,Cyfarthfa Castle Grammar School 1913-1963;* the Merthyr Express; personal knowledge.

Chapter Three

Was written by Dennis Bennett who was educated at Caerphilly Boys' Grammar School and University College, Aberystwyth, where he gained a Master's degree in Geography. Headmaster of Cyfarthfa High School 1970 – 1990, he came with a wide experience of teaching and administration in Midland secondary schools. In 1985 he was joint author of the Welsh Office publication *Schools in Action.* In 1990 he became Senior Advisor for Assessment with Mid Glamorgan Education Authority. In 1988 he received the O.B.E. for 'services to education'.

The sources were Headmaster's *Reports* to the Governors' Quarterly Meetings; Speech Day *Reports;* HMI Inspection *Report, 1983;* the *Merthyr Express;* communications from former teaching staff; and personal knowledge.

Chapter Four

Trevor Jones was educated at Ferndale Grammar School and Aberystwyth University before becoming an English master in a number of Rhondda schools including Ferndale Comprehensive, Tonypandy Grammar School and Mid-Rhondda Comprehensive. In 1980 he was appointed Head of English at Cyfarthfa becoming Deputy Headteacher in 1997. He retired from teaching in 2010 and now lives in Brecon.
The sources were largely personal knowledge and discussion with colleagues.